Praise from Kirsten Chapman's *Columbus Dispatch* readers:

"Honest and heartwarming columns—words that always remind the reader that the world of our families and our friends, both now and in our memories, is a rich one, worthy of examining and cherishing."
—Norman Carmichael

"[Chapman] share[s] so many of the feelings I can't put into words, and [her] compassion and nostalgia along with a down-to-earth style moves me."
—Alyce Danielson

"If there is any one thing which ties all [her] essays together, it is love in a loving family."
—Donald W. Bolin

"The heartache and frustration a family experiences, especially a spouse, sons and daughters, is so exhaustive. [Her] insight and deep understanding must have been a great balm and encouragement to those who struggle with loved ones trying to cope."
—Freida M. King

"When [Chapman's] column appeared, I was drawn magnetically to it . . . . [Her] willingness to tap into [her] memories and feelings, and to share them with others, has been an inspiration."
—Chuck Postlewaite

"[Her] article regarding Lake Michigan was wonderful. I read it to my wife and she said, 'Let's keep it to enclose in our Christmas cards.'"
—Craig Williams

"Golden nuggets like these should be captured in a book. I hope [she's] writing one."
—Don Sebastian

What happened to the
brave Indian guide?

"Almost home"
The Tired voyagers
rest — Bonja took
pictures —

LEIF LOKVAM
Summer 1947

Home Again

Kirsten Lokvam Chapman

Illustrations by Patti Sharpe

Copyright© 2006 CHI, Inc.
Published by Third Tree Press
ISBN-13: 978-0-9665767-1-9
ISBN-10: 0-9665767-1-3

Third Tree Press
P.O. Box 331504
Nashville, TN 37203
www.kirstenchapman.net

THIRD TREE PRESS

To Tia and Tyler,
with love and gratitude.

Acknowledgments

With special thanks to *The Columbus Dispatch* for allowing me to reprint the essays included in *Home Again,* all of which (with the exception of "Mrs. McQuestion" and "Summer Son") originally appeared in the newspaper.

And to Luke Feck, Bob Smith, Mike Curtin and Ben Marrison for publishing my work.

To Gary Kiefer for championing my first articles in *Capitol* magazine.

To T.R. Fitchko and Tracy Lemmon, and to Kirk Arnott, Joe Blundo, Margie Breckenridge Lewis, Diana Lockwood and John McNeely for their editing during my 21-year tenure.

And to Barth Falkenberg, Mike Harden, Kitty Harriel, Diana Hill, Jewell Johnson, Becky Kover, Jim Massie, Scott Minister, Evangelia Philippidis, Lisa Reuter, Mark Siple and many others for their help over the years.

Special thanks to Patti Sharpe, whose illustrations carry me home again, and whose use of my mother's paintbrushes moves me beyond measure.

To Bill Kersey who aptly designed and produced this book, and to his assistants Sara Anglin and Megan Kersey.

To Diana Lockwood, who edited it with precision and grace.

To Toni Carter and Karen Updike for their careful readings.

To Kelley Helton and Dawn Thrasher for their assistance.

To dear friends for their encouragement and support.

And, finally, with special thanks to family — the Chapmans, Coburns, Debeses, Flynns, Lokvams, Murbachs, Owenses, Pierottis, Sawyers, Spallatos and Updikes, and especially to Chip, Tyler, Judith, Miles, Tia and Alberto — for inspiring the essays.

"To us, our house was not unsentient matter—it had a heart, and a soul, and eyes to see us with; and approvals, and solicitudes, and deep sympathies; it was of us, and we were in its confidence, and lived in its grace and in the peace of its benediction. We never came home from an absence that its face did not light up and speak out its eloquent welcome—and we could not enter it unmoved."

MARK TWAIN
(1896, in a letter to his
friend Joseph Twichell)

In the Fullness of Time

Oh incremental slowness,
I love watching you spread green
dotted lines over winter-plowed fields.
I love watching you creep
a brilliant yellow up ligularia spires,
and bulge tight knots of hydrangea
into creamy billowing blooms.

In your time, in your time,
the vine lengthens and twines,
the Labrador violet curls
farther along these rocky cracks.
I see Irish moss sending forth
its stars, feathered grasses
unfurling their plumes,
milkweed pods swelling with silk.

Oh slow steady force unfolding the world,
you have blessed me and given me peace.

KAREN LOKVAM UPDIKE

Contents

A River Within 1

A Father's Legacy 3

A Sisterly Trinity 5

A Changing Family 9

Sunday 11

Drum Majorette 13

Family Biographers 15

Favorite Teachers 17

Miss Learn 19

Vesterheim 22

Amanda Johnson 24

Turi Kampestad 26

Halloween 28

Family Songs 30

Parents' First Christmas 32

Wrapped With Care 34

A Happy Christmas 36

Storybook Dolls 38

Gifts of Insight 40

Easter 42

Spring Break 44

Standing Up for a Parent 46

Glory 48

Mrs. McQuestion 50

A Taste of Summer 53

Dog Days 55

Summer 57

The Best Gifts 59

Ownership 61

Before the Back Door 63

Summer Camp 65

In Search of Self 67

Lake Michigan 70

The Fourth of July 72

A River Within 74

He Is Speaking Still **77**

A Pitcher That Never Empties 79

The Magic Tree 81

In Praise of Teachers 83

Conversations in the Car 85

The Gathering 87

No Thanksgiving? 89

A Talking Christmas Tree 91

Letter Carriers 93

The Spirit of Christmas 95

Early Christmas Morn 97

Epiphany 99

Frozen Flowers 101

Bird at the Window 103

A Valentine's Day Gift 106

The Man From Boston 109

To Make—or Not To Make—the Bed 111

Recipes 113

About Face 116

Spring-Cleaning 119

Lilacs 121

Inga Torgeson 124

Summer Son 126

The Ladies of Bullitt Park 130

Train Ride 132

Blackberry Farm 135

A Journal 138

Maybe 140

Two Dads 142

Visit to the Hospital 145

Retirement 148

Thelma Lien 150

Dad, Age 7 152

"A Child's Garden of Verses" 154

Hospital Rounds 156

My Father's Voice 158

A Sense of Home **161**

Civil War Letter 163

Letters Home 165

Erie D. Chapman Jr. 167

Martha Chapman 170

Molly Chapman 172

Letter to Washington Irving 174

The Headless Horseman 177

Thanksgiving's Portal 180

November—a Fitting Month 183

Mother-in-Law Restores Order 185

The Unopened Gift 187

A Feeling as Old as the Flag 189

Here I Stand 191

The Music Plays More Softly 193

"April Is the Cruelest Month" 195

A Sense of Home 198

Forget-Me-Not **201**

The Night Air 203

Wisdom Compensates 205

The Scorched Diploma 207

The Faintest Graphite 209

Hiding Shoes 212

A Skirt Versus Pants 214

Dec. 31, 1999 217

Changes 219

Blue Forget-Me-Nots 221

Turning Points 223

Free as the Wind 225

Like Mom 227

Gardening Takes Root 229

Roses Ever Bloom 231

Legacy of Love 233

"The Razor Edge of Danger" 235

The Little Bank 238

Saved Letters 240

The Line From Mother to Daughter 242

A Tablecloth of Thanksgiving 245

The Perfect Thanksgiving 247

Angels 249

A Time of Thanksgiving **251**

Grandchildren 253

Dining Out With Children 255
Rites of Passage 257
Wedding Presents 259
June 23, 2001 261
Journal of a 90-Year-Old's Birth 263
Homecomings 265
Grandmother-To-Be 267
Letter to a Grandson 269
Baptismal Heirloom 271
Cradle Song 273
Attachment Parenting 275
Birthmark 277
Godparents 279
Time Recaptured 281

"In the Fullness of Time" **283**
How Young Are You? 285
Beauty 287
Apache Ceremony 289
Home Alone 291
Karen's Cabin 293
Grand Canyon 296
Tia's 28th Birthday 298
"Do as the Romans Do" 300
Turning Tables 302
A Romance Language 304
Wedding-Dress Shopping 306
Well-"Tamed" 308
Christmas Past 310
June 25, 2005 312

Italian Fairy Tale 314
College Reunion 316
Halloween Ghosts 319
Thanksgiving Chairs 321
A Blue Basket 323
Christmas Blue 325
Love Remains 327

About the Author 331
About the Illustrator 332

And then there were four:
Chris' homecoming, 1950

A River Within

*By and by, we try to find
our way back to the raft.*

Sonja, 7th Avenue, 1943

A Father's Legacy

*H*ow strange to hold my father's baby shoes in the palm of my hand.

The brown high-tops, size 2, once launched a journey. Now they lead me back along a path.

The power of a parent lives on. Although my dad died six years ago, the dialogue continues.

"What are you doing?" I once asked as he dug a hole in our boulevard.

"Planting a tree for your brother," he replied.

"Why him and not me?" I countered. "He's just a baby."

"I did plant one for you when you were born—the apple tree in the back yard at the other house—and, before you, a cherry tree for Sonja; and before her, in the front yard, a flowering crab apple for Karen."

I grew taller that day, my feet more rooted in family.

Recently, I came across the words "He plants trees to benefit another generation" and better understood my father.

No other siblings arrived, but my brother's sugar maple was joined by two more maples. In the back yard, a cherry, apple and crab apple filled in for those left behind at the other house. Even a pear tree and a family of birches took up residence.

After retiring as a general surgeon, Dad continued to make rounds, visiting his trees the way he once checked on his patients. Then, with care, he administered the correct spraying or the necessary pruning.

So, too, he once measured us, taking stock of our growth—nipping here, encouraging there, grafting insight and experience.

Even now, some of his (and his generation's) favorite phrases conjure up his memory:

"I'm off to fight the wars."

"Let that be a lesson to you."

"Hold the fort."

"Shake a leg."

"Put on your thinking cap."

"Now you're talking."

"Sooner or later, they'll get their comeuppance."

"Let's get down to brass tacks."

One day, I asked him what had been the happiest time of his life. Retirement? Childhood?

"When you children were young," he said, "and I thought life would go on like that forever."

When we were young, our father looked so youthful that the fortuneteller at the fair always guessed his age wrong.

"I can still see his young hands," my older sister said, "getting a good grip on a bottle cap I couldn't open; . . . showing me how to tear the gauze down the center to tie off a bandage before taping it, . . . folding his hands from long habit, even when he was not praying.

"If only we could go this year," she said, "to let the fortuneteller guess wrong again."

Dads become larger than life, lingering as long as their kids live—casting shadows, for better or worse, like towering trees.

One autumn, as the three sugar maples wound their way to red, my father's journey of 85 years ended.

Sometime later, I discovered his baby shoes in a box in my parents' attic. I hadn't seen them before; rubbing a thumb across their smooth leather soles, I realized how much I didn't know.

So I keep returning to what I do know: the image of a large boot pushing down on the spade, a crunch of metal meeting earth, a sapling settling into the scooped-out spot.

Fathers can become myths.

How do I know? I am not only my father's daughter; I am the third tree.

A Sisterly Trinity

$\mathcal{M}$y world always held them. Karen, born three years before Sonja, and Sonja, three years before I, witnessed my life at the start, sharing and shaping the universe.

For seven years I was the baby of the family. When our brother was born, I not only lost the role, the family moved to a larger house. As adults, my sisters and I would sometimes view our first home and old neighborhood and marvel at how small everything had become, as if it would fit inside a teacup.

There was nothing small or fragile, however, about our experiences in the morning of our lives. Those generous, unbreakable moments— exploring the overgrown woods behind our house, the sand dunes lining Lake Michigan, Hannan's farm where Karen boarded her horse Glory— cemented our sisterhood, bonding us together. In play, as much as birth order, we found our lifelong parts: Karen's firstborn leadership; Sonja and I, happy to follow.

Each of us, sharing the same parents, was a variation on a theme, a separate act in a three-act play.

Not only did we not look alike; we didn't behave alike. Karen was boisterous and a tomboy, riding bareback, climbing trees, building forts. Sonja was quiet and artistic, preferring drawing, painting and ballet. I guess I was somewhere in between, struggling toward a kind of balance.

5

Our differences complemented one another. Together, we created something stronger than each of us alone: three in one and one in three, a sisterly trinity. In that sense, we were "the Lokvam girls," more than just Karen, Sonja and Kirsten.

Such closeness had been hard won—forged by the same rivalries, hurts, bickerings and even the fights so familiar to many families.

One summer day, over an issue long since forgotten, I did what so many siblings do: I made my sister angry. Usually shy and calm, Sonja chased me outdoors, yelling and screaming. I shouted back. Karen, trying to break it up, chimed in with her own shouts just as our mortified mother pulled into the driveway.

"Girls! Girls!" Mom called out, leaping from the car.

"I could hear you all the way down the street. What must the neighbors think?"

That settled it. As much as we'd been ready to choke one another, whenever it was us versus "the neighbors" or an outsider, my sisters and I drew our wagons together in a tight circle.

Back then I would never have guessed that someday each would view me as an equal, not merely the youngest, tag-along.

"For so long the wedding seemed very far off and now it's nearly upon me," Sonja confided in a letter on June 3, 1967:

"Generally I've held up quite well until about a week ago. Since then I've found myself wound up . . . and a little sad. I've been told that this is 'normal,' however I hadn't expected to react this way. If I'm completely honest I would say also that I'm a bit afraid."

When sisters are the closest of friends, nothing sustains more than sharing secret joys, darkest fears, all kept safe inside the bond.

Within our circle, we took turns listening and being heard, being heard and listening. What had begun in the bedroom of childhood, the whispering of confidences after "lights out," had survived, overcoming decades and distances.

When Sonja died suddenly at 36, my world shrank. I remember thinking, "Now we're no longer three."

Ring around the rosy. Ashes, ashes. One fell down.

In that sad and stunning moment, I realized I had lost more than a sister. Our magic circle was broken.

"That's what I miss most now," Karen wrote in a poem to Sonja, "the way you listened / my sense of being heard. / It wasn't just your secrets / you carried to your grave / but the chance to tell you ours / Although you are now so silent / I am speaking still."

6

Karen continued to talk, in poem after poem. Poetry rose up to meet her the way the fields did when she rode horseback. If one door had closed, forever shut, it forced her to open another—and write. Unbeknown to us, we each had turned to writing. In a way, it was Sonja's last gift, helping her sisters write through grief.

At first, Karen's poems would arrive in letters. Now, two decades later, they appear, magically, fresh from the poet's fax. Creeping downstairs in the morning and finding a new poem always reminds me of when Karen would lead Sonja and me downstairs to discover our presents on Christmas morning.

Ring around the rosy. A pocketful of poems.

Karen's poetry explored new paths or, rather, veered from the path: "Riding where no one / goes at all / between planting time / and harvest in fall / I find in fields / too far for herds / grain swaying high, grass growing tall. / When I see some hollowed into a nest / I wonder, / who circled down to rest? / Who, cradled in these grasses deep, / was swirled softly off to sleep?"

Recently, Karen confessed that in trying to write a poem, she often begins a letter to me which she never sends and, sometimes, even "trashes." Hurt at first, I now view it as a high compliment. She is "talking still," I realized, not just to Sonja, but, perhaps, to both Sonja and me, combined "sisters," a confidante, a place to pour her poetry.

Curious, I asked whether she had any examples. She sent reams from her computer.

"This printout is typical of un-mailed Kirsten letters," she wrote across the top of one:

"Dear Kirsten," it began, "I am writing to you in hopes of getting a poem under the most peculiar circumstances."

Page 3 contained her creation *Try To Write at Least an Hour a Day*.

"I can't believe how much I miss having you to talk to and listening when you talk to me," she wrote in January.

This spring she shared: "It seems I always write to you when I feel I have no one else to tell.

"I have been horseback riding several times. Freya is calmer, which is lucky for me, for I am weaker in the thigh and need a tree stump to mount. . . . I love being 'old.' I can go with what other people need so much more easily. What is in their nature I can forgive so readily."

Her next sentence, "Oh incremental slowness I love watching you spread fine green dotted lines over winter-plowed cornfields," became the first four lines of a 20-line poem, *In the Fullness of Time*, which ends:

7

"Oh slow steady force / unfolding the world, / you have blessed me / and given me peace."

Wouldn't Sonja be shocked to see Karen, one of Dad's "brave Indian girls," now 61, a published poet, a teacher of writing, needing a stump to mount her horse? And me, at 55, having given up riding all together?

And Sonja? Whenever we think about her or see her photograph or reread one of her letters, she is with us. She is reflected in the next generation, too, not only in my children's appearance, but in my son's and nephew's love of art, my daughter's and niece's love of ballet. And she lives on in Karen's poems, the poems which she inspired:

"Remember, in the dusk, after dinner, / in dusty spots, on cool cement sidewalks / or on lawns where the sprinkler didn't reach, / how we played our block games? Kick the Can, / Round the Moon, Run My Good Sheep, Run? / . . . Sometimes I like to think you're out there now / in the dusk and long grass, waiting to be found, / but I keep on playing our game the old childish way; / I'm still cautious and cheat. / I will be here, still hovering around goal, / when you give up and don't want to hide anymore."

Our world holds her still. The circle survives.

A Changing Family

A photograph makes us pause.

There we stand, wearing snowsuits or hiding behind another year's Halloween masks, frozen in time. Although we continually change, a snapshot keeps us "preserved for posterity," as Dad used to say.

We find comfort in studying the fixed reflection, which puts an edge on eternity: Time flowed before us, and time will flow on without us. Yet for one moment, Moses-like, we part the waters—push them back on each side—when we take a picture or look at one.

Typically, the photographer and subject agree "to hold still."

A print that shows unwanted movement, even as slight as the blinking of an eye, is discarded. A shot too honest or unflattering—a disgruntled look, a stern expression—is rejected.

We demand perfection in photos. For posterity, we prefer censorship over reality. But what if we're missing from the picture? One day, about a year ago, I got an eyeful. Rummaging in my mother's basement, I unearthed a framed 8-by-10 photo.

It showed a family of four, my then-young parents and two sisters—as much a family as any other, as much as my own.

I hadn't seen the picture before. Until then, I hadn't viewed a formal family portrait that didn't include me or my younger brother and me.

Yet I wanted that photo all the more, for it reminded me that, if I hadn't been born, my family still would have been complete.

Where do we come from, "out of the everywhere into the here," emerging like a photograph in the darkroom's developer?

And how much difference does our birth make? Do others fare better or worse when we enter their picture?

Sonja, the baby, became a middle child when I usurped her position, before our brother arrived seven years later. Would her life have changed if parental time, energy and attention had not been divided among four children?

Karen, the eldest, eventually helped with three siblings instead of only one. And my parents? They had more mouths to feed and college tuitions to fund.

Does what we bring to the world make up for what we take?

Today, more than ever before, families are pulling up stakes, replanting them. Yet, even when they stay put, they're constantly moving, changing like a mobile: A baby in one photo is a teen-ager in another, a father in one portrait is a child in another.

Each touch of the family mobile makes us move in relation to the others: In separate scenes, a sister, then a brother, enter stage right. In later scenes, a sister, then a father, exit stage left.

We are four again—different but the same.

Upon returning from the war in Thornton Wilder's *The Skin of Our Teeth*, Mr. Antrobus is relieved to find that his books have survived: "The steps of our journey are marked for us here."

Our steps are preserved in photos, too. Ever since homesteaders first posed outside a sod cabin, we've marked our moments.

Today, humans race to the photographic studio before each Christmas dawns or grab a camera when the extended family gets together.

Which, of all the photographs, gets hung on a wall? Which is added to an album or becomes the holiday card?

Although I wanted the old picture I'd found in an art-deco frame, I figured that my mother and older sister had the greater claim. So I settled for the negatives from that "pre-me" sitting. Holding them up to the light, I saw plenty of rejects but not that from which the image was made.

I did, though, choose a negative to be developed—one, I later discovered, in which Karen's eyes look blurred and my father far too stern.

Still, I'll save the picture as a reminder: We think we photograph life, yet life focuses on us, for better and worse, frame after frame, until our role is spent.

Sunday

$\mathcal{T}$he splash of a tide and the return of a day give a rhythm to life.

Thus did Sunday emerge from the churning, sea-tossed week like an anchor.

An island unto itself, Sunday remained apart from other days—its pace slower, its glance turned inward to home and family.

Once a week we climbed into its generous and welcoming lap to find rest and renewal.

After church and Sunday school, we lay on the living-room carpet and read the funny pages while a roast-beef dinner cooked in the oven.

Relatives came round, or, during a Sunday afternoon ride, the family visited them.

Rarely did the day pass without an outing for a chocolate sundae or a search for a caramel in a Whitman's Sampler.

Most of all, the day consecrated the "we" of family 52 times a year.

Today, more and more, Sunday resembles a weekday—a chance to run errands, buy groceries, work.

Where did we lose Sunday and with it a sense of peace? In stores with longer hours? In the driving pace of a seven-day workweek? In the need for busyness?

"There is more to life," Gandhi warned, "than merely increasing its speed."

Wayne Muller—who wrote *Sabbath, Restoring the Sacred Rhythm of Rest*, published in 1999—agrees.

"In the trance of overwork, we take everything for granted," Muller writes. "We consume things, people and information. We do not have time to savor this life, nor to care deeply and gently for ourselves, our loved ones or our world; rather, with increasingly dizzying haste, we use them all up and throw them away."

Folks have become lost in a world "saturated with striving and grasping, yet somehow bereft of joy and delight," he says, by forgetting the Sabbath and the necessity of rest.

"Sabbath time—or sacred rest—may be a holy day, the seventh day of the week, as in the Jewish tradition, or the first day of the week, as for Christians. But Sabbath time may also be a Sabbath afternoon, a Sabbath hour, a Sabbath walk—indeed, anything that preserves a visceral experience of life-giving nourishment and rest."

The goal, he says, is to find the balance "at which, having rested, we do our work with greater ease and joy, and bring healing and delight to our endeavors."

Muller reminds us that, if "we forget to rest, we'll work too hard and forget . . . those we love, forget our children and our natural wonder."

Sabbath rest is so important, he says, that it is considered "not a lifestyle suggestion but a commandment as important as not stealing, not murdering or not lying."

He tells of a secretary who grew up in the country and misses her life there.

Several times a week, she makes a "Sabbath meal" from scratch and invites friends to join her. "It is time away from work and responsibility," she notes. "It becomes almost sacred, sacramental, the way food and hands and friendship all work together in the warmth of the kitchen."

The traditional Jewish Sabbath begins precisely at sundown, Muller points out.

"It is not dependent on our readiness to stop. We do not stop when we complete our phone calls, finish our project, get through this report. We stop because it is time to stop."

Without the Sabbath or a Sabbath moment, we would never stop—because we are never finished.

On long-ago Sundays, whenever I left home to return to college, I was reluctant to let go of the sense of time standing still or deep. Yet, as soon as I arrived at my dorm, I felt more invigorated and rested because of that grounding.

Let the other days of the week blur into one another. Let Sunday be singular like the sun.

Drum Majorette

Studying a shadowy negative, I recalled at once the photograph.

I had to make another print. I had to see my sister once more, standing in the sunlight proudly holding her silver baton. Outside camera range, lurking in the shade, I am invisible—which is exactly how I felt on that long-ago day.

Yet, as I relive the moment, I see myself all too clearly.

Let me paint my picture, an unflattering portrait: As my sister posed, displaying her new baton and majorette outfit, I sulked nearby.

Confusion colored my envy. If it wasn't her birthday, if it wasn't Christmas, why did Sonja, even at three years older than I, rate such a surprise?

When I saw the white, satiny jacket with three rows of brass buttons, a little red skirt and a matching red-and-white cap, I suddenly wanted to have my own—and to be a drum majorette, too.

Her desire, however, had increased with each passing year.

In an age when one couldn't easily find a pre-made uniform, Mother asked a seamstress to sew one. Dad had a baton cut to the right size. Most of all, my parents found someone who could give Sonja lessons.

Half a century later, I understand why she, a middle child, wished to be first in line, leading the parade: Karen, the oldest, and I, the "baby," too often stole the spotlight. No wonder Sonja strove to shine alone.

My parents tried to honor her, as they did with all of us, by affirming her interests.

A 5-year-old doesn't care about such nurturing, of course, unless the nurturing concerns her.

That my interest in horses years later would result in a riding outfit didn't matter. That afternoon, I wanted what Sonja had found when she wandered into our bedroom and discovered the baton and outfit on her bed.

Her joyous squeals sent me running up two flights from the basement. "Who bought her those things?" I demanded.

"Santa," said my oldest sister, hoping to silence me.

The rest of the day and well into the next, I marched up and down the stairs, repeating aloud so that he and my parents would be sure to hear, "I wish Santa would bring me a surprise."

To their credit, they didn't budge. Nor did he.

Sometimes the gifts that stay with us the longest are those we didn't get—or give. They teach hard lessons.

Year after year, in a home movie, I hear my daughter, then 5, wish for "Baby, Baby, Thumbelina and Katy" on Christmas Eve before going to bed.

Oh, Baby, Baby, why didn't I buy you? Did I want to give my daughter an old-fashioned, cuddly doll like Katy more than a newfangled one requiring a battery in her bottom? Although she considered you as lovable, or more so, as a traditional doll, you were nowhere to be found on Christmas morning.

Fortunately, the next year my sister Sonja set me straight when she suspected that the dollhouse I was having made was as much for me as for her niece. She also urged my husband and me to buy our son the Earthquake Tower that we thought was too flimsy and, therefore, not worth the money.

"It may not end up in your attic as a family heirloom like the dollhouse," she said. "It may last only a few days. But it will make Ty's Christmas."

"Look at it this way: He realized you couldn't care less about an Earthquake Tower. But if you give it to him, it will show that you honor and respect his values, even if they're different from your own."

How could Sonja, who had no children, have been so wise?

Did she remember being given her dream? Did she recall standing in sunlight before an imaginary band?

Seeing her again, ready to lead the parade, I think I know.

14

Family Biographers

*M*ost of us have no biographer taking notes, no life review, no showing of how this led to that.

We read that Lincoln suffered melancholia; that Emily Dickinson turned from an outgoing girl into a shy, retiring genius; and that George S. Patton resurrected his military career—but find no mention of ourselves.

The famous attract attention, even scrutiny. The rest of us escape unnoticed.

Yet, when we were growing up, our parents sometimes praised or marked a moment.

"By looking at the inner side of a tapestry," Anne Morrow Lindbergh wrote, "one can often uncover patterns and colors that reveal a complexity and meaning invisible on the surface."

A parent senses that other side of the fabric, the texture, even the threads tying it together.

Who among us—however old we've become—doesn't wish for in-depth news from our childhood? Too often, though, a parent, or the parent's memory, slips away before such an account is written down.

On my older sister's 12th birthday in 1952, my father took time to record some thoughts:

"My dearest Sonja, Now you are beginning to enter another phase of your life, and gradually, over the next few years, you will change from a sweet young girl to a very sweet young woman.

"It seems only yesterday that you arrived on the scene. What excitement and rejoicing to think we had another little girl. . . . Mother and

15

Daddy carried you home in the big basket, . . . (which we put) on the chair in the dining room. Karen was only 3 years old . . . and must have thought you were just another big doll."

Dad recalled a bout with pneumonia, which, "with God's love and help," Sonja had overcome, growing "nice and plump and happy."

Eventually, her sweet disposition ("except occasionally when you would say, 'Boy, I'll sock 'em one!'") had earned her the nickname "Sunny."

He placed her birth not only in the context of family but also, biographically, against the backdrop of history:

"The war had not yet started for us. Because of recent events caused by the death of King George VI, I think of a young girl at the time of your birth who was then your present age. That little girl was Princess Elizabeth, just 12 years old. Now, only 12 years later, . . . she has become the queen of her country.

"You are my queen, Sonja. Continue as you have in your interests and work; develop your talents (of which you have many) in dance, art, music; . . . and God bless you all the days of your life."

With my son's 30th birthday on the horizon, I had wanted to write a similar letter celebrating his three decades—which began with his birth and my rebirth.

Recently, while driving along Bryden Road, I saw crepe paper blowing in the wind and a yard sign proclaiming: "Holy cow / Jessica is / 18 now."

"Holy cow," I thought. "Tomorrow is Ty's birthday, and I still haven't written my letter."

Rushing home to begin one, I planned to send it by overnight delivery. I discovered an e-mail from him first.

"Can you believe it's been 30 years?" he wrote. "The fact you were only 25 at the time sounds more and more remarkable to me. You were only three years out of college! And only seven years out of high school.

"I wish I could go back and talk to you then as I am now. . . . I remember you so vividly as a 27- or 28-year-old reading me stories. Still, it would be fun to talk as peers and hear the kinds of things that were going through your head as you thought about your teaching career and being a young mother."

He continued, exploring the tapestry of years, giving me news of myself on the eve of his birthday—and proving that parents don't have to be our only biographers.

Our children often tell the other half of the story.

Favorite Teachers

$\mathcal{T}$he schoolhouse door never closes completely.

Instead, it stands ready to welcome our return.

How easily we slip inside whenever we trace our thoughts on memory's blackboard.

Again we cross the freshly waxed floors and inhale the brand-new smell of a new grade: varnished desks, clean chalk, even the leather of unscuffed shoes.

All my elementary-school teachers are gathered, seated in the first-grade classroom.

Mr. Perry, the Durkee School custodian, steps through the doorway.

No, he isn't late; he just had to ring the school bell.

He made us feel 10 feet tall by letting us take turns. His every act, stoked by kindness, warmed our days; from him we surmised that teachers, often the best ones, come in many guises.

Their names, most of them, rush back to me: Miss Weibel, Miss Schultz, Miss Gardner and Miss Irving. "Look. See. See all the teachers."

We learned from them.

Yet, surprisingly, we already knew so much: which teachers deserved the title and which fell short, which ones were sincere and which only pretended to be (especially when our fair-and-square principal, Miss Nelson, or our parents entered the room).

With a child's insight, we understood that a great teacher honored the whole child; that even the strictest teacher, with underlying compassion, merited admiration.

What they taught us wasn't as important as how: For better or worse, it often determined what we thought about ourselves and carried with us afterward.

Some, just by sharing their light, made us grow and reach new heights.

Miss Gardner, the kindergarten teacher, still seems patient and kind, just as she did on that first day when my mother pointed to a toy telephone.

"Oh, look," Mom said, "why don't you call . . . "

Call whom? Whom did she mention that made me let go of my grip and turn my attention, if only for a second, away from her?

Miss Gardner stopped the tears, nudging me along the scholastic path.

Oddly enough, I often return to the first-grade room when I visit the schoolhouse that never closes.

Why? Because, given that the years hold endless beginnings, we go back to the start of another first?

Or because our mean-spirited teacher, who was relieved of her duties halfway through the year, represents a terror—inexplicable anger around the next corner—that I haven't resolved?

Fortunately, as I look about the room, I don't see her.

After recess, when I take my seat at my second-grade desk, I encounter Miss Weibel—my favorite teacher—reading from *The Boxcar Children.*

She made us fall in love with stories—and with her.

Once, years later, I asked my mother why she'd invited her to our house for tea. I wished she had invited her more often.

"Miss Weibel called and asked if she could stop by," Mom said. "I assumed something was wrong. But it was nothing—nothing wrong, that is.

"Whenever I mentioned your new brother, she'd turn the conversation back to you, asking you questions and telling me how much she enjoyed having you in her class.

"It wasn't until months later that it dawned on me what she'd been up to. She must have sensed you felt displaced or jealous when your brother was born and tried to make you feel special."

As another school year dawns, I can't help feeling thankful for the beloved Miss Learn, who taught my mother for eight years in a one-room schoolhouse on the Koshkonong Prairie; for the teachers who brightened the school days of my children; and for all the Miss Weibels of the world.

Miss Learn

A 1921 letter from a district clerk to "Miss Susie Learn" of Cambridge, Wis.:

"I am writing to ask if you would like to teach our school for the coming year. Our school is not very large (28 students). Equipment is very good—basement, furnace, cistern, hot and cold rainwater for children to wash in, one swing, two trapezes with rings and rug underneath in basement. This school is called the Carpenter School. Miss Weisman (the superintendent) advised me as to your ability. Please give me some idea what wages you expect. I am waiting for an early reply."

Even as my grandfather, farmer Gust Owens, wrote his letter, the one-room schoolhouse was vanishing throughout rural America.

Yet my mother, like a later-in-time Laura Ingalls, attended the Carpenter School for eight grades before beginning high school.

Her education from Miss Learn was a gift, just as the teacher was a gift to the prairie.

"She taught us reading, writing (the Palmer method) and arithmetic," Mom recalled. "She emphasized literature and science, too. In agriculture, we learned where to put a well on a farm . . . and how to recognize different kinds of trees and crops and when to plant and harvest."

Cardboard signs with advice were hung on the walls: "Sleep with your window open." "Drink more milk."

Miss Learn even had green window shades installed to pull over the blackboards.

"On them she wrote the names of national, state and county officers for us to memorize in our spare time," Mom said. "The last period on Friday, we always had a spelling bee. It was our treat, but it kept us studying all week long."

Miss Learn taught music appreciation, too.

"Since she had no instruments and no budget, she started the Toy Orchestra. Using paper over combs for the melody, triangles and homemade drums for the beat and bells for interest, she decked us out in crepe-paper uniforms—and a proud-looking sash spelling out 'Carpenter School.' "

It takes a village to raise a child? It takes a Miss Learn to raise a village.

Her schoolhouse, a center of learning, became a community center when decorated for parties in the evening.

She started the parent-teacher association and the girls' auxiliary club. She organized plays and taffy pulls, square dances and box socials, fruit-basket raffles and debates ("Resolved: That all women should bob their hair").

She taught the girls how to embroider doilies to give to their mothers and how to make crepe-paper sweet peas, fastening them to wire stems and dipping them in wax to earn money for the school.

Like many other great teachers, Miss Learn knew that the best lessons are often rooted in reality: For credit in arithmetic, students traveled to town to deposit money. For the sake of journalism, students took turns contributing school news to the *Edgerton Reporter*.

"The older boys and girls are acting as big brothers or sisters to the first-graders," one article said. "They help prepare seatwork, fill out their health cards and give them any assistance that they may need. This aids the teacher, the first-graders and us, for we are glad to be of service to someone.

"No school was held here Friday as the teacher attended the National Dairy Show. . . . The upper grades are busy making posters (to be shown in store windows in Madison) for 'milk week,' which begins Oct. 27. . . . The Toy Orchestra journeyed to the Albion Town Hall last Wednesday evening and gave a concert.

"The Halloween party given by Miss Learn . . . on Friday night was enjoyed by all. Some 80 guests were met at the schoolhouse door by ghosts. Candy made and sold . . . from an autumn-trimmed booth went like hot cakes."

And the outcome of the debate, on the night when the fathers entertained at the PTA meeting?

"The judges decided the question a tie and to let those who wish to bob their hair do so," one of the young reporters wrote.

"Miss Learn was a remarkable educator," Mother said.

"Some of her students became lawyers, scientists, teachers, . . . and some were even elected to office—the kind written on Miss Learn's green window shades."

Vesterheim

*D*uring our Wisconsin childhood, my sisters and I used to love to hear our dad read *Little House in the Big Woods,* Laura Ingalls Wilder's book about the pioneering spirit.

Our father, born in a Minnesota log cabin to Norwegian immigrant parents, and our mother, daughter of first-generation Norwegian-Americans in Wisconsin, kept some of the ways of the old country: They sang folk songs in their ancestors' tongue and dressed us in sweaters knit by nimble Norse fingers. Each Christmas, Mom baked *fattigmanns bakkels.* Yet mostly—as many of their generation did—they tried to assimilate.

Hoping to learn more about our heritage, my sister Karen and I recently drove from Wisconsin, crossed the Mississippi River at Prairie du Chien and headed for Vesterheim Norwegian-American Museum in Dakora, Iowa. In letters back home, Norwegian immigrants had called their new land Vesterheim, meaning "western home."

Containing more than 21,000 objects, the museum says its collections are the "most comprehensive from any 19th-century group in this country." Founded in 1877, it also claims to be the first folk museum in the United States, predating Massachusetts' Sturbridge Village and Michigan's Greenfield Village.

The main building organizes its displays around three themes: life in Norway, the migration and the immigrants' life in the United States.

"In 1825, the Restoration, the first ship of Norwegian immigrants, arrived in New York with 53 passengers," said Marilyn Peterson, our guide of Norwegian descent.

"It was about 25 more years before they started (crossing the Mississippi and) coming heavy in this area. . . . Most of them were farm help. That's what they knew. They worked for someone as the hired hand, the hired girl."

We recalled how our father's "Auntie Karen," the woman who had raised him, had worked first for a "Yankee" family in Wisconsin. And when we heard that crowded ship bunks often held a family of five, each member lying on his side, we thought of our mother's great-grandparents, who had endured a three-month voyage with their eight children. Eventually, ship owners ripped out the beds on the return trip so supplies could be brought back to Norway.

Passengers' sea chests contained many essentials, including food and cheese for the long voyage. Great Auntie Karen's trunk, her name—and "America"—on its lid, took on even greater meaning.

A spinning wheel, Peterson said, was made of removable parts so it could be easily broken down to fit in a trunk. Finally, I understood why our spinning wheel, which had intrigued me as a child, was made of many "puzzle" pieces.

We surveyed wooden trunks, pitchers, bowls, boxes and plates—all covered with exquisite Norwegian rosemaling, or decorative rose painting, that began in the late 18th and early 19th centuries. The artwork reminded us of home, too, as more recent counterparts had decorated the kitchen of our youth.

So steeped in Norwegian history is the museum that Peterson recalled how once "a . . . visitor threw up his hands in mock disgust, saying, 'You're more Norwegian than we are.' "

At the end of *Little House in the Big Woods*, Laura hears Pa's fiddle playing and the wind's lonely sound.

"She was glad that the cozy house, and Pa and Ma and the firelight and the music, were now. They could not be forgotten, she thought, because now is now. It can never be a long time ago."

Regardless of heritage, visitors to Vesterheim can remember that "now" from long ago.

Amanda Johnson

I knew the books by their orange covers and their black-and-white illustrations.

Combing the library shelves, I'd lose hours perusing *Clara Barton: Girl Nurse, Abe Lincoln: Frontier Boy* and *Dolly Madison: Quaker Girl.*

The historical figures are known to all—but what about our ancestors?

Do compelling stories lurk on the branches of our family trees?

Jane Addams: Little Lame Girl had escaped my attention.

Not until I became a parent did my mother share the information—or, perhaps, did it register—that her aunt Amanda Johnson had lived and worked with the social reformer at Hull House in Chicago.

I wondered recently whether an earlier awareness of Johnson might have empowered my growing up female.

None of my grandparents went to college.

Yet she not only graduated (in 1893 from the University of Wisconsin) but also was awarded a Phi Beta Kappa membership after the chapter formed at her school.

In 1895, Addams became the garbage inspector for the 19th Ward in Chicago. Her appointment marked the first time that a woman held such a position.

Given that complaints about sanitary conditions had gone ignored in that ward for years, Addams hired an assistant.

"I have arranged with a Miss Johnson of Pittsburgh, a graduate of Madison (Wis.), to take charge with me," Addams said in an April 30 article in the *Chicago Times-Herald*. "She is very clever and thoroughly efficient."

Addams drove a reporter and newspaper artist "in a two-seated trap, drawn by a lively little nag," to investigate conditions in the ward.

The group found many alleys impassable because of piles of garbage and manure, and dead dogs and horses.

With nowhere else to play, children were thus exposed to filth and disease.

By July 29, however, the *Chicago Evening Journal* reported:

"A transformation has taken place, . . . and the Nineteenth Ward is as clean as any ward in the city—cleaner than most.

"Every morning at half-past 6 o'clock, Miss Addams or her assistant, Miss Johnson, starts on her rounds. They find out where the (garbage) teams are going and follow them . . . and see that the work is properly done."

Addams and Johnson were described as "essentially businesslike in manners and thoroughly conscientious. The result is that they have achieved wonders."

In 1896, Addams was preparing "to be absent in Europe for several months," according to *New England Magazine*.

"Miss Johnson, who had been acting as her deputy, took the first civil-service examination offered under the new law, passed at the head of the list, and was appointed vice chairman. Miss Addams resigned."

"Your resignation was tendered to me," inspector chief John C.W. Rhodes wrote on May 26, 1896, "which I gladly accept on account of your deputy, Miss Amanda Johnson, to whom I have given the credit of being the best of all the 24 inspectors."

"A case can be made that Amanda was the first female civil servant for the city of Chicago," said Scott Feiner, a Wisconsin Historical Society researcher.

Before women were granted the right to vote, she accomplished so much.

And I almost missed knowing about her.

Turi Kampestad

*W*ind rustles like taffeta skirts. Night is as black as a cape. And the golden moon, like a locket, hangs from a strand of stars. Could it be old Turi Kampestad roaming the midnight road?

Restless in life, she is elusive still. What was it about this wandering woman—whom I never knew—that created such an impression? Today we can move in and out of a neighborhood and scarcely be noticed. "Let's see," others might ask in two years, "were they the ones who . . .?"

Turi was 88 when she died in 1938. More than half a century later, people still speak of her as if they saw her just last night. Have they? Or I? Or did a prophecy, spoken over a newborn baby, come true?

"She was homeless," some say, "and wore six skirts at once."

Others say, "Her house was on the left, two doors down from the church. The choir practiced there in winter."

Everyone agrees she was wealthy and carried her valuables in the pockets of her skirts.

I first heard her name in 1978 in a country church's cemetery bordered by corn. Walking among the aging, tilted tombstones of Norwegian immigrants, my mother said, "Look, there's Turi Kampestad's grave," as if I'd known the woman all my life.

As a little girl, Mother had been frightened by the sight of her—dressed in black—walking by the farm. "That's just Turi," her mother told her. "She visits people for a week or two and moves on."

During the summer of 1993, when corn plants waved like small green flags, Mother and I revisited the cemetery. Unable to find Turi's weathered marker in the spot we remembered, we joked that she must have picked it up and moved on.

"Yes, I knew Turi," said Susie, my 86-year-old second cousin whom I met for the first time that afternoon. "Down the lane from our farm I'd see a dark speck grow larger and larger and shout, 'Turi's here.' We children loved her to stay, because she told us stories in Norwegian."

Susie remembers the swish of taffeta skirts, Turi's flat black shoes and the red silk lining of her black pocketbook. In winter, Turi wore a black velvet bonnet over her gray bun; in summer, a black straw hat with ribbons that tied under her chin.

As afternoon sun curled up on the farmhouse carpet, Susie began a strange tale: "When my mother was born in 1877, Turi came to call.

" 'She's the most beautiful baby I have ever seen,' she told my grandmother. 'She must have something beautiful—so she will remember me.'

"Searching through her pockets, lifting one black skirt after another, Turi passed up gold bracelets and pins and rings, until she came upon a golden necklace with a locket and ruby. " 'This is perfect.' "

And so it was—forever clasping the past to the present, the present to the past, it made prophecy come full circle.

Susie left the living room and returned with the gift given more than 100 years ago—the necklace of delicate, intertwining leaves holding the front half of a locket whose gem was missing.

"Mother wore it for her confirmation," she explained, "and every Sunday thereafter. One day she discovered it had disappeared from her neck. Four years later, a farmhand found it in the dirt—its locket broken. The back was gone, along with the ruby."

Engraved on the winds were Turi's words: "Remember me."

In October, when skeletal corn stalks rattled together, Mother and I returned to the church cemetery a third time.

The middle-aged secretary startled us by knowing Turi's name at once, as if the funeral had happened yesterday. She showed us on a faded file card that the grave was purchased for $50 in 1938. Though we spotted the exact location "FE 38" on the church map, and though we searched and searched, we couldn't find the headstone. When we returned to the office, it was locked.

As in life, Turi was neither here nor there. Her grave, appearing and disappearing like the necklace. Missing, like the ruby.

Half a locket can hold a whole mystery. There's something about suspense that won't let go—shadows in a photograph, a half-revealed face in a painting, the tension of not knowing who's behind the mask.

Yet I know where Turi is. Whenever wind rustles like taffeta skirts and night is as black as a cape, I remember.

Halloween

*T*he Halloween masquerade lingers longer than fall leaves, hangs on through the holidays, snoops around even in summer.

Oct. 31 may lie in the basket of discarded days, but Halloween hovers.

Once, after morning kindergarten, I rooted through a ball of knotted costumes, shaking out a cape here, unsnarling a mask there.

After sneaking out the back door, I knocked at the front.

"Why, hello there," said my mother, pleasantly surprised. "I have a girl just your age. She was here a minute ago."

Calling my name, she looked expectantly over her shoulder—so believably that I peered around her.

"Trick or treat," I dared.

"Halloween was a long time ago," she admonished, then softened: "Still, I'll give you some candy.

"But don't you go to any other house until it's really Halloween. And if you see my little girl, tell her the same thing."

A few minutes later I bounded into the kitchen, where she told me all about her visitor.

Imagine, she said, going trick or treating at a time other than Halloween. Hadn't the girl's mother taught her better manners?

I knew, even at age 5, that she knew, and I sensed that she knew that I knew. Still, we played our parts.

A generation earlier, when Mother was a young girl, she would wait for her Grandmother Julia to return from town with groceries.

"My dad would offer to take her in the car to Edgerton," she said, "but to the end Grandmother insisted on hitching up the horse to her buggy and driving the 9 miles each way for supplies. What she brought home always seemed more exciting than our shopping."

My mother would look for the buggy to reappear at the four corners and turn right on the East Koshkonong road. Then she'd spurt from her farm down to her grandmother's, where she watched her unhitch and feed the horse, and put away the buggy.

"It seemed like forever," Mom recalled. "Grandmother knew I wanted a store-bought treat, and I knew it, but neither of us would mention it. I'd finally be allowed to help her into the house with the bags, and I could smell the bananas and cookies and doughnuts.

"Then she took off her hat and put it in a hatbox, took off her black coat and hung it in her closet; all the while she would look at me and smile. At last, when we were cozy and seated in her kitchen, she would give me my treat."

From time to time, we find ourselves in such charades but pretend otherwise. Or, sometimes, we don't know any better.

Recently, realizing that my daughter wouldn't be at her apartment, I sent a box of her clothes to her workplace.

She had to attend a function on her way home, and she takes the subway, so she decided she'd leave the package behind. Still, she wanted to wear one of her suits the next day and tried folding it into her briefcase.

"There was no way that suit was going to fit inside my briefcase," she told me, "but there I was, stuffing it in. It reminded me of when I was 5 and tried to put my black-cat costume inside the doll suitcase I used for my crayon box. I felt, if I just pushed hard enough, I could do it. Amazing that I'm still doing the same thing."

Suddenly, I remembered the scene: my daughter on her knees in a friend's front hall, and the crayon box flung open, as she tried maneuvering the furry costume and tail. Waiting to take her home, I wondered when she would give up.

Recalling the moment, I was struck: Sometimes we force ourselves into a box that doesn't suit us. Or we keep wearing a part we've outgrown.

If only we could follow the path of least resistance. If only we could slough off old roles as easily as a child her costume, instead of hanging onto a person, a place or a job that no longer fits.

The Halloween masquerade is past? It merely hides in our different disguises.

Now that's scary.

Family Songs

$\mathcal{N}$ow and then, when my parents would briefly turn their eyes from the road to look at each other, I'd catch their profile.

I'd get a rare glimpse of them more as a couple than as my parents.

Knowing we had a place to go and, more important, a home to which we would return, I couldn't help feeling thankful.

Do any families yet drive over the river and through the woods to Grandmother's house?

Do any remember leaving home with the pies placed in a basket, side dishes packed in a cooler, suitcases jammed into the trunk?

If so, they might want to sing.

A jetliner doesn't exactly encourage travelers to break into song, even when they're caught between the moon and New York City.

In a darkened car, the rising orb alongside, I couldn't help joining in when Dad began, "Shine on, shine on harvest moon up in the sky."

Almost as much as Thanksgiving itself, the long road trip represents a part of American culture.

Heritage rolls along on a song, from one generation to the next. Eras come and go, "yet the melody lingers on."

"And you'll always know your neighbor, you'll always know your pal, if you've ever navigated on the Erie Canal."

I liked hearing our voices blend during *Tenting Tonight*.

So might have Union and Confederate soldiers whenever their voices united above campsites: "Many are the hearts that are weary tonight, wishing for the war to cease."

Growing up, I didn't know that *The Blue-Tail Fly*, with its abolitionist leaning, was favored by President Lincoln. (He asked that it be performed at the ceremony where he gave the Gettysburg Address.)

And none of us kids knew that Katharine Lee Bates, an American poet, wrote the words to *America, the Beautiful* in 1893 after seeing the view from Pikes Peak. Yet we saw her "spacious skies" and "purple mountain majesties," her "fruited plain" and "amber waves of grain," merely by singing of them.

Even the youngest chimed in on *Yankee Doodle*, a Revolutionary War tune, originally called *The Lexington March*, that energized militias at battles such as Lexington and Bunker Hill—and energized us, too, on the endless ride.

Sometimes the three in the front seat took turns singing with the three in back, trading among *Clementine*; *Hello, Ma Baby*; *Home on the Range*; *I Want a Girl (Just Like the Girl That Married Dear Old Dad)*; *On Top of Old Smoky*; and even *Jingle Bells*.

One by one, we'd begin to tire and look out the windows.

Here and there, like falling stars, lights punched holes in lonely farmhouses.

Images flashed by of a barn, a windmill, a three-store town.

Hoping to revive us, a single voice, feeling alone despite our crowded car, might hum *Beautiful Dreamer*. Unknown to us, days before his death, Stephen Collins Foster had written the song in the poverty ward of Bellevue Hospital in New York.

A familiar tune gives a sense of place to the outward-bound. And so it does to a country about to experience a turn-of-the-century Thanksgiving.

We Gather Together will always remind us not only of our Thanksgivings but of the first celebration in the New World.

Whenever we remember, even though the song was based on a Dutch hymn from the early 17th century and wasn't translated into English until 1894, we picture grateful Pilgrims at their first harvest.

With a mix of melody and memory, songs stitch us together, passing around American history as much as servings of turkey and cranberries.

Sometimes, asleep in the back seat, I'd awaken to hear my parents softly, so softly, singing in the front.

Mother would harmonize with Dad (just as she did in child-rearing) as they sang, "Let me call you sweetheart, I'm in love with you."

Parents' First Christmas

*T*he glow from Christmases past lights the path to the present.

My parents' reminiscences are as real to me as when I used to sit on the staircase, watching Mom trim the banister with boxwood and bows. I feel as if I, too, "recall" the evening angelus ringing over the fields on Christmas Eve, the sleigh rides warmed with buffalo robes, the candles burning on trees.

This year, as if unpacking a treasured ornament, I hold the memory of their first married Christmas. I see in the reflection snow on the sills and frost on the windows, and a frail, young man asleep on the sofa. Not far from the front door, Lake Michigan slams the shoreline during the record-breaking winter of 1935-36.

Two months before, driving north of town, the newlyweds found fall's foliage brilliant. How romantic, they thought, to rent a small house overlooking the water. "House" was too kind a word: Built to accept breezes, not blasts, "summer cottage" was a better name. Still, the faulty furnace and poor insulation were far from their minds on the autumn day they signed a year's lease. They had their love, after all, to keep them warm.

Steeped in the Depression, they were soon steeped in cold and snow.

Mother wore a snowsuit indoors, huddling by the registers. Some nights she threw a rug on the bed for extra comfort.

When roads became impassable, my father, a fledgling physician, slept on the examining table at his office.

"If he did get home, but had to make a house call during the night, he'd have to shovel his way to the road," she later recalled. "There were buses, but even they couldn't operate sometimes because of the severe weather."

Yet she knew that life could get worse.

And it did.

The pace eventually wore down her 28-year-old husband. He became ill, running a temperature and experiencing pain that doctors from Milwaukee to Chicago were at a loss to diagnose. Weeks and perhaps a month passed before time and "the dear sisters" allowed him to hope he would go home from the hospital on Christmas Eve.

Earlier in the day, his grateful, 21-year-old bride scurried about — first visiting a store to buy him a bathrobe. Strapped for cash, she summoned up what scant confidence she had and asked whether she could charge the robe, then pay for it, month by month, out of her grocery money:

"Please, please, send the bill to me and not to my husband," she pleaded.

The store owner, bemused or busy, told her not to worry. And so she was off, gift in hand, bells ringing in her heart, to search for a small Christmas tree. Had she realized that it would become the first of 57 trees that they would share through the decades, she might not have worried so about his health. All she knew was that they were lucky to celebrate at all.

After putting up the tree, she placed her wrapped gift beneath it and brought her husband home.

He could barely open the surprise and put it on before he fell asleep that night on the davenport.

The first of the month, to her everlasting embarrassment, Dad received a bill for the bathrobe. The laughs it gave him far outlived the garment. Best of all, each time he wrapped himself in the memory, he was warmed by her love.

Wrapped With Care

*M*y father-in-law used to send an annual package to each of his children.

From "a wonderful but actually poor family," he recalled often lacking a dime for the streetcar.

That helped explain his "Christmas care packages, which hopefully contain items you will find useful," he said.

More than the stamps, rolls of quarters or other items, the care he put into the boxes is what touches me today.

His daughter Ann waited almost six hours last month to have Chris Van Allsburg autograph her grandson's copy of *The Polar Express.* When she neared the front of the line, she gave Kyle an early Christmas present by calling him on her cell phone so he could "meet" the author.

Such ambassadors of the season are the ones we remember through the decades, their acts still shining with each December.

And so I remember my mother.

Because of her, peace permeated the house: She played carols on the piano, burned bayberry candles in the dining room and hung mistletoe in the front hall.

About the only thing she couldn't do was speed up time. Advent was a month of waiting—to open the next window on the Advent calendar or bake cookies or decorate the tree.

More than anything else, though, it was a period of waiting to visit Santa Claus—and, even before, to be taken shopping.

Not much taller than the counter, my purse clutched in my hand, I waited to be waited upon, with Mother—my translator—at my side.

Inside the store, beyond the outdoors as black as a cave, hung twinkling lights, illuminated globes and, nearest to the ceiling, pneumatic tubes whisking cash and paperwork to the business office and returning change and receipts.

Adding to the happy hum, a speaker shared *We Wish You a Merry Christmas*.

"Let's see," I thought: "an angora collar for my sister, a handkerchief for my dad, an angel for my aunt."

The angel, I realized later, was Mom, who made me feel unhurried when I took forever to choose something.

Before each trip, she showed care with a list of chores for me: I could earn the money—and self-respect—when gifts made by hand would no longer do.

I wanted to be like my sisters and parents, offering store-bought presents prettily wrapped.

How did she accommodate me, what with three other children all receiving, in turn, the same undivided attention—not to mention a busy husband and other demands of the holidays? Yet I never noticed any impatient shifting from foot to foot, any sighing or yawning.

She offered merely a respectful "Where would you like to go next?" or "Whom do you have left on your list?"

She didn't do any shopping herself, although she must have had some to do.

My shopping became the most important task in the world.

How could she have known she was giving me a lasting present, one that wouldn't melt like the snow?

Years later, even before she developed Alzheimer's, she may have forgotten about such an experience in the bustle of other holidays, but how could I?

I still see the swaying candy canes decorating the streets and hear the Salvation Army bells.

Although my bills are all spent, she lets me donate some of hers—rounding out my feeling of good will.

My presents have yet to be hidden or handed out on Christmas morning, their effect still waiting to be determined.

All is full of hope and promise.

From boxwood boughs tied on the banister to, most of all, time given to a child, the merriest Christmases come wrapped with care.

And, anything but fragile, they never break. Instead, they endure forever.

A Happy Christmas

Christmas couldn't always be left up to parents—or even Santa Claus.

Sometimes an 8-year-old boy had to take matters into his own hands, especially when what he wanted most was a Dick Tracy toy.

My brother, Chris, kept a No. 1 rule in mind: Begin to wear down the opposition in early December.

"A gun that shoots plastic bullets? Why, that's no plaything," my father announced at breakfast. "It could put an eye out."

The toy didn't become safer as the month gained momentum—only more familiar. Thanks to my brother, it showed up more often in family conversation than the names of relatives.

Did the rest of us know, for instance, that it came with a shoulder holster? Did we know that it came with a Dick Tracy wallet and badge?

Rule No. 2: To increase the chances of receiving your heart's desire, add more items to your "wish" list.

By constantly updating and padding his gift suggestions, Chris hoped that our overwhelmed parents would remember only one item—the one that mattered—when they stood, confused, in the toy store.

Rule No. 3? My brother was about to teach us.

In his day, instead of having to be driven to a faraway mall, all that Chris had to do was walk several blocks to the toy store.

Parting with his own hard-earned money was difficult. Even more so was getting the Dick Tracy toy and all its glorious trappings through the back door without being detected.

Luck was on his side: Chris entered unnoticed and crept down to the basement.

Next, as luck further had it, a family tradition came to his rescue.

Each December, to protect anyone who might be wrapping presents in the recreation room, anyone else had to ask at the top of the basement steps, "Is it OK to come down?"

"No," came a squeaky response to my inquiry that day. "I'm wrapping a present."

My brother was speaking the truth.

"The package took a long time to wrap," Chris recently recalled, four decades later, "because I had to make it look as if an adult had done it. I tried making my handwriting look old, too, when I signed the card 'To Chris / From Santa.' "

Who knows when he slipped his prized possession under the Christmas tree, beneath the other presents? It remained hidden, though, until something occurred that he hadn't expected.

Each Christmas Eve, the children were allowed to open one gift apiece.

"Look, Chris already has one from Santa," one of us said as the others were sifting through the pile, trying to decide what to open.

"From Santa? How could that be? Santa doesn't leave presents until later tonight," another said—in case our brother still believed.

Chris stayed cool: Better to wait until morning, he cautioned himself, and open his gift amid the confusion.

And so, early on Christmas Day, during a tumultuous moment of merrymaking, his voice suddenly rose above the racket.

"Wow—thanks, Santa!" he shouted as he strapped on the holster.

My mother shot an accusatory glance at my father.

"Don't look at me," he seemed to say, returning a similar look.

Both parents then studied their three daughters, who shrugged their shoulders.

That left only Santa.

We marveled at the mystery of Christmas—all of us, that is, except Dad, whose irritation rose.

"Never aim that toy at someone," I heard him scold above the din as my brother set us—and the season—in his sight.

That night, a tired but happy "Santa" clasped under his pillow the Dick Tracy holster set, badge and wallet.

He had plenty of years left to learn that giving is better than receiving.

Storybook Dolls

*F*ifty-five isn't nearly as sobering as 56—the numeral "6" underscoring that the leap to 60 is that much closer.

Only yesterday I was in my late 40s, still fooling myself that life was infinite.

Then, the future was mine to plan; now, the future is making plans for me.

What happened?

Where did she go—the person who ran off with my time?

Who is the new acquaintance inhabiting my old skin? Perhaps each of us is merely a series of strangers.

Why does each new me disappear just as I get to know her?

Half a century ago, I could say exactly what I wanted for my birthday. I never thought to wish for a long and healthy life or parents who live forever or lasting world peace.

Instead, when I was 6, I pined for a Storybook Doll.

Actually, I wanted every single one in the Nancy Ann Storybook Doll display at Barden's Department Store: Little Betty Blue, Polly Put the Kettle On, Daffle Down Dilly and One, Two Button My Shoe—all of them and more.

My nose to the case in the girls' section on the second floor, I prayed that Mother would get lost in the nearby notions department. I could never tire of gazing at the 5 1/2-inch beauties, I told myself.

If my parents really loved me, why wouldn't they want to give me all those polka-dot boxes, each one holding a diminutive doll in a dainty outfit?

Ginny Vincent seemed to have half the collection lined up on her bedroom shelves.

If I owned that many dolls, I thought, I'd never want for anything else. I promised myself that, when I grew up, I'd go back to Barden's and buy every one—even the display case, lights and all.

In the era before Barbie, cars had more flat tires and the milk was delivered by a horse-drawn wagon. Ladies wore hats, as did well-dressed gentlemen, while girls covered their heads with babushkas on a cold March day.

Our school desks still bore the holes for long-forgotten ink bottles, while our classrooms bore the holes of missing students.

Though young, we knew about polio and tuberculosis and an iron lung.

Our homes sometimes displayed "Quarantine" signs in the windows and received visiting nurses.

When we dreamed about Storybook Dolls, though, we escaped that world of terror. When we received one of the dolls, we were transported.

Yet, after the ribbon and wrapping paper were off and the lid was removed, after we and our birthday guests had oohed and aahed, we faced a conflict: whether to leave the cellophane seal intact.

I could forever preserve my porcelain doll like a sleeping Snow White. Still, in the end, after listening to the urgings of my friends and my inner self, I'd rip off the transparent covering and seize my new toy.

My hands couldn't resist touching her bisque face, moving her jointed arms, playing with her lovely hair—and putting her in a pocket.

My travels left her scruffy and worse for wear—flowers fallen from her hair, a wrinkled dress—but, oh, the adventures we had.

Some 50 years later, the memory of a Storybook Doll still hovers: It reminds me that having the experiences, even the mistakes, is better than remaining intact, never taking risks.

Did I ever receive all the dolls? No, only a few.

Today, even if I wanted to keep my childhood promise and collect them in one fell swoop, I couldn't find them to buy.

Other dolls are sold, of course, but not those dolls—all new and lined up in a case at Barden's. In fact, the store no longer exists.

Nor does the girl who used to dream there.

Gifts of Insight

*W*e enter the world unable to talk or walk—or wrap a present.

And we don't always conquer the third.

The parental gift-wrapping service was one I took for granted during an era when birthday parties reigned—until the day my mother suddenly relinquished the role.

"But, Mom, I'm already late," I wailed. "Besides, I don't know how."

"Then it's time you learned," she said, "because I won't always be around to do things for you."

Such a response was out of character for a "Why, sure" and "Certainly, dear" mother who seemed as consistent as a clock.

She talked me through the task the first time.

For the next occasion, however, I had to fly solo.

Racing home from elementary school before a birthday party, I found myself staring into a drawer holding only holiday wrap.

Digging deeper, I unearthed a handmade Christmas card showing a painted white angel on blue construction paper.

I could turn the card inside out, allowing only the plain blue to show, I thought—although I couldn't find any tape.

So I simply folded the paper around the gift, a diary, and secured it with a ribbon.

Arriving late to the party, I buried my gift under a pyramid of presents.

Then, at the appointed moment, I hunkered down with the other children in front of the birthday girl, who sat on the sofa.

Her mother, starting at the top of the pile, plucked one present after another.

As luck had it, the first time that my mother hadn't played a part in the wrapping, other moms had gone "all out."

The birthday girl turned each unopened gift this way and that, heightening the effect.

The rest of us oohed and aahed as if watching a fireworks display.

One mother had created a doll on the front of a large box wrapped in plain paper, using yarn for the hair and fabric for the dress, and coloring the face, arms and legs. On the other side, she had even made the back of the doll.

Another one had secured sugar cubes to pink streamers cascading from a bow: "To a Sweet Birthday Girl."

And still another had wrapped a large nest of boxes, one inside the other—until the smallest held a surprise.

Mine was the final gift to be opened.

The room fell silent, as if the best had been saved for last. Then a giggle erupted—and another and another.

As the ribbon was untied, the angel was revealed.

"It's not Christmas," someone whispered.

"Let's sing carols," someone else mocked.

"Angels aren't only at Christmas; they're here all year," said the mother, an angel herself for trying to rescue me.

Late in her life, Mom unwittingly tied up some loose ends.

She began talking about her older sister.

"Florence was so sweet, so dear to me," she said. "We were only a year apart and as close as two sisters could be.

"But one day she said I needed to be more self-reliant, not forever asking her what to do and how to do it, because she wouldn't always be around. Her tone was so different that it hurt, although what she said was probably true."

And, down a long corridor of years, I saw my clumsy fingers struggling to wrap a present.

Gifts of insight, unadorned, appear out of nowhere.

Easter

$\mathcal{M}$y father always went to church, but he didn't like going on Easter Sunday any more than he did on Christmas.

Every time the lost sheep were berated for attending only on such occasions, his aversion grew stronger.

"No wonder we won't see those folks again until December," he'd say to Mother on the way home, with the children in the back seat. "It'll take that long for their ears to cool off before they show up for another tongue-lashing."

The minister, Dad theorized, must have anticipated the two holy days just so he could deliver his tirade.

"If he were more interested in saving souls instead of scolding them, there'd be standing room only on most Sundays," my father continued. "Why send them away feeling worse than when they came? Why not give them hope?"

I always enjoyed the post-sermon more than the preacher's lesson.

Whether it was the pastor or the coffee served afterward, something got Dad going: He didn't drive home so much as be propelled by the fuel of his monologues.

One thought I took away from his sermonizing as I sat in my back-seat "pew" was his belief in salvation instead of damnation.

Through the car window, I needed only to look out on the sprays of forsythia, the stir of crocuses and daffodils, and the leafy spires of tulips to know that something good was happening.

Such sights, then and now, are offered as gifts—deserved or not—year after year: They alone make us want to turn over a new leaf or start down a fresh path.

Someone—or something—thinks enough of us to provide the second chance called "spring."

And who doesn't pay homage to spring? We explore the outdoors, and arrange bouquets inside our homes, while celebrating the riotous shades of green, yellow, pink, purple and blue.

Filled with the renewal of the season, we summon the courage to quit a dreaded job or propose marriage to a loved one.

Spring fills us with the possibility that we see shimmering on the next hill.

During my childhood, the Easter baskets awaited after dinner.

My catch one year still looms above all others, from the time Easter fell on my birthday: A cardboard and cellophane box held the largest chocolate, cream-filled egg I'd ever seen.

Not only its size made it noteworthy: The candy bore the letters of my name written in white frosting.

Growing up with siblings, one struggles to stand out.

The egg gave me hope, then, regarding my uniqueness—because someone had taken the time to recognize it.

And what was Dad trying to convey so many years ago on the drive home from church? That everyone is special and deserving of another chance.

Perhaps hope is what Easter, what spring, promises most of all.

Spring Break

*B*efore jets or superhighways, a slower-paced trip in the family car reigned.

During many a spring break, my father relied on the automobile to show his children not only our country but its history.

"By the rude bridge that arched the flood, / Their flag to April's breeze unfurled, / Here once the embattled farmers stood / And fired the shot heard round the world."

In a distant April, we stood on the same Massachusetts soil when Dad—thanks to a former teacher—recited Ralph Waldo Emerson's *Concord Hymn*.

Yet, most of all, I remember our trips South—when we left weary Wisconsin, still trapped in the throes of ice and snow, and dived into spring.

We would make our escape in early-morning darkness. Sometimes we'd drive only a block, then stop at Mrs. Schulte's for breakfast so Mom wouldn't have to clean up afterward.

Before the dawn of fast-food restaurants, friends did such favors for one another—making something, say, for the picnic basket packed in the trunk.

Our car, therefore, became our movable house, the only tangible link between the unknown and all we knew of home.

Like Aslan, the regal beast in *The Lion, the Witch and the Wardrobe*, it sped along, freeing us from the wintry spell of the White Witch.

As Wisconsin faded away, towns such as Cairo, Ill., and Marion, Ohio, took shape.

Our shouts announced the first sightings of green grass and dancing daffodils. When we reached Kentucky and Tennessee, our eyes rested upon hills fringed in green and dotted with dogwoods and redbuds.

Given the lack of drive-through windows, we'd stop at markets for cold cuts and milk, and absorb the atmosphere. Farther along the highway, we'd find a roadside table for a picnic lunch and, at day's end, a cafe or diner. Later, in that era before air conditioning, we'd open a window in a motel cabin and welcome the fragrant night.

My first trip South, 50 years ago, was made so that my oldest sister could visit the horse farms of Kentucky.

Before the growth of tourism, one could drive up to Calumet Farm and observe a morning workout on the track.

Gone are such opportunities, but so, for the most part, are the flat tires—and the mule-drawn plows and spittoons.

Gone, most fortunately, is what I discovered at a filling station when I noticed the signs—"Whites Only," "Colored Only"—above drinking fountains and bathrooms.

"What do they mean?" I asked and learned about the ugliness of segregation before reading about it in textbooks.

As he drove, Dad often told stories of the Civil War, making it come alive. At Shiloh in Tennessee, however, I sensed only death: All that remained from the battle of April 1862 were common graves holding the bodies of more than 10,000 Union and 10,000 Confederate soldiers.

The war seemed centuries away, but it had ended only fourscore and seven years earlier.

Throughout the journey, our family of six sang old camp songs. We dubbed ourselves "the happy cottagers." We took turns wearing a straw hat—for whatever "honor" I have long since forgotten.

We four children quarreled, too—and we were asked to play the silent game, to appreciate our siblings. In such cramped quarters, we had to get along: Each of us needed a shoulder on which to doze.

We were inspired by the nation's history, and, as we traveled, we made family history.

Eventually, as the trip neared its end, spring slipped away again. The White Witch returned, carrying cold rain, leafless trees and despair.

Not until weeks later—with a whiff of apple blossoms in the air—did we roller-skate in the driveway. We arrived at our second spring, a return to real life.

The image comes to mind each Easter—and whenever the heart blooms again.

Standing Up for a Parent

$\mathcal{A}$s adulthood advances under the weight of worry, parents easily forget the burdens children carry—the frustration of trying to put on boots, wanting to play with the big kids, seeking to protect parents.

My son, then a 4-year-old, one day heard me anguish over the willy-nilly way the city had planted new trees in our Toledo subdivision. Holes had been dug at intervals along the boulevard, without a thought to existing landscaping. In our yard, for instance, a tree ended up standing right in front of another.

A day or two later, a frantic neighbor called to say my son was chopping down a tree in her front yard.

Impossible, I assured her. Then I rushed outside.

Horrified, I saw him attacking a sapling. Two trees in our yard, I later discovered, already had gash marks.

"Why would you do such a thing?" I demanded.

"You didn't like them," he said, between sobs. "I wanted you to be happy."

My young knight had gone out into the world to slay dragons. Instead, he had to apologize to all around.

Once, when I was a child, a neighbor looking out her window might have witnessed my own attempt to protect a parent. It all began innocently enough when Miss Schultz announced that our class would visit Hawaii.

"Not a real trip," she emphasized, and we fourth-graders groaned.

Sitting at our desks, beneath a flag of 48 stars, we listened to our teacher explain that Hawaii wanted to become a state.

"We'll have a luau at the end of our unit," Miss Schultz announced. "We'll even invite Mr. Mauer, the superintendent."

I gave my mother the teacher's note requesting a food donation.

"We're going to shove all our desks out of the way and sit on the floor like at a real luau," I told her breathlessly, adding that Mr. Mauer, the superintendent, whoever he was, might be there.

"How special," she said, after my buildup. "I'll make that lime Jell-O recipe. It'll look tropical and pretty."

My heart sank halfway to Hawaii. I didn't know how to tell her that I didn't like the shredded carrots lurking inside; that, although the Jell-O looked inviting, I didn't think it tasted sweet; and that, worst of all, I didn't prefer the mayonnaise dressing to whipped cream.

The day of our luau finally arrived. As proudly as I could, I carried into the classroom my mother's prized green-Jell-O concoction in its white enamel mold.

Two tables beneath a row of windows held rice, fruit, salads, brownies, cupcakes and cookies. Students kept arriving with more food, shoving my mom's Jell-O farther to the side.

Miss Schultz didn't notice. All she worried about was the superintendent: Would Mr. Mauer really attend? None of us cared much one way or the other, except that we weren't allowed to "luau" until he did. She tried preparing us—or herself?—that he might not make it. He might be too busy, she said, to visit one classroom out of all the classrooms in the district.

Suddenly, a man filled the doorway. Miss Schultz gave a nervous laugh, then introduced the superintendent and encouraged him to help himself to the buffet. Maybe he'd try some of my mother's salad, and I could tell her.

He passed it by. So did everyone else.

After the luau—despite our program and speeches—Hawaii still wasn't in the union and my mother's Jell-O still wasn't touched.

Inching home, I carried the full container. She'd made a salad, I thought, and not one person, not even her daughter, had eaten any.

What if—and I looked about to see if anyone was watching—I disposed of the evidence by dumping it in some bushes?

"Here," I said, rushing through the back door and handing my mother the empty mold. "Yours was the best."

Like mother, like son—like every child.

Glory

*I*f I wanted to go inside the horse trailer, why didn't Glory, my sister's horse?

I was reminded of the childhood scene during this year's Kentucky Derby when a Thoroughbred balked at entering the starting gate. Instead of trying to "hand the horse in"—with two men locking wrists behind the hocks—why didn't they use the trick that Walt Hannan taught us more than 40 years ago?

The Hannan clan, with a love of horses running through their lifelines, came from Ireland in 1830, before my childhood town was a city, before Wisconsin was a state.

When we met descendants Walt and Bill Hannan in the late 1940s, the brothers, retired farmers, had retired from harness racing. A track beyond the barn, and their tarnished trophies in the tack room, testified to former fame.

Now they rented the empty stalls, boarding horses such as Glory.

Good-natured, they enjoyed teasing others—especially my father, who, in his early 40s, was just learning to ride. Once, they convinced him that Glory's hay belly was a pregnancy.

"Well, Doc," they ribbed my worried dad, "looks like you'll be boarding two before long."

Not until he took his stethoscope into the stall to hear the extra heartbeat did they double up with laughter and confess.

Early one Saturday we arrived at the farm, our old Packard pulling a rented trailer. While Karen used a currycomb to ready Glory for her first horse show, my parents talked to Mary Hannan, Walt's wife.

Left alone, I explored the empty van. Trotting up and down its lowered ramp, eating imaginary oats in the trough, I wished I were tall enough to look out the round windows on each side. Glory, 16 hands high, would soon see the world pass by.

I'd always wanted our car to pull a trailer—but one with beds and a place to cook while on a trip. My parents had said no.

Glory was lucky to have the chance.

"Let's get the show on the road," Dad called out to Karen, who was leading her horse from the barn.

Years later, she wrote: "The frustration of heading one sullen mare into the narrow trailer is no less than rounding up hundreds on the open range, in the thick dust, the thundering hooves."

Because unloading Glory had gone smoothly, Dad and Karen assumed that loading her would be just as easy.

That was before they learned about the art of loading a horse. That was before they discovered that each trainer has developed a technique. That was before Glory's ears flattened backward and her forelegs—like a newborn foal's—splayed sideways to resist the ramp.

Then, churning back, back, back, she suddenly reared up and pawed the air, neighing in fear. Again and again the scene repeated itself as I wrapped my arms around my mother's waist, half hiding my face.

Bill rushed up from the field as Walt flew around the side of the farmhouse. In slow tones that Glory understood, they calmed her before Walt disappeared into the tack room to get a blanket.

Approaching her again, Walt slipped the cloth over her eyes. Blindfolded, she quietly followed his lead into the van.

After all these years, like the sound of the tailgate thundering shut, it strikes me: Glory's horse sense makes sense.

The reason we can climb the ramp of time is that our sight is shrouded.

Why would anyone choose to enter tomorrow's door with perfect vision? To see not only coming triumphs but failures, even disasters? Not only births but deaths, even our own?

Staring the future in the face, who wouldn't flail like Glory?

Had Charles Lindbergh known that his fame would lead to the kidnapping and death of his firstborn son, would he have tried a solo flight across the Atlantic? Had John F. Kennedy foreseen Dallas, would he have sought the presidency?

Better to know some things, but not all, so we can still have hope.

Without hope, days turn like a merry-go-round instead of running free like the horse.

Mrs. McQuestion

"*W*here do your find your strength?" is what I wanted to ask Mrs. McQuestion over lunch that day.

"A strength that fills your slender body with a powerful contralto rising to the church's rafters? A strength that saw you through the death of a young son, then a husband, and, finally, your adult son without your becoming broken and bitter?"

What I asked was, "How did you and Mr. McQuestion meet?"

She put down her fork and said, "That's a long story." Listening, I understood—21 years to be exact. And, I discovered, quite by accident, where strength began.

I had known my parents' old friends, Everetta and Henry McQuestion, all my life—as well as any of us "know" our parents' friends when we're absorbed in growing up.

Mr. McQuestion, jolly as Santa, had a strong handshake. Mrs. McQuestion, a wisp of a woman, sang each Sunday in the Lutheran choir while her husband and children attended Roman Catholic Mass. Now a widow, she still lived in the same white house on a corner in Kenosha, Wis.

"In 1915," she began, "when Henry was only 17 years old, he quit his job at Nash Motors and literally rode the rails out West—lying above the tracks and beneath the box cars. When a train came to a stop, he'd stay overnight in the nearby jungles where the hobos camped.

"In North Dakota, the railroad police caught him. With one foot on the engine and one foot on the tender car, he was forced to stoke the engine's coal-burning furnace—shoveling his way to Columbus, Mont., and freedom.

"Back then it was only a two-street town—a livery stable, saloon, barbershop. Henry—dusty and dirty—made his way down the street when a tall Dutchman approached and offered to buy him a bath, a haircut and a shave. Later, over supper, he offered him a job: 'I've got a ranch that needs a lot of fencing.'

"Henry followed the stranger 12 miles out of town to his home. The first time he entered the ranch house, he saw a baby girl asleep in a wash basket. That Dutchman was my father," said Mrs. McQuestion. "And. . . ."

"The baby in the basket was you?" I blurted out.

"Yes," she smiled. "I was a few months old and we'd just moved into the frame house my father had built with help from neighboring ranchers. Until then we'd lived in a drafty homesteader's shack where on the ceiling he'd attached two pulleys, tying a rope to each of my basket's handles. Every night, for the first month of my life, he'd pull me in my basket up to the rafters because it was warmer there."

Under its own ceiling of big sky and mountains, the ranch spread— from 160 acres to 3,000, which Henry, hired hand and cowboy, helped tame.

"I adored him," she recalled, "and followed him everywhere—out to the barn, out to the fields."

Once, when she was 3, "Henry was driving a team of horses, and, of course, I was right up there with him. When he turned to fix a loose tarp, the horses took off, crashing toward the granary. Rearing up, they stood the wagon on end. It threw Henry out and me . . . and I broke my leg."

It didn't hurt half as much as when several years later her childhood hero returned to his hometown—where he married and entered business. Eventually her father gave up ranching and settled his family in Springfield, Ohio.

"My parents and Henry remained close friends and always corresponded." When he divorced, the stage was set. During one of his visits to her family, something magical happened—he and Everetta fell in love. She was 21.

"Long after we were married," she said, finishing her story, "Judge

Drury would tease us at parties—'Henry went all the way to Montana to pick out his wife from the cradle.'"

By lunch's end, I saw Everetta McQuestion as if for the first time—as if I stood atop the Beartooth Mountains, with a view reaching toward the horizon. Or at the place where the headwaters plummet, falling into focus.

Daughter of homesteaders, raised among looping ropes and rivers, she had learned her lessons from the land. She knew of fruition and want, of being lost in a blizzard and surviving the night in a haystack, of life and death. And in her basket of infancy, she found a metaphor for life—to rise above.

That's what made her strong, I decided: the imprint of being pulled skyward.

Author's note: Mrs. McQuestion died Aug. 9, 1998, at the home of her sole surviving child, Marilyn M. Pearson, and her husband, Dr. Thomas Pearson, in Helena, Mont.

Recently the daughter shed new light on her mother:
"I can hear my mother's voice and see her smile as she is relating this memory to you. She shared it with me frequently and I share my parents' love story with my friends.

"Did you know that while my mother practiced her Lutheran faith, sang in the choir, as well as was a soloist for the church, she was also the cantor for the Jewish temple?

"Her Friday evenings were spent singing at the Beth Hillel Temple, and her Sundays were filled with her going to Grace Lutheran Church and then coming home and attending St. Mark's Catholic Church with us as a family. Her faith and her strong family commitment, roots and experiences gave her the resilience to survive losses many others couldn't."

A Taste of Summer

Long ago, in the midst of a breathless summer day, we'd hear the ring-ring of a bicycle bell.

Pedaling a huge tricycle with a white freezer in front, the white-suited Sammy Man would wind his way through our leafy neighborhood.

We summer-stranded children couldn't help rejoicing: Our delivery in the form of chocolate-covered ice-cream bars lay close. Scrambling into our houses, we'd clamor for coins until our beleaguered mothers came up with change.

During World War I, British soldiers called their American counterparts "Sammy." Afterward, in Wisconsin, the veterans who sold ice-cream bars became known as "Sammy Men."

In my youth, after World War II, the name still stuck for such vendors.

Knowing nothing of the derivation, we wondered from where our bandylegged bicyclist had come. And where did he go when he rode away?

He appeared and disappeared at will, like fate, as he navigated the circumference of our childhood.

We never knew on what day he would arrive or at what hour—sometimes, before lunch; other times, in the afternoon or even after supper.

Worse than having "to go to bed by day," as Robert Louis Stevenson wrote, and "hear the grown-up people's feet / Still going past me in the street" was hearing the ring-ring of the bell after my parents had tucked me in for the night.

Because we lived where town met country, where the wood grew as wild as our green selves, the Sammy Man rarely ventured our way.

Like a mirage rising from the street, he'd suddenly show up.

The magic multiplied as we raced toward him, watching him slide off his seat to open the lid of his freezer.

Like a dragon guarding the frozen treats within, the treasure chest puffed plumes of smoke. Its arctic tongue licked our faces as we enjoyed the blast.

We gladly gave up our pennies for the sweet slice of summer that only the young know how to buy.

Eventually, my childhood was traded for that of my children—and the bike and its bell were replaced by a truck and its tune.

Waiting for the ice-cream van, my daughter recalls, she would meet a friend in the dead end, where they'd pop tar bubbles with their Keds.

Now and then, "a faint melody" would send them "spinning toward our piggy banks. . . . Invariably, Lesli and I would return with our money to a barren curb—duped yet again by Mrs. Claxton's clattering wind chimes.

"There was just one thing we'd spend our 35 cents on: the raspberry screwball—a plastic, funnel-shaped cup with raspberry sherbet on the top and a gum ball at its tip."

Once too small to leave the curb, my son had to let the truck come to him.

He would hear "the tinny music, faintly at first—so faintly that you weren't sure if you actually heard it or if you were just imagining."

When his grandmother recognized a melody, repeating some of the words, he thought of "kids in antique clothing and a pier with a carousel."

Don't we all, each in our own time, buy a taste of summer? And, instead of melting, it lasts forever.

Dog Days

"We're bored," we chorused in the depths of summer.

I can still hear our whine, winding its way through childhood. Oh, how the days dragged on in a deadening routine. We could hardly move in the hazy heat, let alone make our minds leap at an idea.

By August, long before we learned about "the dog days of summer," we lingered in limbo: The old school year was centuries old; the new one crept toward us with glacier speed.

Our parents may have worried about the quickly passing season, but we kids didn't think about it. We were worn-out.

So my older sister Sonja, our friend Mary Ann Gallagher and I plopped down on Mrs. Gallagher's living-room davenport. Little did Mrs. Gallagher know we'd hung around the penny-candy jars at Allendale market until the exasperated owner snapped, "Don't you kids have anything better to do?"

"Why such sad faces?" she asked with extra cheeriness, calculated to deliver a bolt of energy.

"There's nothing to do," we moaned, raising our feet as she vacuumed beneath.

Our fathers went off to work; our mothers cleaned. All we had to do was play. And we couldn't even hold up our end of the bargain.

"What about a lemonade stand?" she proposed, offering to stir up a pitcherful.

"No," we groaned, staring straight ahead like three birds roosting on a fence.

Recalling previous stands, we weren't interested. All that endless waiting for a "customer" to walk by or a car to stop was followed by sweet humiliation: Our parents turned out to be our best (and only) clients.

If we had to wait, might as well wait right where we were—on the sofa.

"What about thinking up a play?" asked Mrs. Gallagher, coiling the cord of the vacuum around the handle.

"No," said my sister and I, our wrangling over the role of queen still fresh in memory. Worse yet was the scolding we and our other sister received for "hosting" a production with our friends in the basement: We invited neighbors and charged admission, yet failed to tell our parents.

Our mother, walking in on the scene, was so horrified that she served popcorn and refunded the money.

"How about another swim?" Mrs. Gallagher inquired.

Just that morning we'd trudged the few steamy blocks to Lake Michigan and returned, covered in sand, to our back doors. Under the sun, near the pier pilings, we'd played in the waves until, finally, we felt played out.

Even the idea of playing softball in the empty lot didn't move us. Nor did creating a campsite in the woods. Once, my oldest sister, at the suggestion of "the big kids," had buried her prized stash of marbles there. Days later, she dug and dug, only to realize her treasure had vanished.

"What about your trading cards?" Mrs. Gallagher suggested.

"I'll watch," I told the others, afraid I might be talked out of my favorite horses.

I loved the smell of my old cigar box that held my hoard, just as I loved the scent of mowed grass through the living room's window. A breeze stirred the curtain. I could have sat there forever, hearing the ticktock of the cuckoo clock.

I enjoyed how we could slip so comfortably into each other's houses, seeing how other people lived—such as Mrs. Gallagher, with her cooling rack outside the kitchen window for pies and pastries; her victory garden, where we pulled carrots; and her dining-room table, always with enough room for another chair.

In her infinite wisdom, she knew how to cure our ennui.

"I know," she said: "You could help me fold the laundry and iron the shirts and. . . . " Suddenly we sprinted across the street, out of reach.

Oh, what I wouldn't give to be so "bored" again.

Summer

Summer—always the same, yet different.

The last horse in the dairy's stable delivered milk up and down the block, the rhythmic clip-clop calling kids from play. Coos from homing pigeons drifted down, colliding with the clucking of hens in backyard pens.

Although the war had ended, victory gardens continued to grow.

Mrs. Gallagher across the street had one; when I asked for a cookie close to supper, she'd have me pull a carrot instead.

Outside her kitchen window, high on a metal rack, she cooled her pies, cakes, cinnamon muffins and bread.

The country encroached where the bus reached the end of the line: Pumps waited outside back doors with a handy tin cup; shy strawberries hid under vines; ladders lingered beneath cherry trees. Towering above farms, windmills gently turned and clouds plied the skies.

Summer—always the same, yet different.

Screens came out of storage. Windows closed only for rain. Every now and then, a breeze played hide-and-seek with the curtains.

Most of the time, fans moved from cool room to warm room or whirred from above like a fluttering of wings at the night window.

Woolens hibernated in mothballs. Cottons and white shoes—worn only from Memorial Day to Labor Day—made up the uniform of the day.

Grass, petal-soft underfoot, seemed greener.

Before the splash of pools, lakes invited swimmers: Brown Lake, Lake Geneva, Twin Lakes, Paddock Lake and, most of all, Lake Michigan with

Southport Beach, Eichelman Park, Alfred Park, Simmons Island—each, in their turn, aroused temptation.

The cove, a natural beach without benefit of lifeguard or supervision, most lured us. Prompted by an older sibling, we couldn't wait until we, too, could go there on our own.

The retreat—with seaweed clinging to old pilings, breakwater rocks creating secret caverns and the curved arm of sand—was just right for teenagers daring to break away.

The new transistor radios, competing with lapping waves and laughter, played alongside sunbathers on granite outcroppings.

Summer—always the same, yet different.

Telephones had their place; they didn't travel in cars or go on picnics. Nor did fast food—which didn't exist.

"Home-cooked," slow food—fried chicken, potato salad, coleslaw and cake—was slowly savored. And Cracker Jack always came with a surprise.

Push mowers never had trouble starting; only the operator did.

The yard could wait, though, when the circus moved into town.

The big top didn't go up without many pairs of eyes to supervise. With or without spotlights, an empty field, hardly noticed before, became the most exciting place around.

Evening fireflies fought for space in the back yard. Barefoot, we chased their shimmering beacons and, later, wished our way after them from the bedroom window. Sometimes they lighted our way home from a family outing.

Burma Shave signs, too, lined country roads before more and more drivers took to the interstates.

Suddenly I glimpse a windmill still spinning high above a white farmhouse. An American flag waving from a pole. And pink roses maneuvering for room on a pasture fence.

I see fields of wildflowers and red poppies and, along a creek, orange day lilies. And, edging the road, a blur of blue flowers interrupted by the showy white delicacy of Queen Ann's lace.

Everywhere, cylinders—silos extending toward heaven, waiting rolls of hay—take shape.

The rain comes and goes, along with lightning. Here and there, an old barnacle of a barn gives up the ghost while a cornfield stretches in the early light. And in a meadow, near a lush growth of trees, the cows stand as solemn as Sunday.

Summer is like the rest of us—different, yet always the same.

The Best Gifts

One day when I was 7, my father took me with him to St. Catherine's Hospital.

Under a big top of blue sky and billowy clouds, the auxiliary had its annual, fund-raising carnival—Barnum & Bailey to me.

Dad gave me a little spending money before he disappeared inside the building to see patients.

I hoarded my meager funds, resisting everything from pony rides to cotton candy so that I could play something called roulette: I wanted to win one of the prizes—a baby's cap and kimono trimmed in blue ribbon.

"Made by a lady in the auxiliary," said the man turning the wheel. "Pretty clever, pretty clever."

My mother had recently given birth to her fourth child—and only son. I thought I had somehow slipped outside her orbit, and I hoped to give her something that would restore me to lofty heights.

Try after try, I watched my money dwindle. Finally—miraculously—the ball landed on my number; applause and scattered cheers rippled overhead.

Later, holding the present as I rode home with Dad, I felt curiously older: I was carrying a real gift instead of a fistful of wildflowers or one of my school-made efforts. As I burst into the house, I begged Mother: "Open it now."

Suddenly, to my horror, the hard-won gift came apart before my eyes. As Mother removed the cap and kimono from a box, we saw they were dishcloths—dishrags.

"Why, how clever," said Mother, trying to stop my tears and salvage the situation. "And I needed new ones."

The gift was the first I had given—and remains the worst.

Ever since, I've considered gift-giving—like the roulette wheel—a game of chance.

The presents we give, through no genius or fault of our own, can please or displease: Selecting them carefully, we hope they will convey thoughts such as "I love you" or "I remember."

Yet we never know how the overtures will be received.

When Bexley resident Deborah May was growing up, she always tried her hardest. The second of five children earned A after A after A.

Yet, for such high marks, "I was never rewarded materially, "she said. "My parents always wanted me to know they loved me for who I was, not for the grades I earned."

Then, in typing class during her sophomore year in high school, she received her first C.

"I was devastated," she said.

Her father, however, bought her a silver charm, in the shape of a typewriter eraser, for her bracelet.

"I want it to remind you," he told her, "that you don't always have to be the best. It's OK to be less than perfect."

His gift of permission, she said, "was the best present he ever gave me."

Sometimes, though, gifts may not be desired.

"I can't buy my mother anything," I overheard a middle-aged woman tell a friend outside a gift shop last week. "She says she doesn't want *things*."

My mother made the same plea several years ago. So, instead of a birthday present, I gave her an experience—art lessons.

This time, in the gift-giving game of chance, the ball landed firmly on my mother's lucky number.

She continues to take the classes.

"Your mother is one of the most enthusiastic students I've ever had," began a report from her teacher. I felt proud, as if I were her parent.

Mother knows all about paints, the tooth of the paper and sable brushes. She has made new friends—of her teacher, the neighborhood children who go to her door to paint and the family who owns a framing business.

The past two Christmases, she has shipped to our home a wooden crate filled with 10 framed watercolors for the family.

Purely by chance, I thought of the painting lessons for Mother. Purely by chance, she was enchanted.

I'm not sure she would consider the gift of lessons the best she has received. For me, though, it's the best I've ever given.

Ownership

*N*ippy, like most everything else in my childhood, was a hand-me-down.

Yet, for a few years, I "owned" her—or, rather, the black cocker spaniel allowed me to think I did.

Just after my birth, I'm told, my father surprised my sisters by bringing home a puppy that he urged them to discover in his overcoat pocket.

He had picked her out, at a patient's request, as payment for a house call. He had chosen the runt of the litter because he thought no one else would.

His reasoning softened Mom, who—reeling from a 6-year-old, a 3-year-old and a newborn—was about to put her foot down.

When the puppy stared up at her, the contract was sealed.

The name "Nippy" was conferred by my older sister, trying to capture the brief behavior of puppyhood.

Instead, the kind-spirited dog tolerated my tugging her every which way and pulling her about in a wagon. She nipped at me only once—for offering food, then withdrawing the dish one time too many.

"Never fool with an animal while it's eating," Dad cautioned.

His tone implied that anyone dumb enough to do so deserved what she got.

Nippy guarded us, the house and even our neighbors faithfully, not with indiscriminate yapping each time the doorbell rang but with radar-like instincts.

One lazy Sunday afternoon in the back yard, our peace was broken only by barking—as Nippy ran back and forth along a picket fence separating our lawn from the neighbors'.

"Must be a rabbit," my father figured.

With Nippy ignoring his verbal commands, Dad rolled up a newspaper and cracked it in his hand to silence her.

Our neighbors later appeared at the door: Had we noticed anything suspicious?

Nippy, it turned out, was the only one who had.

She had done her best. We, however, had failed her—and our neighbors.

As I watched a detective dust a grand piano for fingerprints, I felt proud knowing that, besides being a chaser of rabbits and motorcycles, Nippy was a "police dog."

Rabbits led her into the woods, where burs clung to her like Velcro—or toward the dunes, where she'd emerge from the lake smelling like fish.

Motorcycles teased her down the block, away from our screaming lungs, as she scolded a rear tire, trying to teach it a lesson. Thunder drove her upstairs to hide, trembling, under a bed.

Yet she was fearless in protecting us: When my brother was a toddler, a neighbor's German shepherd (usually confined to an outdoor pen) plunged into our yard. Nippy, a quarter of its size, leapt between the intruder and my frightened brother for a showdown—and won.

Nippy displayed similar courage to find her way home.

One winter, after piling kids and sleds into the car, Dad drove off, forgetting that she was still bounding through drifts. Although we tried to find her, not until the next day did she make her way up the drive.

Another time, after she was missing for more than a week, we figured that someone had stolen her,

"You have to accept that she's not coming back," Dad told us as we cried over Sunday dinner. "There's Nippy!" we interrupted, pointing to the window.

Rushing out to meet the bedraggled mass, we watched her collapse, exhausted.

Soon she resumed her place by my side, exploring the woods or waiting for me outside a friend's back door.

The summer I was 7, however, she found new purpose: Forsaking me—and, for a while, even rabbits and motorcycles—Nippy guarded my baby brother with her life as he slept in his crib or napped outside in his buggy.

Stout of heart, the least of the litter, our family dog lived 16 years.

She rests now in time's pocket, where I discover her again and again.

I did so the other evening during a thunderstorm, which sent me under a bed—not to hide but to find, still hidden inside a tin, a dog tag:

"Nippy / I belong to Kirsten Lokvam, Kenosha, Wis. / Phone 3711."

She was ours, not mine, but each of us knew we owned her.

Before the Back Door

$\mathcal{A}$t the evening of middle age, I stand before the back door, full of cockleburs, the way my dog once did.

Nippy, my cocker spaniel from childhood, loved to chase rabbits in the woods behind our house. No matter how loudly I shrieked her name, no matter how strongly I whistled against the wind, she heeded a deeper call.

My protestations couldn't make her pause after she picked up a scent.

Sniffing and snorting, her nose to the ground, she'd twist and turn, following this lead, then that, as she sped off toward the sand dunes.

Hours would limp by before she'd stagger into the yard, sand and burs clinging to her hair.

"Clean her up," my parents would admonish me.

So a sister and I would set to work, trying to untangle the matted coat.

Sometimes our pricked fingers, bloodied by the thorny business, made us yelp as much as Nippy.

A bath in an old metal tub left her shivering and sheepish. A towel would help fluff her up.

Still, wriggling free, she'd nose about the yard for a perfect spot, then fling herself down and roll around until, eventually, she felt more like her old self.

Once, she pursued a skunk.

"Oh, Nippy," we groaned with a "How could you?" tone, distancing ourselves as much as possible.

I must have "removed" myself altogether because I cannot remember how the situation was resolved—only that now, unlike what I predicted at the time, the scent is no longer with me.

Her most alarming backdoor appearance occurred after she was singed in a field fire. Her black coat had all but disappeared, exposing patches of gray skin.

My dad, a physician, helped return her to health, all the while shaking his head—in disbelief and pride—that she had survived.

The loss of her hair made Nippy seem more embarrassed than proud, though.

She mostly hid in the basement until her coat grew back. Whenever she encountered us, she made herself as small as possible.

Remarkably, none of the mishaps diminished her passion for rabbits.

Not until old age—she lived for more than 16 years and ran a good race until close to the end—did she spend more time by the fire than on the run.

Still, whenever we saw her legs move in sleep, we could guess at her dreams.

Who, at times, hasn't returned home with cockleburs—the slights and setbacks, "the slings and arrows"—still clinging to oneself? And who, at times, hasn't tried or wanted help in removing what hurts?

After we've retreated for a while, after we've suffered in silence, after we've recovered, who doesn't want to re-enter the fray?

Sooner or later we resume chasing rabbits, try maneuvering safely through the fire. And, sooner or later, we experience another setback, another lesson on the seesaw of life.

When a disappointment seems too great, like a bur too deeply enmeshed to pull, we try cutting it out. Sometimes we succeed.

We may get singed, we may hesitate to collect our bearings, but eventually, with luck, we regain the urge to participate.

One answer might be found in a quotation I read long ago.

I have since forgotten who wrote the words but not what they mean:

"Any man can sit by his fire and solve problems, but to make a machine or build a building one has to love something better than his own ease."

Nippy loved going after rabbits.

Some of us climb mountains; some become doctors; some take on the responsibilities of parenthood.

Burs make the going rough.

Yet, badgelike, they provide proof that we did live, we did try, before we had only to sit by a fire—rather than start one.

Summer Camp

Going to camp was like being reborn—we left behind our familiar world and stepped into a new family circle. For a week or two months, the experience was framed by forest: We entered woods, letting the city slip away. When we departed, we tried to keep some of the wilderness.

An echo remains the rest of our days—of the splashes and shouts rising from "swim point," the creak of oars, the whisper of a paddle in water.

Yet my echo is more than a sound—more than the reverberating voices from across the lake, more than a lone bugle playing taps. Mine is the memory of packing my suitcase and duffle bag for the first time, of thinking I was on my own because—pioneerlike—I was the only member of my family to be in that place at that time.

The first days were hardest: A stranger among mostly strangers, without relatives to help smooth the way, I was included or excluded on my own merits as I tried to form new friendships, pave new paths. Staking out my bunk and a place to sit at mealtime, I discovered a new malady: homesickness. Everything felt unfamiliar—from nighttime rituals to camp rules for setting and clearing the table.

Like Winnie in Natalie Babbitt's *Tuck Everlasting*, I realized that eating was "a very personal thing, not something to do with strangers. Chewing was a personal thing. Yet here she was chewing with strangers in a strange place."

Rest time proved melancholy, too: Lying on my bunk, I wondered whether my parents missed me as much as I missed them. Yet, when I wrote, I tried sounding happy and grown-up, not wanting to admit to them—or anyone else—how I really felt.

Mail call was as much a popularity poll as a school's valentine box. Standing on the rock, a counselor called out the lucky names. When hands shot up, letters flew their way. Groans greeted the ears of the kids who received more than their share.

Again and again, I left mail call empty-handed. Finally, a friend looked up from one of her letters and said, "Your sister Sonja's in the hospital. She has something called diabetes. She was in a coma and almost died. But my mom says she's OK now."

"What's diabetes?" I wondered aloud.

"I don't know," she said.

I worried a lot during my short stay. When I saw my parents again, I blurted out, "How come you didn't write and tell me?"

"Because we didn't want to worry you," they replied.

I tried to tell them—while fighting back angry tears—that knowing would have been better than hearing the news from someone else.

Had I not been separated from them, however, I might not have gained such an insight. Or realized that, though we belong to family, families are made up of individuals, with different points of view. Or that within our separate circumstances we strive for balance.

My mother, who heard country creeks sing her into spring, dreamed of living in the city; my father, reared in the city, escaped Huck Finnlike on a raft—and floated down the Mississippi River with a friend.

Just when I found my balance at camp, just when I was sure of my footing, the session was over. As my son would say at the end of his first season: "My only regret is that I signed up for one month instead of two."

The last days of camp can be the best. My new friends and I went from beginning "red caps" in swimming to intermediate "blue caps," with the hope of becoming "white caps" the next summer. We overcame stage fright when our turn arrived to put on a skit. We learned how to fold a flag and to raise and lower it. We felt content clamoring into the mess hall each morning and snuggling into our cots each night.

Even now I can hear the faint singing around a campfire, echoing down all those homesick hills into a happy valley, and see sparks spiraling upward into the dark yet starry future.

In Search of Self

$\mathcal{A}$ hot attic conjures up running rivers, the splash of a lake, the shouts of youth.

"Dear Mother, Thank you for your letters," my eldest sister—full of enthusiasm and youthful spelling—wrote decades ago from summer camp:

"I am learning how to swim. I can do the crawl pretty good . . . . Tell Daddy we don't go fishing out hear, so I can't get him a fish."

And, from another year: "I made this stainary (stationery) in handy craft . . . . I am learning to spring when I do the swan dive . . . . Please save this paper. Are you coming out Sunday?"

Who doesn't pine for adventure, only to long for the very people—and the home—you've chosen to leave? The tug between family and the unfamiliar is as eternal as the tide: to be a part and yet, at the same time, to be apart. Youth, especially, feels the dual pull.

Almost as soon as I got to camp, I sent word:

"Please write!! I had my throat painted by the nurse! . . . . We are going on a breakfast cookout. I love you. Please write."

At first, that's how all my letters began—and ended. It's not that I didn't like sleeping in a cabin or using an orange crate for a bureau—or even waiting on tables when it was my turn to be "hopper." I was enthralled by it all—rowing a boat, eating berries by the vine-covered tennis courts, drinking cold water from a pump. Still, I missed my family.

Then, several years later, I wrote in a note: "I would like to stay up over Labor Day weekend if OK with all of you. Could you please send the money if I can? Most of the kids are staying, so may I?"

Despite the rare show of independence, my letter still ended with: "I haven't got any mail for three days. I feel awful but understand you must all be very busy."

My sister Sonja, a counselor at another camp, felt a similar ambivalence, although she was "loving every blessed minute. . . . I'll be sad to leave this place, but I'll be glad to get home!"

The attic yields letters of other generations, too—among them, reports from my daughter of her canoe trip on the Pine River, her visit to Sleeping Bear Dunes National Lakeshore, her "water fight with another sailboat. It was a blast."

"See ya in eight days," she wrote from camp. "P.S. I would like to leave early in the morning on Fri. instead of Thurs. night."

Thus we practice exiting the nest before our official departure.

"We just had a natural disaster," she noted, describing a re-enactment during the summer she attended Girls' State: "Then the bridge fell—I was on it so I'm (supposed to be) 'dead' . . . . for 45 min. I've been wanting to write you, so I figure now, while I'm dead, is the best time. Cause if I really did die there are so many things I'd want to tell you. I know you know I love you but I really do."

Why does going away allow us to see more clearly what we're leaving behind? Distance—like a telescope, or old letters and scrapbooks—offers perspective.

In a picture from a long-ago river trip on the Chippewa and the Mississippi, I see my father—then a teenager—on bended knee. With one hand he's eating an apple; and with the other, leaning on his ax handle. A friend is stirring a pot over the open fire while another takes the picture. In the background is seen a pitched tent with a clothesline and lantern, and the U.S. flag. The campers put forth so much effort, even as they merge with the wilderness, to create a homeplace.

"Oh, how like the old pioneer and shades of Daniel Boone you are, midst the woods primeval," he wrote on the back of a snapshot.

In search of self, we try to lose ourselves in something larger than ourselves, larger than our families—whether it be an experience at camp or in the great outdoors.

That's why an image of Mother still touches me. Growing up on a farm, she lived too far from town to join a camping society. Yet that didn't stop her desire. A $10 bill she found on the way to school went unclaimed. It was returned to her at the end of the year. That summer she ordered a Camp Fire Girls uniform from the Sears catalog:

She belonged—to a troop of one.

Lake Michigan

"*I* own everything I can see," my mother would say.

In that sense, she and therefore Dad "owned" Lake Michigan, thanks to the two houses where they raised their family. Neither home, however, was on the water. The first, where I lived from birth to age 7, sat seven blocks away. The second one, only three.

During the leafless winter, I could see from my bedroom window an expanse grayer than the sky, whitecaps and sometimes sheaves of ice.

Had I grown up in the hills of middle Tennessee, I'd now yearn for undulating land. Had I come of age out West, mountains would be my lighthouse. As it was, the lake, along with its stretches of sand dunes and prairie, carved my childhood.

If you have lived near water immense enough (in a child's mind) to be an ocean, you know what I mean. And if you find the sound of a foghorn as reassuring as the call of a train whistle at night, you can surely grasp the impact.

The lake was as much a presence as a close and playful friend or, sometimes, a respected elder. In later years, a visit home for my siblings and me would have been unthinkable without taking a "swing by the lake"—often before first pulling into the driveway.

Its fragrance and mist permeated our days. With a logic I never had the patience to fathom, my father liked pointing out why living near a large body of water kept us "warmer in the winter, cooler in the summer and made the roses thrive."

On frigid walks to school, I didn't notice its benign effect. Yet there was no mistaking a refreshing breeze to stir the bedroom curtains during sweltering nights.

The lake was always there: from my first forays into the water, held securely in a parent's arms, to inching my way on my own, deeper and deeper, testing its depth and my bravado, to the teenage years when my friends and I, with transistor radios blaring, languished at the cove.

Exploring its cavelike formations, watching water spray against mossy pilings—emerald in the summer sun—was better than any fun-house amusement.

We learned to "ride" the lake in the way one learns to master a horse. There were tame days, rough days. Some were so wild we weren't allowed to swim but had to wait until the waters settled.

Still, the lake demanded of us a certain courage—when we accepted its challenge. As often as possible, we wanted to push our limits with diving and swimming.

The lake taught us another side of nature, too, showing off its bounty and beauty—sunrises reflected in its swells, stars spilling over its shimmering bed. We knew the water then as a magical being who offered up beach glass, worn smooth by its pounding; fish, made strong by its currents; and afternoons turned happy by its placid pools.

My friends and I saw the seven stages of man, or at least his moods, mirrored in our lake right up to winter. We didn't visit much then, keeping our distance until some dramatic temper tantrum of ice and spray sent us lakeward to catch the display.

Some days, sitting in school, I could barely concentrate what with the waves pounding the breakwater. At night, I'd sometimes still hear the crashing and subsiding of their force.

I've long since forgotten how many seconds would pass between foghorn soundings, counting those instead of sheep as I fell asleep to the intermittent lullaby.

Yet I remember that four years have come and gone since I've stood at the shore. And how many more times that since I've put my feet in the water or gone for a swim? Still, the lake goes on. And will long after we've gone.

"I own everything I can see," Mom used to say.

Only now do I realize that the great lake owns me.

The Fourth of July

$\mathcal{S}$ometimes, on summer nights, my brother slept on the back porch.

A sleeping bag on an Army cot served as his bed.

Surrounded by the light of fireflies and sound of crickets, Chris would drift off—dreaming, no doubt, of bigger adventures beyond the back yard.

The place held a few of its own, especially on the Fourth of July.

One year, a teen-ager from down the street wandered near.

"What do you have there, Eddie?" asked Dad, barely looking up while puttering in the garden.

"Something I made," Eddie said. "Let me show you."

My 8-year-old brother knew: a firecracker.

"He no sooner touched the match to that thing and pitched it— like a baseball—than it exploded," Chris recalled. "It was only about 10 feet away when it went ka-boom!' It was the loudest firecracker I'd ever heard."

Even before the confetti settled over the lawn, our father, a doctor, fumed:

"Eddie, you shouldn't be doing that. I've seen fingers taken off, hands blown off."

Afterward, Dad scolded Chris.

"Let this be a lesson to you: Don't ever let somebody give you a firecracker. Don't ever light one of those things."

In those days, my brother said, "Everything was 'Let this be a lesson to you.' But I didn't mind it that time, because I knew I wasn't in trouble. . . . I liked to see Dad mad—when he wasn't mad at me."

"Honey," said Dad, heading inside to tell Mother, "do you know what just happened?"

"He was correct, he was right, but he wouldn't stop ranting," said Chris, who, basking in his rare innocence, had followed Dad indoors.

Mom, in her calibrating way, soothed him: "Yes, dear . . . . Why, that's terrible, dear."

The next Fourth of July, the family lingered over supper on the back porch.

Night drew Chris into the yard, where he lighted sparklers.

Running like a comet, holding a trail of snapping light, he would whip a sparkler into the air, then watch it nose-dive into the grass.

"Don't do that; it could poke your eye out. Just hold it in your hand," Dad warned through the screen, then returned to the table.

Unable to resist, Chris eventually lobbed another that, instead of hitting the lawn, landed on the canvas.

He came clean at the first curl of smoke.

"Hey," he yelled, "a sparkler landed on the awning!"

Our aunt, seeing a flame licking down, stood on a bench, goblet in hand, and flung her water.

Everyone got into the act, emptying their glasses, and even the pitcher, before dousing the blaze—and themselves.

My brother was grateful for the help and for the audience.

"Dad didn't want to be too harsh in front of the company," Chris said, chuckling. "Instead, he said things like 'Thank God it didn't land in your eye.' "

Becker Awning repaired the damage by sewing a square patch.

From then on, whenever Chris fell asleep on the back porch, the last thing he saw was the patch—a constant reminder of the night Dad didn't explode.

A River Within

A river within runs free.

We become Huck, riding the life force that no parent, not even a Pap, and no teacher, not even a Miss Watson, can tame.

Overflowing in youth, the spirit eventually encounters bends and turns, snags and shoals, and, sometimes, shimmering peace.

Other girls like me must have identified more with Huckleberry Finn than with Becky Thatcher—whose life seems circumscribed, not free.

Huck, though a boy on the brink of manhood, rises above gender, embracing our human condition.

Who doesn't know or remember the feeling of being "all cramped up" in society's conventions? Or the need to "light out for the Territory" before becoming "sivilized"?

Summer after summer, my father and his teenage friends fashioned a raft and headed toward the Mississippi from Eau Claire, Wis. Fishing offered them far more than food, the forests so much more than scenery. Each night, the explorers—young like the century—settled their raft in a new place.

Their sky was Huck's—"all speckled with stars, and we used to lay on our backs and look up at them, and discuss about whether they was made, or only just happened."

"And sometimes on the water you could see a spark or two—on a raft or a scow . . . and maybe you could hear a fiddle or a song coming over from one of them crafts. It's lovely to live on a raft."

A generation later, before summer sunrises, two friends and I would steal out of our houses. We'd lug a black griddle and breakfast fixings, and head for a cove along Lake Michigan. At water's edge, our backs turned away from shore and civilization, we'd watch our fire duel with the dawn. The lake led to the unknown, summoning the future; we'd answer with a swim, feeling more alive than those in the sleeping houses.

Before the sun ascended to its rightful throne, we owned the cove.

We were like Huck, who said of Jackson Island, "I was boss of it—it all belonged to me."

Author Mark Twain was once lord of his uncle's farm near Florida, Mo.

"It was a heavenly place for a boy to be," he recalls in his autobiography. A brook "sang along over its gravelly bed and curved and frisked in and out . . . and yonder in the deep shade of overhanging foliage and vines—a divine place for wading, and it had swimming pools, too, which were forbidden to us and therefore much frequented by us."

My son was a camper or counselor for some 12 years at a century-old camp on Lake Champlain.

Each summer, he goes back to feel "reinvigorated."

"There's a sense of going home again," he said. "I definitely feel more alive, more conscious of my humanity, when I'm around rushing water, mountains and open space . . . . Natural forces . . . remind me that, whatever power I am, I'm part of nature, too.

"As a child . . . you do a lot of dreaming. It's nice to re-connect with those dreams, re-evaluate them."

Twain offers a bridge between then and now, a bridge between who we once were and whom we long to be again.

Perhaps it is no coincidence that the author was middle-aged (41-48) when he wrote *The Adventures of Huckleberry Finn* from 1876 to '83 or that the country was 100 years old when he began.

Twain not only captured his childhood but also set the novel about 50-60 years after the country's founding. He revisited not only his youth but the nation's.

Huck on a raft remains a sturdy metaphor for an individual floating through time.

Forests fall and malls rise as outward signs, perhaps, of a soul's journey—a layering over, a putting up with, a compromise.

By and by, we try to find our way back to the raft.

Rereading *Huckleberry Finn* is one way to begin.

"There warn't no home like a raft," Huck tells us. "Other places do seem so cramped up and smothery, but a raft don't. You feel mighty free and easy and comfortable."

Dad, age 7, 1914

He Is
Speaking
Still

*Deep and resonant, filling the hills
and valleys of my childhood, his voice
lulled me to sleep at night.*

A Pitcher That Never Empties

*T*his is a tale of to have and to hold, of milk pitchers and music.

Two pitchers carry significance in my family: the pewter one (which Mother set on the table three times a day, every day, throughout our growing up), and a small ceramic one (which I received for a shower gift shortly before my marriage in 1966).

Today, Mom's pitcher sits on my kitchen shelf, full of childhood memories. Likewise, several years ago, as a trophy from his youth, my son claimed the white ceramic one.

The latter has a cow painted on the side. It's the perfect size for a small child's hand. It sat in front of him, my firstborn, and later, my daughter as each of them joined the table.

I had no recollection of opening this present at a party given 33 years ago until recently, when I found a snapshot of myself happily holding up the new pitcher for all the room to see. Surprised to glimpse the instant at which it entered our family life, I sent off the picture to my son.

"1966 probably doesn't seem long ago to you," he responded, "but think how much the world has changed—and your life. Someone meeting you now might not even recognize you in the picture. Your outfit, plus the hairstyle, really put you in the '60s.

"You and the country had no idea what was in store: Vietnam, social upheaval, Watergate."

Thanks to a camera capturing a scene, my son and I were able to visit a moment that occurred two years before his birth.

If only we could be like a lens, letting time stand still for a second, think what we might notice and learn.

"Do any human beings ever realize life while they live it—every, every minute?" Emily asks in Thornton Wilder's *Our Town*.

"No. The saints and poets, maybe—they do some," the Stage Manager answers.

And once in a while, so does my mother.

Two days before my marriage, she asked whether I would listen to the organist practice the wedding music.

Take time out to just sit? Why, I had to finish packing, write thank-you notes, do a dozen details before I walked down the aisle.

Yet how could I refuse the one thing she'd asked of me in the months she'd spent helping to plan the wedding?

While I sat next to her in the almost empty chapel, the organ's deep tones spiraling down from the choir loft, I remember thinking, "When will this end so I can get out of here?" I tapped a foot impatiently, as if I were doing Mom a favor.

I was none too happy about it. Besides, why did she need me to check up on the organist? If the woman made a mistake, Mother, who had selected the music, would know before me.

All the while, Mother kept her dignity and sat serenely—lost, I assumed, in listening. Eventually, I followed her lead, slowing down and settling in.

I noticed the sunlight illuminating stained-glass windows and the worn pews where my sisters and I had once sat at the start of each school day. I looked at Mother's hands, no longer as young as when they'd turned the pages of our storybooks, and I recalled so much of what they'd done.

Never again, I realized, would things be exactly as I knew them, nor would we.

By the time the organist finished, I had quieted down enough to want to keep sitting, the way I'd often felt as a train pulled into the station.

All these years later, a mother myself, I realize what she wanted: not so much to listen to music, perhaps, as to have time together, where we could close out the day-to-day world and say goodbye to our world as we knew it.

To have and to hold, in the crush of years, I revisit that moment more and more. Though there is no picture of it—like the one of me holding up the milk pitcher—its imprint fills me with peace.

Like a pitcher that never empties, Bach's *Arioso* continues to pour forth, as does Purcell's *Trumpet Voluntary*, but most of all, a mother's music.

The Magic Tree

*I*t wasn't a hazel branch—the magic wand of folklore—that turned the tree into something special. It was my young son and his father.

They created a "magic" one in the woods behind our first house.

"Older and stronger than human beings, trees present us with the eternal image of powers," Marie-France Boyer writes in *Tree-Talk*:

"In the fourth century A.D., Arnobius, while traveling through Tunisia, described in his journal some magical trees covered in strips of cloth, representing wishes.

"In the 15th century, the Black Death stopped at the elms of Senarpont, between Paris and Le Touquet."

In the 20th century, on New Year's Day in some parts of Japan, "Little pieces of paper are hung on branches of trees to bring good luck."

Yet sometimes a tree, like the tree in our woods, "exerts its power merely by existing."

My son and his father left no offerings, tied nothing to the branches for good luck. They merely visited the tree and talked to each other—and continue to talk.

What drew them was how the tree fashioned the first leaves in spring and how, each fall, its fingers waited the longest to fling them free.

"I felt that was something most people never noticed and that we had a special bond with the tree," my almost 30-year-old son recalled. "We'd stop to see its magic, while others probably thought it was just a regular tree. It was as if it could sense our appreciation."

"His legs were barely long enough to work his way along the path," my husband said. "Sometimes I would hold his hand and lift him.

"What I remember most about the tree was not its magic but the magic of the child who stood before it—his stunning imagination, his trusting belief, a belief so strong that because of him . . . the tree somehow, along the way, actually did become magical."

My husband first pronounced the tree "magical" to focus a 3-year-old's attention for a photograph.

"He certainly had a wonderful expression in the photo—looking off into a world richer than I could have seen as an adult," his father said. "He must have thought that elves might appear on the limbs or angels might fly out of the bark."

"When Dad talked about the tree," my son said, "I felt that he . . . was revealing one of the mysteries of the world . . . . It wasn't some kind of tooth-fairy ruse he was trying to put over on me. . . . He talked about nature being magical in general. He implied, too, that you can imbue something with magical powers by the way you respond to it and appreciate it."

As our son grew older, he became "a little disappointed" that the tree didn't really resemble one in a book or cartoon.

"Even as a 4-year-old," he said, "I knew; I understood because he actually took time to explain it. I think he really enjoyed talking with me and hearing what I had to say. That, to me, seems like the ideal parenting attribute."

Someday he might carry on the spirit of the magic tree with a child of his own.

"As the story *Yes, Virginia, There Is a Santa Claus* makes plain, there is a Santa Claus as much as there is a magic tree. Helping a child understand how that can be so is to contribute to raising someone who is capable of having a more broad-minded, sensitive, large-souled approach to the world."

Does the tree still live? I wonder. Does it still stir the stars? Does summer's moon slumber in its branches? Does it wait for another child and parent to discover the universe?

Or, in the name of "progress," does a parking lot stand where it once did?

"Twenty-six years later," our son said, "I still think of that tree and what it represents for me about life and my relationship with Dad. I can't imagine anything more magical."

In Praise of Teachers

*L*et us now praise teachers who give praise.

The ones who provide the best adulation—not the blanket compliment easily announced (and easily dismissed) but the well-placed expression that encourages progress instead of contentment.

My sister, a speech therapist for young children, used praise even as an alternative to punishment.

With an unruly girl who threw herself on the ground, she would say, "You're too nice to be down on that dirty floor"—and urge the girl to rejoin the rest of the group.

In *How To Win Friends and Influence People*, Dale Carnegie observes:

"I can look back in my own life and see where a few words of praise have sharply changed my entire future."

My son could say the same, all because one teacher "kept her eyes and mind open," he noted recently.

In math, reading or any other subject, he had thought of himself as "in the middle."

Then, at the end of his first quarter in fifth grade, Mrs. Mikesell called him to her desk, as she did with all other students, to review his report card.

"I remember looking at . . . (it) and a smile creeping across my face," he said, recalling B's and B-pluses.

While he felt appreciation for his marks, she expressed disappointment.

"You can do better," she said. "You're better than these grades."

"I am naturally a very lazy person who often is inclined to be content with B effort and B results," my son said more than two decades later.

"I had had . . . great teachers before her, and, for some reason, I had not decided to push myself in the way I did after.

"I interpreted . . . (her comments) as challenging, supportive and complimentary. I was honored . . . and from then on I was determined to prove that she was right."

That moment, backed up by her teaching, contributed to his academic success in high school and college.

He remains grateful to the teacher who made him want to try harder—when "She could have just continued handing out B's and let me sail through her class."

And so do I.

Asked to meet with Mrs. Mikesell before school one day, I fretted:

Had he started a fight? Did he cause trouble in class?

I was surprised by her concern for his grades. Yet, when she commended his ability, I saw his potential in a new light.

Only the exceptional teachers, often pressed for time, worry about students in the middle.

And only the most exceptional do something for them.

A measure of praise, carefully bestowed, earns my eternal thanks—and praise.

Conversations in the Car

To live in suburbia means to chauffeur.

If only I had broadened my mind—reading or writing—while I enabled my children to broaden theirs.

Growing up, my daughter tried art, piano, violin, ballet, tennis, swimming, horseback riding and gymnastics.

Each endeavor spawned other outings: Ballet, for example, translated into further trips—for *Nutcracker* tryouts, and, with luck, rehearsals.

The kicker was the violin: Beginning at age 3, she studied the Suzuki method with a pint-size instrument.

Her teacher insisted on two 15-minute sessions a week in addition to Saturday play-alongs.

The drive to class took more than 30 minutes each way—after a drive home from nursery school.

Therefore, with one lesson and the preparation needed just to get out the door, at least 90 minutes vanished from my life;

"Couldn't we just make it one half-hour lesson a week?" I pleaded.

"Frequency is important at her age—and brevity," the instructor said without even a hint of sympathy. "We wouldn't want to tire her, would we?"

I grew up in a small town—close enough to the downtown area that eventually I could get there by bus or bicycle, or on my own two feet.

Even when she worked as a teacher, Mom insisted on only one car.

"Otherwise," she said, "I'll turn into a taxi driver."

Not until I started my senior year in high school did she relent.

Until then, whenever my three siblings and I wanted to go somewhere, we got there on our own: the library, music and sports lessons, the movies.

To ride horseback, for which we had to reach the countryside, we transferred on buses to the end of the line, then walked the rest of the way.

Before the age of car pools, the sharing of chores drew children and parents closer: planting crops, removing storm windows, hanging clothes on the line.

Doing something together, such as driving a nail or drying a dish, eased communication—without the need to make eye contact.

The modern lament "Whose turn is it to load the dishwasher?" does not inspire the give-and-take that took place before the appliance was invented.

More and more, such bonding moments occur within the cocoon of a car—free of television and other distractions.

My father-in-law cherished the opportunity to drive our children to school and elsewhere.

He craved only one reward: time with his grandchildren.

Who doesn't recall enjoying a child's budding sense of humor or quelling another one's tears?

To hear a hurt hurrying to the surface or a triumph standing tall before it shrinks into the familiar "Oh, nothing" or "I don't know" is to gain an unexpected dividend.

This school year, the annual carousel is more than half-completed.

Parents have juggled getting their children to school and to after-school activities.

Some shoulder the burden alone; others organize car pools with friends and neighbors.

All hang on at a galloping pace.

In the years to come, so many of them will acknowledge, when discussing their grown children, "We had some of our best conversations in the car."

The Gathering

The season bends to the gathering: apples in a bowl, leaves at the curb, firewood in tidy stacks.

Cookbooks collect on counters. Ingredients fill a list. Groceries accumulate in the cart.

Thanksgiving, like a guest who shows up year after year, expects to be entertained in the same fashion.

"Something feels different," the Spirit of Thanksgiving seemed to whisper earlier this week as I stood in an uncluttered kitchen.

My conscience rushed to explain:

"I thought we'd go to a restaurant where they fix a turkey for each family. Then, afterward, we take home the leftovers."

"Leftovers without the fuss? You mean a 'pretend' Thanksgiving?" asked the spirit, incredulous. "Isn't that like having a concrete goose in the yard instead of a real one?

"It won't be the same. In the middle of our reliving that story about Aunt Alma, a waiter will interrupt to describe the dessert tray. We'll never get to the punch line. Even if we did, we couldn't laugh until we cry in a place that public."

"Some years," I countered, "what's wrong with making it easier on the hostess?"

"Remember that Thanksgiving when your sister visited her fiance and her future mother-in-law served instant mashed potatoes? Thirty-eight years ago, you thought it scandalous. Now, you're turning the whole ritual into something instant. I say, 'The more you put into something, the more you get out of it.'

"I realize," I acknowledged, "that the Pilgrims didn't sit down with the Indians and give thanks over someone else's meal. They rejoiced in the shared triumph of their planting and harvesting.

"Yet times have changed. My mother grew up on a farm in an era when most other people did; today, most of us aren't eating food we've grown. And we have less time to prepare an elaborate meal.

"I see nothing wrong with honoring the day, some years, by going out. What's important is gathering together, right?"

"Of course," the spirit answered, "if you want to put it that way. Why do you think each November I cause winds to blow, driving families toward hearth and home? My celebration is more than just a meal; it's all day long and, sometimes, all weekend.

"Thanksgiving can be attending a church service and delivering food to the hungry. Or opening the back door and finding firelight within. Or lingering over stories and leftovers, watching football and talking far into the night."

The voice trailed off—tired, no doubt, from witnessing so many Thanksgivings, including some from a childhood before mine.

"Thanksgiving was most memorable—new socks, new Mary Janes, new petticoats and new dresses," my mother has often recalled. "Everything smelled new. And we started early for Arlington and Aunt Charlotte's."

Her family would arrive after what seemed like hours of driving, and Uncle Arthur would be making ice cream—turning and turning the crank, adding and adding ice.

"Children were king," Mother said. "We had all that the grown-ups had and more. We were asked to give performances, sing, dance, make up plays and play games."

Again I tried to perk up the "visitor" for the big day ahead by saying, "That's why you're the favorite holiday for many people."

"Really?" said the spirit, surprised and grateful.

"Yes, you encourage the common bond—instead of presents, the presence of people," I said. "At your table, you help children find their place among the generations."

In the scarf of days, things gather together: stars in their constellations, people in their families.

And, within each November, Thanksgiving—our Plymouth Rock.

No Thanksgiving?

What if Thanksgiving were canceled?

What if merchants and consumers prevailed, insisting on the day off for most workers—but only as a jump-start for holiday shopping?

What if sports fans turned the fourth Thursday in November into a national football rite? People would attend games or watch nonstop TV coverage rather than take time out for church services or even the traditional dinner.

And why not? ask those who consider Thanksgiving far from a "real" holiday.

It doesn't include gifts or greeting cards, dizzying parties or frantic to-do lists, or fancy fireworks.

In fact, Thanksgiving is so unpretentious that the observance could slip away unnoticed. Or could it?

The family cook would welcome the respite at first.

Other relatives would be relieved not to have to make long-distance trips.

"The holidays are just around the corner," they'd reason. "We can visit then."

Yet, as Thanksgiving went unobserved, an unsettling feeling might emerge, inspiring the thought of something missing.

No amount of shopping, spectating or going to the movies would take its place.

Thanksgiving, we'd eventually realize, had fed not only our stomachs but also our souls.

We would feel diminished just from skipping the annual ritual. As more unnoticed Thanksgiving holidays passed, the more impoverished we might become.

Thank goodness for Thanksgiving: By providing at least one day of the year to show our collective appreciation, it allows our nation to nurture the habit.

"Gratitude is a fruit of great cultivation; you do not find it among gross people," British writer Samuel Johnson observed in 1773.

Whenever a family or country gathers in gratitude, its strength builds in number and also in appreciation.

Only if the holiday were to be threatened would we grasp that bounty isn't guaranteed.

Nor freedom. Nor life.

A land that forgets to give thanks might soon be forgotten.

Many of us put aside our unique demands to attend a Thanksgiving celebration or to make one happen.

Afterward, we return to our daily lives with a sense of peace and calm that beforehand was frayed.

The table is our touchstone, giving us renewed insight into our shared journey: Pilgrims all, we are reminded again that none of us achieves anything without the help of family and the support of loved ones.

Perhaps, like other blessings, Thanksgiving would be truly valued only if it vanished.

Then we might understand that the day isn't so much about wanting something more as about appreciating what we already have.

A Talking Christmas Tree

Standing under summer suns, sleeping beneath midnight moons, the evergreen grows to the height of a Christmas star. It hears the creak of other trees as it waits to be found by a family trooping through the woods.

Or it stands at attention, one amid a regiment under a rigging of lights.

"Pick me; pick me," it whispers with the north wind.

Year after year, we set out to claim the Christmas tree. Yet the tree actually claims us, making us stop and finally say, "That's the one," without knowing why.

For, even as we change through the years, the tree remains unchanged—its scent of deep, cold forests and aroma of gingerbread ornaments permeating the house.

Once, when I was very young, and again during my adulthood, the tree—different but somehow the same—seemed to speak to me.

Did I awaken in the middle of the night or just before dawn, the fragrances drawing me downstairs into a living room illuminated only by starry lights? There, the lucky herald of Christmas got to wait up for Santa Claus and watch him work.

My heart, sensing that Santa had just left, skipped rope. Beneath the boughs crouched some presents.

I saw my mother nearby, lying on the sofa because of a throbbing tooth.

"Yes," she said, caving in without a fuss, I could open a gift before the others woke up.

After a quick reckoning, I ripped off wrapping paper and tore apart a box. Inside I found a tea set.

Santa had remembered.

"Look," I squealed to my mom, placing at her side the tiny teapot and dishes. "Don't they look real?"

"Huh?" she responded groggily.

Then I heard the tree:

"Let her be. Let her be."

Scooping up my gift and retracing my steps, I sat sheltered under the lower limbs, playing tea party and waiting for the others to awaken, as now and then I offered the branches a sip.

Many years later, my son—was he 2 or 3?—hung ornaments for the first time.

I held the box of decorations, and he carefully withdrew and placed each one—all on the same branch.

The weighted bough groaned to the floor.

Did he want to remove that ornament and put it here? I asked. Or that one and put it there?

"No, no," he said, happy with his work.

Later that evening, as my son and husband slept, I crept down to the living room.

"Let me be," said the lopsided tree.

But I couldn't resist; I couldn't leave all the ornaments clustered on one branch. So I removed all but one, hanging them on other boughs and even using a ladder to reach the loftier heights.

I was wrong, though, to worry about what visitors might think.

If only I'd listened. If only I'd realized how many more years were left to try for perfection.

Oh, that we could skim the slopes and revisit long-ago Christmases.

If I could do everything again, I'd leave each ornament on the crowded bough. I'd invite each guest to admire my son's handiwork.

Never before, my friends and I would agree, had we seen such an unusual tree. And, drawing near, we'd hear it proclaim:

"Along with Christmas, a child lives here!"

Letter Carriers

*L*ike Dylan Thomas, I remember the mailmen of my youth.

"With sprinkling eyes and wind-cherried noses, on spread, frozen feet they crunched up to the doors and mittened on them manfully." If we delayed in answering, a "thunderstorm of . . . Christmas cards" slid through the mail slot, tumbling onto the hardwood floor.

Better than any calendar, the white drift in the front hall grew larger each day. When it piled up twice a day—once in the morning and again in the afternoon—it told us Santa was just around the next chimney. Time to write letters, addressed to the North Pole, and turn them over to our tall and trusty letter carrier.

"Don't you worry," he said, slipping them into his big leather bag. "I'll make sure these get there." And when we saw our presents, we knew he had made sure.

The letter carriers of my childhood were "fond of walking and dogs and Christmas and the snow." And children. Long before I sent away for my 1 square inch of land in the Yukon, I'd often sit on the front stoop awaiting the mailman's arrival. He always had a word for me, always patted my cocker spaniel and even said "nice horsie" to my lassoed tricycle.

Our mailman was the human thread joining us to a larger tapestry. He brought word from grandparents in south central Wisconsin, relatives in Virginia, friends in California. Crisscrossing his way through our days to deliver the mail, he kept a hand on a family's pulse—surmising births and birthdays, weddings and anniversaries, illness and death.

And so it was that one summer day he sat down next to mopey me. He made me feel important, so important that I forget I had a new baby brother, forgot I was no longer the center of my parents' attention.

93

The mailmen of my children's youth were also "fond of walking and dogs and Christmas and the snow." They stood "in the little, drifted porches and huffed and puffed, making ghosts with their breath, and jogged from foot to foot like small boys wanting to go out."

"It's Mr. Springer, Mr. Springer," squealed my 6-year-old daughter, peeking out the front hall window at the sound of the doorbell. A blizzard, canceling school for the day, had trapped us inside our igloo, where a batch of springerle—our first attempt at the German Christmas cookie—baked merrily in the oven. From the family room window, I saw our mailman's footprints stitched across the snow, and I hurried to the door.

In stomped Mr. Springer, carrying packages and Christmas cards. He had knitted us to the world even before our daughter was born—letters from Vietnam, notes from family, cards at her birth.

Delirious in her freedom from first grade, my daughter twirled about, singing, "Come in, Mr. Springer, and have some springerle." I was sure he couldn't, wouldn't—he had never stepped beyond our little front hall. In his hesitation, however, I sensed acceptance.

"Please do," I urged, while she tugged at the tip of his long wool scarf and led him toward the kitchen. Was it 10 minutes or 15 that he stayed and put his feet under the table, that he sampled our cookies and sipped the coffee, that he laughed at her antics and made us feel good?

"Goodbye, Mr. Springer-lee," my daughter chirped when he left, a name that held forever after. As we watched him disappear down the street, "he wagged his bag like a frozen camel's hump, dizzily turned the corner on one foot, and . . . was gone."

Like her mother before her, my daughter discovered that letter carriers can do more than move the mail. The best can lift the spirit, and even mend it.

The Spirit of Christmas

The stockings hid in the attic until Christmas Eve. Then, amid much excitement, we kids would pull down the attic stairs and ascend into arctic air, past bushels of Jonathan apples, kept fresh in the cold.

Our mission was to retrieve the box with Mom's homemade Norwegian Christmas cookies and to find our Christmas stockings. Jingle bells, stitched to the socks' toes, announced our happy descent into the warmth of the upstairs hall.

Sometimes, the red-and-white stockings would offer up a memento from the Christmas before—a gift card wedged in a heel, a brittle pine needle or two, a piece of clinging yarn.

And so it was, after dinner and church, after our stockings were hung, I liked to reminisce about Christmas around the fireplace. I'd coax Mother, for instance, to tell more stories so I could stay up late, watching flames turn to embers.

"An orange in the toe of a Christmas stocking was a prize, indeed," she said, when fresh fruit in winter was a rarity. "Besides, if you have less, a little is a lot."

Tobacco was the main crop, she said of her prairie youth on a Wisconsin farm. Even on holiday from her one-room school—where during blizzards the fathers took turns coming for the children in sleighs filled with "sweet-smelling hay and large buffalo robes"—she and her siblings had to work hard.

Yet at 5 p.m. on Christmas Eve, when the church bell chimed the evening angelus, they could stop stripping tobacco in the cold shed and begin to celebrate.

"The smell of Christmas bread, turkey, pies and candies greeted us as we came into the house. Then I'd take up my watch for Grandmother, hoping she'd bring a doll."

Years later, on other Christmas Eves in front of a fire, I'd tell my children stories of their ancestors—how even before my mother's family farm was lost during the Depression, Aunt Hulda in Oregon would send black wool stockings, not toys, because that's what Mom needed.

Who knows whether Tia, my daughter, recalled any of this the year she was in seventh grade and I asked her what she wanted for Christmas.

Rather than presents, she suggested that any money that might be spent on her could instead be added to what she'd already saved: "That way I'll have enough to feed a hungry child for a year."

Touched, I told her that we most certainly would do that.

"Still, it won't seem like Christmas," I pleaded, "if you don't have at least one present to open."

"Mom, I've already told you want I want," she said more firmly. "Besides, just think how happy I'll feel waking up each morning knowing that because of me, a child won't go hungry."

Because of Tia, I was fed the spirit of Christmas—and, again, the following year when she found her dollhouse in the attic.

"Let's give it away," she said. "Let's take it to the thrift store."

She filled each room with her doll furniture: a brass bed a grandmother had given her, a Duncan Phyfe table found on a family trip to New Orleans, a Chippendale highboy. I bit my tongue, saying nothing in the face of her generosity. But when she put in the miniature Christmas tree with its tiny, wrapped packages, I could bear it no longer.

"We always use that to decorate our gingerbread house," I reminded her. "Don't give that away. That's the best of all."

"Isn't that the whole point?" she said. "Isn't that what Christmas is all about?"

From her dresser drawer she took a $5 bill, folded it over and over into a little square, then placed it and a note in a drawer inside the miniature highboy:

"I know you've been a very good child, so I send you this to spend in any way you wish. Merry Christmas! Love, Santa Claus."

Early Christmas Morn

*T*he light comes at Christmas just when stars turn to embers and wind snuffs out the moon. Smoky gray slips through the windowpanes. Just as silently, an older sister nudges you awake; you and she tiptoe down the stairs to see whether Santa has visited.

A pounding heart drowns the sounds of a ticking clock and a creaking step as you, lighter than air, float barefoot into the living room. Adjusting your eyes to the dimness, you detect its evergreen scent.

Yet it's the fireplace that pulls you, where plump stockings hang, and a roomy chair that draws you, where Santa has arranged some toys.

"This chair will be mine," you'd said before going to bed, "so Santa can leave my doll."

As if feeling for braille, your fingertips inspect tissue-covered packages until they touch a face with eyes that open and close, a nose and a rosebud mouth. Clasping the doll close, you breathe in her newness— and kiss her quickly before you scamper back upstairs and pretend to be asleep.

My sister and I were the only ones, I thought, to find that gray-lighted land between Christmas Eve and Christmas Day. Each year, it emerged out of mist.

When my father-in-law, as a small boy, discovered the time between times, he found a pop gun under the Christmas tree in the parlor. He dropped onto his stomach, crawling scout-style, and promptly shot off most of the tree's ornaments with the gun's cork.

When a friend's brother, a toddler, woke up before the rest of his family on Christmas morning, he opened all his presents—and all the others. His mother, finding scattered gifts and cards, didn't know who had sent what.

When my mother, as a child, slept in her farmhouse bedroom, she could peer into the parlor below through a heating grate in the floor. On Christmas Eve, she'd select a chair directly beneath the grate, where she hoped Santa would leave her presents; then, in early light, she could see whether he'd given her a doll.

I revisited that time between Christmas Eve and Christmas Day years later, when I stayed up late to put the finishing touches on my children's presents. A log's last ember glowed before it, too, like the moon, gave way. When all the world seemed one, a still house and stiller streets filled a silent night.

Climbing upstairs, I would meet my young self, a wispy ghost of Christmas past, descending. She and I would re-enter the fragrant living room, the still-lighted tree pulling us closer. Its little white lights were magical, but not nearly as magical as the colored ones I had loved in childhood, especially the blue bulbs. Whenever I had lost myself in their coolness, they transported me to tundra and the North Pole and Santa's workshop.

Alone with my young self, I'd lie on my back, maneuver under the tree and look up. Or I'd turn over and stare at the manger scene beneath the boughs. Finally, after unplugging the lights but before going to bed, I'd notice the same gauze of gray from childhood filling the room, settling on the Christmas tree and my children's toys.

On one such Christmas Eve, after I'd gone to bed, I heard snow shift loudly on the roof. My heart raced for a split second: I thought I might be hearing Santa. Then I caught myself, remembering that I'd been up all night helping him to do his work.

Still, a part of me wanted to believe—and did.

I pulled the covers up and snuggled down. I couldn't wait to open Christmas Day once more.

Epiphany

$\mathcal{N}$o one slams the lid on Christmas; it just winds down. Before the music stops, there are lessons to be learned.

Year after year, we're tempted to orchestrate the holidays at full blast. Like a music box wound too tightly, we go faster and faster.

So here we are, at the 12th day of Christmas, reassessing the chaos we've just put ourselves through.

Scoring only 12 points on a 100-point stress scale compiled in 1967, the Christmas season today has soared to 56 points. It produces more anxiety among women than a son or daughter leaving home (41 points), trouble with in-laws (43 points), trouble with a boss (45) and sexual difficulties (53).

"When I asked groups of women how many stress points they'd give Christmas, they'd yell out, '100! 200! 400!'" said psychologist Georgia Witkin in a Knight-Ridder Newspapers story last year.

Revamping the original Holmes-Rahe stress scale, she polled 2,600 women. Witkin's theory on why women today suffer more holiday stress: "Women are working, but they also have to clean, cook, entertain relatives, buy presents and make a traditional Christmas."

"You can't regulate or delegate joy. It just happens," said a friend. Another observed, "It's the spirit of the house."

Wise women.

As children, we know that instinctively. But somewhere along the way, we begin working too hard to produce the Christmas spirit. The holiday isn't difficult; we make it that way.

Like the year my Christmas came late.

That season, scenes from Currier and Ives and Norman Rockwell didn't just dance in my head. They stalked me like ghosts from past

99

perfect Christmases. As the determination to create the ideal holiday mounted, so did the anxiety. By Christmas Eve, I was at least 56 points stressed.

"Dinner," I chimed just as the phone rang. It was my daughter's friend whom she'd been trying to reach all day.

"Mom," she said excitedly. "May I run down to Hope's and give her my present?"

"No," I answered.

"But, Mom, she's leaving . . . . "

"Certainly not," I said. "One night out of the year we should all be able to sit down at the same time."

She burst into tears, ran up to her room and slammed the door. In the time it took to coax her to come back down, she could have delivered 10 presents. Dinner was cold, the atmosphere colder.

Fast-forward two weeks. Our daughter had a basketball game. Her brother and dad and I went to watch. Afterward, we ordered a pizza for dinner. Slapping down the cardboard box on the kitchen table, we huddled around, passing plates and napkins, filling one another's glasses. The conversation flowed—a joke here, a compliment there. In the intimacy of this little scene, a melody began. First one note, then another. We all sensed it. We were family, one in the moment.

Without any trappings or fanfare the holiday spirit arrived softly, like a quiet snow.

Then I realized it was Jan. 6, the 12th day of Christmas.

Even kings—three wise ones at that—cannot bring joy. It glows from within. Christmas came late that year. And with it a gift.

Frozen Flowers

*G*lazed with ice, the pink geraniums startled me. There they were in January beside the barbershop door. Having escaped the shears, they'd been toppled by cold. A spray of blossoms, like a frozen fan, lay forgotten on the ground. Still, they offered hope—that someday summer would return.

We are forever finding or sending messages through flowers. Our experience and the language of legend give them meaning. Chloris, the deity of flowers in Greek mythology, transformed the death of a lovely nymph into triumph by turning her into a rose. The new flower, surpassing all others, symbolized love, youth and beauty.

For my mother, a rose pointed the way. As a young girl living in the country, she found life's direction when she found a "dark-red, perfect, hot-house rose." Looking for neither, she was merely helping her father, the church choir director, by singing at a funeral. After the service, she spotted a fallen flower in the aisle and picked it up.

"It was a city rose—so velvety and fragrant, so long-stemmed and smooth," she recalled. "It wasn't at all like the thorny wild roses that tumbled over our country fences."

If that's what the city offered, she marveled at the time, that was for her.

Years later, my sister Sonja discovered her own meaning within a single rose. "Less is more," she used to tell me when I thought more was more. "The Japanese understand that—in their haiku poetry, in decorating and flower arranging."

On her wedding day, instead of the traditional bridal bouquet, she carried only a white rose.

White on white—like the way she decorated her airy apartment. Because of that, every year at Christmas I'd send her a white poinsettia.

"No, no, not red—white," I told a florist back in 1976. "To arrive this Friday."

In Illinois, a plant showed up at her door—as I learned when she called to thank me—but a red one and on Monday.

"It's the wrong color," I wailed, "and so late."

"It's beautiful," she reassured me. "And I can enjoy it all winter. It'll remind me to keep Christmas year-round."

Two weeks later, in January, the news was sudden—my sister had died. After the funeral, when Mother and I entered her apartment, the first thing I saw was a heap of red poinsettia leaves beneath a withered plant. Grabbing the last gift I ever gave her, I threw it away.

The next month, on what would have been Sonja's 37th birthday, I sent flowers to my parents. Of all the roses in the florist's cooler, a glorious, peach-colored one beckoned.

"It's called a Sonia rose," the clerk said, pronouncing it like my sister's name. "It's new."

Had the Greek goddess of flowers wrought one more miracle? I chose to believe so as I wove my own meaning around the rose.

On the 17th anniversary of my sister's death, I ordered "white on white" altar bouquets for our childhood church in Wisconsin. After the service Mother called to say that instead of taking them home, she'd given the flowers away—to two families whose babies were baptized.

"I hope you don't mind," she said. "It seemed like something Sonja would do."

As she talked, I remembered how finding a rose in a country church had led my mother to the city. And to another church where she also saw a single rose—on her daughter's coffin.

"Yes, Mom," I agreed. "Sonja would have wanted you to give them away."

A white bouquet forever will remind me how a person can influence others long after death. Red poinsettias, like the two that linger in my front hall, no longer make me sad but urge me to try to "keep Christmas year-round." Now even frozen flowers, like pink geraniums, are a gift on a barren landscape.

Bird at the Window

*J*anuary—when the world unmasks itself: Trees stand bare; gardens rest unadorned.

"You can see everything this time of year," said Boris Stanojevic, a Columbus, Ohio, tailor.

He's right: Even birds' nests are revealed. Birds emerge, jewellike, from leafless branches and the drab robe of day—or from evergreens and white snow.

When, except now, does the cardinal's clerical red look so bright on the feeder? Or a blue jay's blue?

A soul can soar watching wings break the bleakness. A heart can melt hearing one winter song.

On a January morning in 1977, my mother noticed mourning doves covering the ground in her Wisconsin back yard. Some filled the magnolia tree; others lined wires. She'd never seen such a phenomenon; yet she'd always heard—while growing up on her family's farm—that when doves gather a death is at hand. Though the flock had left by early afternoon, she couldn't shake a feeling of dread.

The next day, in Illinois, her 36-year-old daughter, Sonja, died unexpectedly. Back in Ohio, after my sister's funeral, I often found myself alone in the living room, face to face with mourning.

One day a sparrow startled me, fluttering again and again against a small side window. Only when I left the room would its wings stop tapping on the icy glass. Each time I returned, however, the bird would repeat its frenzy.

Day after day, the scene was the same.

Was my sister trying to tell me something? I wondered in despair.

Embarrassed, I buried the incident. Years later, though, I mentioned it to a friend grieving over her father's death.

To my surprise, she had had a similar experience: When she drove down her driveway on the day of her father's funeral, a bird kept flying against her car window.

"I felt it was my father's spirit," she told me, "trying to communicate." She shared her experience with a friend whose husband had recently died.

That friend had her own tale to tell: On the morning of her husband's funeral, a bird entered the house through an open door and flew into the master bedroom's walk-in closet—where she was selecting her mourning clothes.

This January the stories swooped back to haunt me, so one day I haunted the library.

I knew that in the Christian tradition the Holy Spirit is symbolized by a dove.

What I didn't know is that "it is a widespread and extremely ancient belief that the soul assumes the form of a bird or, put more extremely, that all birds are human souls." So says Beryl Rowland in her 1978 book *Birds With Human Souls: A Guide to Bird Symbolism* (University of Tennessee).

The Egyptians, she says, "depicted an androcephalic bird as their sign for the soul. In the fourth century B.C., Plato gave an extraordinary detailed picture of the soul growing wings and feathers . . . . In the Roman catacombs the upward flight of the bird was used to represent the aspiration of the soaring soul, released at last from the body. . . . In 14th-century paintings of the Madonna and Child the bird in the plump hand of the Infant was the symbol of the soul which he had come to save."

What really startled me was what I read in Scott Weidensaul's *The Birder's Miscellany*. "Death and birds are inexplicably linked in many cultures . . . . In Europe—and later in America—a bird at the window meant death." How did my friend and I, independently of each other and without conscious knowledge of such a cultural notion, arrive at a similar conclusion? Does archetypal knowledge, such as superstition, rise into consciousness at a certain moment?

When I returned home from the library, I called my sister Karen in Wisconsin. Without giving any information, I simply asked whether she'd ever had an unusual experience concerning a bird.

"Only once," she answered, "right after Sonja died.

"I was horseback riding when an owl hovered overhead down the long corridor of the pass. Its wings almost touched me. You can't imagine how wide the wingspan of an owl is. It gave me the eeriest feeling. I attributed it to Sonja's passing."

Even when the world is unmasked, some things remain a mystery.

A Valentine's Day Gift

*P*ulling his wrinkled pajamas from the dryer, I realize I bought the wrong kind, the kind I'll now have to stand over and press, time and again. Down in the basement, I heat up the iron—and remember:

It's the day before Valentine's Day. During my noon break from jury duty, I'm off to City Center to find a present for my husband. Scores of suited men head in the same direction. High-spirited, smiling, they have a spring to their step. True, the day feels like April, but I sense something more, some male Morse code, of which I'm not a part.

As we converge at the Rich Street entrance, one politely holds the door as I barrel through. Paradelike, we march toward Marshall Field's. With trench coats billowing, in a matched stride of wing-tipped shoes, they quickly leave me behind. My stomach growls as I make the turn, passing the Original Cookie shop. There's no time for food until I've found the perfect present.

In Marshall Field's, I confront a pin-striped sea. At 5 feet 4, I can barely look over the shoulders, let alone the heads, of so many men standing smack in the middle of the intimate-apparel department. They block the panty rack, hide the teddies, conceal the slips. This is feminine turf, yet I feel out of place.

The men—young and middle-aged—all face the same direction, craning their necks, waiting for something to happen. Oblivious to my shoulder pads pushing through their ranks, they enjoy the complimentary sandwiches and sparkling soda. Music pulsates through perfumed air.

It's a "men's shopping event," a saleswoman chortles, "designed to help men shop."

Riding the escalator up to the men's department on the second floor, I hear the loudspeaker: "Informal modeling in the intimate-apparel department . . . . Gentlemen, a perfect time to make your valentine selection."

And I thought men hated to shop. You see, my brother, husband and son would rather listen to Roseanne Barr sing the national anthem 600 times than have to endure 60 minutes in a mall. But they're obviously the exception, judging by today's jammed-packed intimate-apparel department.

Say, if men are this interested in shopping, stores ought to expand the concept. Instead of just gossamer gowns and lacy negligees, invite the men to view the models wearing women's suits and coats, hats and shoes, and the latest in ski wear—things not only their girlfriends or wives might enjoy but also their mothers and mothers-in-law. And what about children modeling children's clothes, so dads can bring home surprises for the kids? And don't forget informal modeling of men's clothes . . . .

Which brings me to the men's department, where I'm standing. I wonder what kind of special "women's shopping event" Marshall Field's has planned to assist us with our valentine selections. The place is quiet. Deserted, in fact. Since I cannot locate a single male clerk, I assume that everyone is downstairs at the informal modeling show.

A workman carrying part of a display crosses my path.

"Excuse me?" I ask. "Do you know where the sandwiches are?"

"Sandwiches?"

"Yes. The free sandwiches," I explain.

"Lady, I don't know anything about any sandwiches."

No sandwiches. No soda. No music, pulsating or otherwise. No male models displaying the latest daring trend in men's nightwear. No sales-men suggesting what to give.

Like some of the men below, I, too, wish to make an "intimate apparel" selection for my spouse. Yet here the pajamas look so specimenlike, so antiseptic in these flat cellophane packages that I feel I need a pair of steel tongs to remove them from the stack.

Rooting about, I find what I think are the perfect pair. But I can't be sure with no one here to model them. No way to see how they cover the chest or drape the leg.

Despite these obstacles, in a moment of sheer, romantic madness, I make my decision. Yes, yes, these I will buy for my valentine. Yet no clerk rushes up to assist or to ask whether I want them gift-wrapped. No one gushes, "My, what a good choice you've made. I know the little mister will like them." No one cautions, "You realize, of course, these are not permanent press."

"Hello? Hello?" My voice echoes off the Calvin Klein-postered wall. "Could someone help me, please?"

Finally, in men's ties, I find a human being.

I take the escalator down and re-enter that world of the familiar tease, of "look but don't touch," designed to separate the men from their money.

Back at the courthouse, a fellow juror clutches his wife's Valentine's Day gift in a Marshall Field's bag.

"Tough decision," he brags. "I couldn't decide which model . . . er, negligee I liked best."

Not only is the iron hot, but it steams.

The Man From Boston

*W*hen I married my college boyfriend, I thought I knew him.

Little did I know—and I didn't learn until many years later—that I had wed the man from Boston.

While growing up, I often heard my dad tell the tale about the "proper Bostonian" who for 30 years, as surely as the sun rose, ate oatmeal for breakfast.

One morning, however, his maid greeted his wife with trepidation.

"Madam, I am sorry to inform you that we have no oatmeal."

"What do you mean, 'no oatmeal'? My husband always has oatmeal for breakfast."

The wife peeked from the kitchen and saw her spouse already seated in the dining room. She braced herself and walked to the table.

"Dear," she began, "I don't know how to tell you this, and of course I feel dreadful, and it will never happen again, but we have no oatmeal."

"No oatmeal?" asked the husband, incredulous. "No oatmeal? Why, that's—that's perfectly all right. Frankly, my dear, I never could stand the stuff."

The story sounded as foreign to me as did tales of trips down the Amazon or of life in Alaska.

I couldn't imagine breakfast in the dining room, a maid and, most of all, a wife who, after so many years, doesn't know what her husband likes.

The story had nothing to do with me. Or so I thought.

Shortly before my wedding day, a family friend slipped me this advice:

"Always make sure you set the table before your husband arrives home for supper. Set it in the morning even, before you leave for a busy day.

"Then, when he walks in the door, even if you haven't started to cook, he'll assume that dinner is on the way."

Thus armed, I walked down the aisle in August 1966—the admonition to "set the table" never far from my thoughts.

"This will be a breeze," I thought.

As one year swallowed another, I taught school, changed diapers, drove car pools. Life slipped in and out of control as I adapted—or didn't—to changing circumstances.

The one constant in the midst of turmoil, as unchanging as the sea, was my table.

Even when dust bunnies went uncollected and mattresses unturned, and cookies for bake sales were bought instead of made, the table was set for dinner—and dinner was "on the way."

The table was ready not only when my husband returned home from work but, on a few occasions, even before he departed in the morning.

Eventually, our children grew up and left home—and with them went meatloaf, beef stroganoff, Richard's chicken and eggplant Parmesan. The table was set less and less, as real cooking gave way to the microwave oven and free delivery.

During one quiet evening, over one of our thrown-together meals, I looked at my husband of 32 years. Summoning up my courage, I told him how bad I felt that I had abandoned the long tradition of having the table set before he walked through the door.

"Oh," he said with an outburst, "I can't tell you how relieved I am that you don't! I hated it."

"What?" I asked, comforted but, at the same time, hurt to the quick. "How could you have hated such a gesture?"

"You know how I tend to run late. However hard I tried to get home early, every time I opened the door I felt guilty: The table was always set. No matter what, I was always late."

I married the gentleman from Boston. Worse, my poor husband married the man's wife.

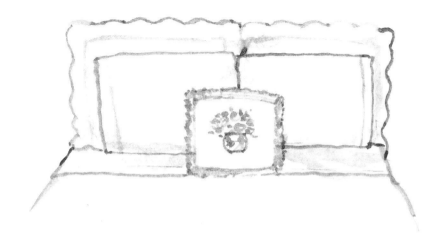

To Make—or Not To Make—
the Bed

$\mathcal{T}$he most intimate of our possessions, a bed is a constant, in sickness and in health, through life's transitions.

A bed, too, is a welcome boat for star-tossed nights.

Sleep, as Shakespeare wrote, "knits the raveled sleeve of care."

More often than not, such mending takes place in a bed, leaving us restored, reborn, ready to meet another day.

Yet, after we rise, the bed itself presents the first daily hurdle, the first brush with reality.

Will we make it? Or, if we happen to be married, who will make it?

"The marriage bed is regal," Alecia Beldegreen observes in *The Bed*. "Even the terms describing its dimension bear witness to this status: queen and king. The marriage bed is a commitment to the future and is usually the first purchase of a married couple. It is more than simply a bed for lovemaking; it is the stage for many of life's dramas. Early weekend mornings it can be a playground for children and parents; late evenings it is a parlor for the dialogue of love and marriage. In a good marriage, the bed is full of memories, children, a life together."

Right from the start, after my marriage in the '60s, the bed-making task fell to me.

I assumed that the simple chore was a given: For as long as I could remember, I'd seen my mother dutifully make hers.

"Who cares if it's not made?" my husband would say as I dashed about, getting ready for my teaching job. "No one is going to see it."

"I care," I thought. "I'm going to see it."

An unmade bed made not only the room seem rumpled but also me.

Why do some of us find the bed, our intimate friend since the crib, too private a place to leave exposed? Better to make it up and keep it under cover, in the same way most of us would rather greet the day dressed than undressed.

And why, late into the '90s, should I, and others like me, still think that an unmade bed reflects more on the wife? Even when both spouses work, women—and not their husbands—are judged lazy or poor housekeepers.

"Why do I have to make it if I'm just going to get back in it tonight?" I used to ask my beleaguered mother.

Rather than nag me, hoping I'd learn by example, she'd make it for me when I forgot. Eventually, I couldn't ignore my unmade bed; I felt too guilty.

My grown daughter learned to reduce her bed-making steps during a similar tug of war.

"When you're tired, the last thing you want to do is rummage through mounds of decorative pillows, all of which are not meant for your head," she explained.

She simplifies the process by using, along with a fitted bottom sheet, a duvet that serves as her top sheet, blanket and spread.

Presto, with almost a flick of her wrist, the bed is made.

Recently, when my husband was away on a trip, something curious occurred: I became less compulsive about making the bed, let alone arranging seven pillows. Why bother, I thought?

One noon, a meticulous friend stopped by.

As I led her upstairs, I recalled, too late, the wreckage inside the master bedroom. Suddenly, I felt no longer like the mother of two grown children but like a child, forgetting again the reminder to "Make the bed."

"Oh, well," I finally thought, trying to ease my embarrassment—"Who cares?"

That night, my husband, staying in an apartment while out of town, called.

"You're not going to believe this," he said out of the blue, "but I've actually been making the bed. I find myself doing things the way I know you would if you were here."

Recipes

$\mathcal{M}$y recipe collection, stored in old folders and a card-file box for 35 years, threatened to boil over.

On Sunday, I tried to remedy the situation.

I spread out the assorted clippings and paper slips on the kitchen table, and began to sort them.

Some patterns emerged.

The fondue fad, at least according to my collection, soon faded.

Other early recipes called more for canned ingredients—such as Korean Salad, made with a No. 2 can of bean sprouts.

Pasta bubbled to the surface in dishes from the 1980s.

By the '90s, beef took a back seat to fish, chicken and vegetarian fare.

Yet not just a culinary history but also a legacy of family and friends revealed itself.

The recipes stretch from Mom's favorites to her mother's, which once filled a farmhouse kitchen; from Dad's tips on the grilling of baby-back ribs, pork chops and steak to his beloved Auntie Karen's jellyroll and doughnuts; and from my first company meal, Chicken and Broccoli Gourmet, to Carole's Hot Tomato Sip.

The nine kitchens I've inhabited range from a 1960s aqua one in a first apartment to the white empty-nest one of today.

Despite the many moves, I still have my original recipe box and, among my folders, the daisy-covered accordion file with which I started.

Both, tattered and spattered, prove I didn't always run in for carryout.

I often meant to type my old recipes, many of which were hurriedly written on the backs of envelopes and greeting cards.

Had I done so, I wouldn't still have some of the birthday wishes that my mother sent—or all the recipes in her handwriting.

I certainly wouldn't possess the page from a legal pad on which, in the late '70s, I copied Pudin de Naranjas.

While I dreamed about such nectar, my daughter expressed a more gnawing need:

"Hi, Mom! Are we having little pizzas tonight?" she had scrawled at the bottom. "I'm extremely hungry!"

(I didn't see her message—oops—until this week.)

Thank goodness I was just as lazy with the recipes sent to me: Years later, I get to savor the notes like fine preserves out of season.

In one letter, written during the thick of my teaching years, my sister Karen offered advice on make-ahead meals:

"Short ribs . . . cook along as you are doing other things. . . . This meat only costs 49 cents a pound, but it tastes like the best roast once done. I wonder if you'll ever make it!"

I didn't, even though I set aside her note, promising myself I would.

After enjoying a tomato bisque at a tailgate party before an Ohio State football game in 1984, I asked my friend for the recipe.

"I'm sorry I don't have any recipe cards to put this on," Phyllis McFarland wrote on Nov. 12.

I'm not, for I have her letter still.

I find from Joanne Bamman the blueprint used in December 1978, when she and my daughter and I made our first gingerbread house.

And from Ann O'Leary, a mother of five, I come across a recipe for finger gelatin; and from my childhood friend Mary Bendle, a prescription for play dough—a lifesaver with my children that awaits future grandchildren.

So many friends and friendly old recipes rush back at me.

Such as Forgotten Cookies, made of egg whites, sugar, chocolate morsels and vanilla: After preheating the oven to 350 degrees, put the cookies inside, turn off the oven—and forget the treats. (Clearly, I did— and numerous others—until now.)

After a few hours of sorting, I realized that I had thrown out not one recipe nor one scrap of paper.

All seem more precious for their longevity.

Even Pudin de Naranjas.

I think I'll finally try to make it—as well as Mom's pie crust and sweet rolls.

My work—no, my pleasure—is cut out for me.

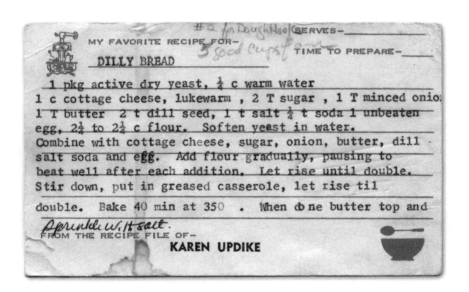

MY FAVORITE RECIPE FOR— #2 for DoughHook SERVES—_____

DILLY BREAD 3 good cups/ and TIME TO PREPARE—_____

1 pkg active dry yeast, ¼ c warm water
1 c cottage cheese, lukewarm , 2 T sugar , 1 T minced onio
1 T butter 2 t dill seed, 1 t salt ¼ t soda 1 unbeaten
egg, 2¼ to 2½ c flour. Soften yeast in water.
Combine with cottage cheese, sugar, onion, butter, dill
salt soda and egg. Add flour gradually, pausing to
beat well after each addition. Let rise until double.
Stir down, put in greased casserole, let rise til
double. Bake 40 min at 350 . When done butter top and
sprinkle w/ salt.
FROM THE RECIPE FILE OF—

KAREN UPDIKE

About Face

$\mathcal{M}$y older sister Karen is one of the least vain people I know. She spends more time on her horse than she does on herself. That's why her phone call took me by surprise.

"My face is bloated and red like a piece of beefsteak," she said frantically. "Don't ever do it. Yesterday I had a chemical peel."

"How awful!" I said. "I didn't know you were planning to."

"I wasn't, " she wailed. "A couple of weeks ago I went in to have a knobby bump taken off near my eye that I didn't like the feel of when I put my glasses on. The doctor removed it in no time. Then he said he could freeze off two large liver spots near my temple, so I said OK. Then he asked what I wanted to do about the mass of other ones.

"What mass?" Karen demanded to know. "So he got out this huge mirror and turned on a bright light. My skin looked horrible: all the brown spots had overlapped. He suggested different treatments, and I liked the sound of a 'peel'—which he said would remove not only spots but fine wrinkles. He actually thought there was something redeemable about my face; that's what was so seductive.

"The fee lured me, too—$135. I thought only people who could afford to go to spas, like Barbara Walters, had peels."

My sister made an appointment for the day after her 58th birthday: "A new face to face the future." she said. "Since the first visit had gone so smoothly, I felt quite sanguine about the whole thing. It never occurred to me to ask to see pictures or talk to people who'd had it done."

116

On the appointed day, Karen ensconced Mother, who was visiting, at a bookstore and dashed off—thinking she'd be back soon and they'd go to lunch.

The doctor told my sister that he'd misquoted the price—it actually was $380—but he would absorb the difference. He recommended a "medium" peel and asked whether she'd cleared her calendar for the next few days.

No, she hadn't. Why?

Her skin, he explained, would have a "sunburned effect."

"Right then I might have realized," Karen said. "But a sunburn makes me look healthy, so I thought it would be OK. Then he asked if I'd brought someone to drive me home. I said no, that I had to drive to pick up my mother. That's when I should have left; it never occurred to me that it would hurt."

Karen, the accidental patient, became more incensed as she described her ordeal: The doctor painted a chemical on her face. Though he said it would sting for about two minutes, she felt roaring flames. Cold compresses helped put out the fire, but she felt intense throbbing for three more hours.

"The whole experience was worse than having a baby," she said, "because it was such a psychological shock—and because you're supported and helped when you're having a baby. When this was over, I didn't even think I could open my eyes. I kept expecting them to do something for me or comfort me, but instead they were all waiting for me to put on my coat and leave."

With flaming face and swollen eyes, my sister drove to the bookstore to pick up our mother. All the way back to Karen's (they vetoed going to lunch), Mother—a quiet, charming, non-controversial woman who was married to a physician for 57 years—kept repeating: "Sue him. Sue the doctor. He should be arrested."

"Never get a peel," Karen pleaded each time we spoke on the phone, threatening to send me gory photographs should I be tempted.

On day three, she announced: "My face looks like withered skin on a frozen red apple."

On day four, she said: "My eyes are so swollen I can barely see through the slits."

On day five she was still reclusive, still spreading on ointments to stave off infection.

A week later, I phoned. Karen sounded serene and elegant—like someone in a movie.

"How does your face look?" I asked.

"Much, much younger," she said. "It's remarkable. Unbelievable. All the dead skin came off and my new skin is like a baby's. You should do it—just make sure you clear your calender, request an anesthetic and take someone to drive you home."

I couldn't believe it. My sister had done a complete about-face.

Spring-Cleaning

*W*hen we compare ourselves with our mothers, my friend Susan Quintenz and I often come up short.

"Women today don't spend as much time spring-cleaning," Susan said. "I remember coming home from school and seeing the coats from the front-hall closet and all our winter skirts and sweaters airing on the backyard clothesline . . . . You could walk up and down the street and see everybody's life hanging on a clothesline."

Spring was the chance, she recalled, "to get rid of all those moments of being cooped up, to air your whole life, to go on to a new chapter."

My mother would plunge into the annual cleaning ritual each February because "you have to be inside anyway." By the time warm weather arrived, she had surfaced in the garden—free to follow her bliss.

The rest of the year, she would either "doorbell-clean" or "deep-clean."

The former involved whisking away this or that, just making things presentable before opening the door. The latter became a thorough attack—room by room by room.

Spring-cleaning was double-deep cleaning.

"Start in the corners," Mother used to say, "and the middle will take care of itself."

So, on a snowy February day, I might find her in the corner of the den, emptying the contents of the bookshelf, dusting each volume. Or I'd see our windows shorn of drapes and the furniture stripped of slipcovers.

Now, as then, we can often find what we've lost while weeding the basement, attic or closet.

Susan recently discovered a $20 bill inside the pocket of a raincoat. In the fall, in the pocket of a jogging suit, she found the key she'd used the spring before to unlock windows for cleaning.

This spring, my sister—who hides her favorite jewelry in the freezer, inside an empty vegetable carton—is hoping to uncover where she stashed some silver tongs and a serving spoon.

Sometimes we come across forgotten things—work stoppers such as a stack of old love letters. Other times, we unearth a treasure we didn't even know we had.

Such was the case for Jody, a Columbus resident who asked that I not use her last name.

In 1962, she and her husband bought an old home and its contents in New Canaan, Conn.

The house, which belonged to an author's agent and his wife, contained everything from the deceased couple's cut-glass goblets to old Christmas cards from Eleanor Roosevelt, Helen Hayes, Marian Anderson, Clare Booth Luce, Eddie Cantor and others.

When the couple decided to restore the 1743 house, they boxed many of the belongings and stored them in the third-floor artist's studio.

Unexpectedly they moved to Pittsburgh and later Columbus, taking along the unopened boxes.

In 1987, when they bought another Columbus home, Jody finally faced the boxes: She invited her grown children to select whatever they would like.

Sometime later, she noticed broken glass on one of the remaining pictures in an open box in the garage. Removing the shards, triangle by triangle, she read the signature: Edward Hopper.

The Columbus Museum of Art confirmed for her the discovery of Hopper's *Night Shadows*, a 1923 etching.

"Magically," she said, "it was another present from the house we bought in 1962."

What would happen if this spring we hung our worries to air on the line? Or threw out certain habits? Or explored the heart's hidden corners?

Deep within, we, too, might find treasure—a forgotten hope, a latent talent. Isn't dusting off our dreams more important than dusting the furniture—and more lasting?

Cleaning always brings rewards—lost money, a painting or a letter.

Or the key to ourselves.

Lilacs

*A*n open door, the yard beyond and lilacs.

"There was a child went forth," Walt Whitman wrote. "The early lilacs became part of this child."

As for Whitman, who remembered when "lilac-scent was in the air and Fifth-month grass was growing," the fragrant flowers with heart-shaped leaves have filled many hearts—Henry Wadsworth Longfellow's, writer Natalie Babbitt's and, perhaps, yours.

One day long before I discovered a lilac bush in my back yard, before I hid beneath its cooling limbs, before I even lived, Abraham Lincoln left this earth.

On April 15, 1865, Whitman and his mother learned of the president's death.

"In a home at Huntington, Long Island," Carl Sandburg wrote of the Whitmans, "they sat at breakfast and ate nothing . . . the son deciding that as long as he lived he would on April 14 have sprigs of lilac in his room and keep it as a holy day."

Whitman's grief was grafted onto lilac branches that later grew into the eulogy for the slain president—*When Lilacs Last in the Dooryard Bloom'd*. His image of the "dooryard fronting an old farm-house" and its nearby "lilac-bush tall-growing" became nearly as common and familiar as the towering Lincoln himself.

For, just as Lincoln was "everyman's" president, the lilac was everyone's flower. Beyond doors and across farmyards, it dotted the land—including Longfellow's fine estate in Cambridge, Mass.

One May, my friend Susan Van Dyke and I found his house by following the haunting scent of lilacs along Brattle Street. The number of bushes showed how Longfellow had adored the heavily scented blossoms. When they were in bloom, he hated to leave his home.

We could see why—and why, in May 1992, the International Lilac Society had given its President's Award to the Longfellow National Historic Site.

Ablaze in purple, his beloved lilacs are everywhere—bordering grounds and sidewalks, surrounding the yellow house, carving out green pathways under a blue sky. We had not experienced anything else so enchanting.

I remember other refreshing bowers, when I hid under the lilacs at Hannan's farm, and other fragrant springs—even those in stories.

"Lilacs," Hercules Feltwright exclaims in Natalie Babbitt's children's book *Goody Hall*. "My very favorite flower. I'd rather have lilacs than all the perfumes of Arabia."

Babbitt spent part of her childhood at 75 W. College Ave. in Westerville, Ohio. Inside her family's album is a photo of Natalie, age 5, and her sister in the back yard by a big lilac bush that was their playhouse. Though the bush is no longer there, its essence lingers in Natalie's books:

"An enormous lilac bush was in full bloom," she writes in *Goody Hall*. "Heavy purple clusters filled the room with their sweet scent."

Another friend, Susan Quintenz, refers to the "lure of lilacs." She and I once picked some in her front yard. When I told her that our outing was one of my happiest memories since moving to Columbus, she remembered another front yard from long ago.

She and her husband had just bought their first house, in Milwaukee.

"We really worked hard to make it look terrific," she said. "But we were always dismayed with the house across the street because of its dilapidated appearance and overgrown yard."

That spring, when the trees had just leafed out and lilacs were in bloom, Susan heard a couple talking as she worked in her front yard.

"I looked across the street," she said, "and realized no one was outside. But a second-story window was open. With the spring breeze, you could hear every word. They were an elderly couple. And the wife was in a wheelchair.

"The husband said, 'Oh, smell the lilacs today.' But the wife said, 'I can't smell them. Where are they?' "

Then Susan saw the husband's hand reach out the window and pull a branch inside.

"Those derelict bushes that I was so disgusted with had grown to the second floor, providing the wife with a moment's rapture.

"It made me realize," she said, "that the way we view our own house may be important to us, but what may be more important to someone else . . . is just the ability to reach out and grab the day."

Beyond an open door, beyond the open window, life, like the lilac, is there.

Inga Torgeson

$\mathcal{M}$any a time Inga Torgeson has come to mind.

Especially when the world is too much with me.

But most of all when my children were small. Then I'd often think of a letter the young mother wrote from her prairie farmhouse on a "Thursday morning a little before 6."

Rising on that day four score springs ago, could she smell lilacs on the wind and hear a bluebird call? Or did motherly concern close her senses to all but the immediate task of writing at dawn?

"Dear Miss Learn," she began, addressing her son's and daughter's teacher in their one-room schoolhouse. Eventually the note would find its way into the Carpenter School scrapbook. Many years later, Miss Learn would entrust the brittle album to my mother, a former pupil.

On that long-ago morning, however, ink and perhaps tears were still wet as Inga continued, spelling her words and shaping the sentences as best she could.

"This is to let you know how I feel about Robert leaving school yesterday. First I like you to punish him in your very own way for leaving without your (the ruler's) permission. At the same time, I think the other two ought to have their share. It is not sense of the bigger boys to tear the smaller ones clothes to pieces or do other bad things, as it is not only the boy that suffers, but also the mother."

Revealing a glimpse of the bygone era, she explained:

"Yesterday I was washing clothes, which meant rubbing by hand till 3:00 p.m. I was also baking bread and making soap for the first time. Do not laugh because I am telling you all these small things; it is to have you understand what kind of a spirit I was in. I had just finished scrubbing the kitchen floor (my mop broke before I got through, so I had to lay on my knees) and in come Edith—mudd, mudd, all over her. So she had a bath, clean clothes and was put to bed for a nap. And I had some more dirty clothes to rubb. My rubbing board had splitt on the rubbing side, so I tore both the clothes and my fingers."

Though Inga's back was aching, she persevered—until, as she wrote, "here comes Robert, crying home from school, and the way he looked. His face, hands and clothes were mudd, all over. By that time, I was so all in, I could not see another thing to do, but to cry. So I sat down and cried with him. When I think of it now, it must have looked a joke.

"Miss Learn, it is hard to be a mother, but I know what it means to be a teacher, also, and I pity you; I just know there is many a time you feel like running away from it all. I felt like that yesterday."

Like mothers everywhere, Inga also was ruled by the clock: "I must close if I shall have my pancakes ready for breakfast."

But, like many of us, she can't resist one more chance to explain:

"I did send Robert back to school yesterday, but he did not go, and he had his treat here for not going. He told me Alfred and Jerome had a rope around his feet, pulled him down and dragged him on the ground and took some marbles. Robert was not feeling any too good in the first place, so I was considering not sending him to school. He had a bad cold, was sick to his stomach and felt very heavy and drowsy. But he went for not to loose any time of school. Hoping that you understand, there is absolutely no blame on you whatsoever for this. I remain your friend, Inga."

Inga's concerns, once so real, have vanished like the woman herself. Gone is her way of life, along with the rubbing board and homemade soap. Yet today on that prairie and in Columbus, Ohio, and everywhere, maternal love—like the letter—remains. We still worry about the same things—children and discipline and kitchen floors and juggling chores. And we still need someone who will listen.

Rereading Inga's letter, I was struck by the closing—"Your friend."

In the same way her children ran home and poured out their troubles, she felt she could confide in their teacher. There are many people who nurture, whether or not they have children—like the late Miss Learn, or Mother Teresa, or a friend.

In large ways and small, these "mothers" offer comfort and understanding. They make life bearable when the world is too much with us.

Summer Son

Summer 1990

One after another they leave: first our daughter, almost 19, to tour Europe with a duffel bag full of dreams. Next our son, 21, to camp on the shores of Lake Champlain in Westport, N.Y. His job, her two-month sojourn take them from us. The house, the yard—my husband and myself, for that matter—are left somber and sedate.

But then he arrives, our summer son, at the back door. Driving almost nonstop from New Orleans, he appears two hours earlier than expected. A call en route lets me know his arrival is imminent, and I rush to finish preparations. A spot on the carpet leaps up. In my hurry to remove it, I rub too hard and end up with a stove finger. It throbs and swells. But suddenly he's at the door, and the finger is ignored.

The son of our close friends, Ben is 19, blond, eager. I see his mother reflected in his face, his father in his gait. A blend of both, he is unique.

Having just completed his first year of college, he's in Columbus for a two-month job. The summer, like a clean, green carpet, stretches out in front of him—and us. Ben and I carry the contents of his car's trunk—

suitcases, tennis racket, sound system, tapes and compact discs—to his new domain, the room above the garage. No mere weekend guest, he's here for the whole nine innings.

Knowing his love of baseball, I try to establish common ground.

"Ever heard of Eddie Mathews?" I ask, summoning up the only player in whom I'd ever taken an interest.

"Used to play with the old Milwaukee Braves," I say, trying to sound casual.

"Sure," says Ben, brightening, as if perhaps this 47-year-old housewife might know a few things after all. I'm reluctant to admit that my interest had nothing to do with Mathews' ability to play third base. Back in fifth grade, I had found him "cute."

Over time, we settle in like family. Yet the routine is different. Instead of the parental urge to change, rearrange, instruct, bring up, I sit back, grandparentlike, taking pleasure in the moment.

Ben and my husband play endless rounds of Stratego, watch *Cheers* and challenge each other in tennis. With the phone ringing and music radiating from his room, life returns to the house.

Off each weekday, dressed in a coat and tie, he returns every evening with his familiar "What's up?" He helps cook dinner and clear the table. Some mornings I find the dishwasher already unloaded.

When you ask a summer child to do something, you need ask only once. And again I experience culture shock each time he does his own wash—sheets and towels included. As he walks by, carrying on hangers his freshly ironed shirts and pants, I'm certain his mother will go down in history, alongside Madame Curie and Joan of Arc. When I see his made bed, I am convinced.

Shortly after Ben arrives, my mother, in Wisconsin, is hospitalized. Both she and my sister assure me long-distance that everything is under control. They insist I not come.

"But what do *you* want to do? Don't you want to be with your mom?" he asks as I put down the receiver. I pick it up again and make flight reservations.

"Call me when you arrive," Ben says, dropping me off at the airport, "so I'll know you got there all right." When a summer son parents, you feel protected.

July 19, at 6 a.m., I look out the kitchen window and am surprised to see his car gone. Then I remember his plan—to drive to Cincinnati and find a seat inside Courtroom 4 of the U.S. District Court.

Summer 1989

Once before, Ben had arrived at our door, the dust of baseball diamonds on his feet. In the midst of a whirlwind eight-city tour to see 117 games, he stayed with us two nights. While living out the dream he had planned for two years, real life had thrown him a pitch more perfect than anything he could have imagined: Pete Rose.

At the start of his trip, he'd watched the Reds beat Houston. After the game, armed with his *New Orleans Times-Picayune* press pass, he struck up a locker-room conversation with baseball's all-time hitter. Rose still had plenty of boy buried inside, for when he heard about Ben's odyssey, when he discovered that Ben would see his Reds play eight times during the next two weeks, the Reds manager kept talking.

After a while, Rose headed to the shower. As Ben started to leave, Rose called after him: "What'd you say your name was?"

"Ben. Ben Banta."

Rose, in the thick of his woes that summer with the federal government and baseball commissioner A. Bartlett Giamatti, was wary of reporters. But not of Ben. The legend must have been disarmed to see the friendly, young face in the midst of professional bloodhounds tracking the fresh scent of scandal. Here was a boy he could talk to, a boy who might mirror the person he used to be.

Time and again, Ben heard Rose, in various states of undress, assess the team between mouthfuls of salad. He watched him shave. He sat on Rose's desk while the two of them watched football on television.

On Aug. 21 Ben hit a home run in the life of a young reporter. Following the Reds' win over the Cubs, he headed to the visiting manager's office at Wrigley Field. When other reporters dispersed, he once again hung around and talked alone with Rose. Later, as Rose headed for the shower, he said, "Well, Ben, I'll see you tomorrow."

"Tomorrow" never came: Rose's wife delivered a baby girl; by Aug. 23 Rose hadn't returned to the park. Scheduled to head home, Ben left him a note thanking him for his help. Before sealing the envelope, he included a congratulatory cigar.

That day, unknown to the public, Rose was signing an agreement in Giamatti's office. The following day, Aug. 24, Giamatti publicly handed down his decision, banning Rose from baseball forever.

On his way to New Orleans, Ben was stunned when he heard. Suddenly, the realization struck him: He'd been the last person to interview a uniformed Pete Rose.

Summer 1990

Until Ben came last summer, I'd never thought much about Rose. In fact, I'm probably one of the few Americans who can't remember where I was in 1985 when Rose broke Ty Cobb's hitting record of 4,191. This morning, however, with Rose's fate about to be determined, I feel an empathy, a connection. And Ben is the link.

Later Ben tells me how he sat in the second row of the courthouse, how he heard Judge S. Arthur Speigel deliver the sentence, how he watched Rose accept it.

"Pete looked at everyone," Ben says. "And his face didn't change. But I'm pretty sure he saw me."

It is still summer. But not the same summer. In the turning of 12 months, both man and boy have moved on.

And so have we. Ben has returned to college. Our children have come and gone.

Now I experience a new ache—a stove heart. For I miss not only our son and daughter, but a summer son as well.

The Ladies of Bullitt Park

$\mathcal{S}$ome 30 years ago, in Columbus, Ohio, the ladies of Bullitt Park gathered on porches, shared stories, talked about the Fourth of July.

Bullitt Park Place, a short street, rests between Broad Street and Bexford Place, with about a dozen houses on each side.

In the mid-'60s, Jean Goldsmith moved to Bexford Place with her husband and their two young daughters. They had bought their home from an 89-year-old woman whose "lady friends" lived right around the corner on Bullitt Park.

"Most of them were in their 70s and 80s," Goldsmith recalled. "I learned early on that first names were not acceptable. These women had known each other for decades, and yet they always referred to one another as 'Mrs. Thompson,' 'Mrs. Crabbe' or whatever the name might be. There was one spinster on the street, and she was referred to only as 'Miss Day.' "

Porches were a must for the brick and stone houses. Some were side porches, hidden from the street by shrubs.

The magnolias that Mrs. North carefully tended not only exuded a heavenly fragrance but shielded her privacy while she enjoyed morning coffee, Goldsmith said.

"Front porches were protected from the elements by awnings of different hues. Mrs. Thompson said, if she had a dime for every time she wound and unwound the awning, she could have lived on easy street.

"It was to her porch I went most often and found the 'bounce' of her metal chairs tranquilizing. Slightly hidden behind the rosebushes, with Mrs. Thompson in the glider pushing it with the toe of her Enna Jetticks shoe, we managed to solve most of the world's problems."

Miss Day had neither privacy shrubs nor an awning. She "enjoyed watching her neighbors come and go. With ankles crossed and a fan in one hand, she held court with anyone wishing to stop and chat."

On Bullitt Park, the day had a pattern.

The women who were still able to drive did their grocery shopping and errands in the morning, Goldsmith said. Social events, calls on the sick or bridge games took place in the afternoon.

In late afternoon on summer days, another routine surfaced.

"It began when Mrs. Thompson walked Miss Buff, her golden cocker spaniel, around the block. Returning home, she settled on the front porch and awaited visitors. Mrs. Babcock emerged from her red-brick Colonial to walk her white poodle, stopping at each porch to exchange news and pleasantries, always ending the 'tour' at Mrs. Thompson's.

"Sometimes they had iced tea or lemonade and, if the day had been especially exhausting, a glass of wine. Confidences were not exchanged, but gossip was acceptable."

One evening, when Mrs. Thompson wasn't feeling well, Goldsmith stopped by with a plate of brownies. She urged the older woman to stay in bed the next day.

"I could never do that," Mrs. Thompson explained. "It would be too easy to get into the habit of not getting dressed. Soon, I would not even care."

The words return to prompt Goldsmith, 69, whenever she debates whether to get up and get going—and she heads for the closet.

"I doubt Mrs. Thompson would approve "of my shorts and sneakers," she said, recalling how the ladies wore their voile and cotton afternoon dresses when they gathered on a porch.

Like everything else, Bullitt Park has changed.

The grande dames either "mercifully died in their beds" or gave in to their children and moved into nursing homes.

"When Miss Day died, her heirs held a tag sale. . . . The other women watched in stoic silence as men in pickup trucks, wearing T-shirts that advertised 'I'm a sex machine,' walked over the grassy lawns to carry away bits and pieces of her life. That was a night that called for a fortifying glass of wine."

Today, many of the porches have been enclosed.

"Skateboards now break the quiet," noted Goldsmith, who moved to a nearby neighborhood 15 years ago. "It is only in the late afternoon, on a lovely summer day, that I venture down Bullitt Park. Once again, I watch for the ladies . . . to promenade. Oh, how I miss them."

Train Ride

"You have to relax and forget about time if you're going to take a train," the woman in line at the station said.

Still, as Amtrak's California Zephyr pulled into Denver a half-hour late from Chicago, time past was on Jean Garza's mind. At 70, she remembered Union Station teeming with troops during World War II; I recalled panting, black steam locomotives barreling down the tracks of my Wisconsin youth before they roared into history.

Sometimes, when I would go on a day trip, I'd hear the train's whistle from inside a passenger car. Yet it wasn't until last weekend that I experienced a train's cry at night from my own berth. I rode Amtrak from Denver to San Francisco—a route hailed by some as "the most beautiful train trip in all of North America." My husband and I ended up traveling further than we ever dreamed.

Flying between airports can make one forget that the nation is more than its cities. A train cuts through the country. Instead of flying over, riders pass through and connect.

America is sunflowers rimming a railroad siding, fly fishermen wading thigh-high in the Colorado River, bedrolls of hay waiting for winter.

America is fence posts and barbed wire, telephone poles and country roads, the Rockies and the High Sierra "purple mountain majesties."

When the original Zephyr, the "silver lady" with its Vista-Dome (better to see peaks, canyons and alpine valleys), entered service in the late '40s, Jean Goldsmith, a friend, was an attendant, one of the first Zephyrettes:

"It was the scenic trip—the long route to California. If you were in a hurry, you didn't take the Zephyr. We didn't have television. People brought books aboard."

My husband and I brought books, too, but, by day, the windows won. In the dining car (where each table had a perfect view, fresh flowers, stainless flatware, china and a linen cloth and napkins) we met other passengers.

Barbara, a print-shop owner from Wray, Colo., and Berna Kay, a rancher's wife, were traveling with their husbands to the Colorado Hotel in Glenwood Springs.

At dinner, Jim, a plumbing estimator from Illinois, and his wife, Sue, a school-cafeteria worker, mentioned the train was traveling 80 mph through the Great Basin but had climbed the steep Rockies at half that speed.

At breakfast we sat with a Sacramento couple. The husband spotted a coyote before the waitress served his pancakes. Earlier he'd seen a buck.

At lunch we met Scott, on his way from Chicago to Stanford University and the start of freshman year.

Now home, I remember Hanging Lake and Grizzly Creek and the Truckee River; I see sage and palomino-colored ground give way to forest floors and the glint of Donner Lake; I recall grazing cattle, the sunset over a mesa and the moon, as silver as our train, leading us toward sleep.

Most of all, I remember the whistle at night as the Zephyr swayed through silent railroad crossings, a light in the distance before blackness swallowed it whole and, finally, pulling back the curtain and discovering dawn.

Did I dream of Indian tribes flourishing from the Great Plains to the Rockies? Of pioneers and railroad tracks pushing west? Of plumes of steam rising to meet the sky? Driven by diesel fuel more than a century later, I felt connected, like cars on the train, moving from past to present.

Saturday night, outside San Francisco, we arrived late in Emeryville. On Sunday we flew to Columbus, switching planes in Chicago. In three hours on a DC-10, we had retraced Zephyr's path. But squeezed into a seat in the center section, I barely saw clouds through the portholes across two aisles, let alone the shake of a pony's tail.

Somewhere below were Salt Lake City, the Rockies' red earth, the Roaring Fork River. Riding a train to the Windy City, I could have seen them all, even a copper spire on a building at Knox College where Abe Lincoln debated Stephen Douglas.

Instead, I ate off a small tray. When I stared straight ahead, I saw *The Truman Show* flickering on the movie screen.

A train takes time. Yet it gives time, too. Disembarking, a passenger holds far more than luggage.

Blackberry Farm

I recently awoke to see mist from the Smoky Mountains rising in smoldering columns to meet the sky. At the Inn at Blackberry Farm, outside Knoxville, Tenn., a magnolia tree's gnarled branches framed my second-story view. Below, in the center of the circular driveway, a lone red leaf on a green dogwood signaled the beginning of the end.

Grabbing the book my daughter had recently given me, I hurried outside to explore.

"Midsummer, this was all green," Jim Gourley, a groundskeeper at the inn, said as he pointed to the nearby trees and surrounding forests. "This time of year, the leaves start picking up spots. Their sugar content starts acting up because it's getting close to fall."

Gourley eyed my leather-bound book: *Trees of North-Eastern America* by Charles S. Newhall. Containing not only descriptions of trees but also natural-size drawings of their leaves, it was published by G.P. Putnam's Sons in 1891 and signed by a former owner—Mary E. Allen—on Feb. 6, 1892. By then, Paul Gauguin had fled to Tahiti, and the first moving picture shows were appearing in New York City. Like mountain mist, that long-ago world has vanished.

Yet trees remain—shouldering the sky, offering shade, witnessing our comings and goings. I wish to bear witness to them, not just give them a passing glance or see only a blur of green. I want to know them—the buttonwood and hornbeam, the sweet gum and chestnut. The closer I grow to leaving Earth, the more I want to identify its contents and know them by name—birds of the air, plants of the ground and, most of all, the trees that join the two.

Someday, I keep fooling myself, I'll try to learn them all. Yet one day I will have run out of somedays—like Mary Allen, whose signature rests inside my book.

So Gourley and I—first on foot, later by golf cart—started down a laurel-lined path to explore some of the inn's 1,100 acres of protected woodlands adjoining Great Smoky Mountains National Park.

"These black walnut trees," he said, "are the first to shed. Within a month, they'll be bare. They're a slow-growing tree. A lot of old folks use the hull of the walnut to stain wood."

Next he pointed out red maples and many kinds of oak—red, white, black, pin, bur and chestnut. Later, I was surprised by the wide, almost square-shaped leaves of a young tree called a yellow poplar or tulip tree that a honeysuckle was trying to overtake. Gourley's copy of an Audubon Society's pocket guide to trees states that Walt Whitman called the yellow poplar the "Apollo of the woods in reference to its graceful, columnar trunk. In spring, the tree produces striking, bright orange and green tuliplike flowers."

Gourley, who has lived all his life in the foothills of the Smokies, observed that, "around here, pines kind of take over the east side of the mountains and hardwoods, the west."

As we passed a stunning sycamore, Gourley shared what his grand-father, a logger, once said—that its wood is almost impossible to split because the fibers are so intertwined.

"Nobody uses it for anything anymore. They used to use it for fire-wood when they couldn't get anything else."

Nearby, he showed me a small chestnut tree.

"That's what all the old log cabins were made of, but it's got a blight. The trees used to be huge. You can still find some tall ones, but most grow only to the height of this little one and die back out."

In quick succession we passed a shagbark hickory (the bark, on older trunks, is usually peeling in shaggy strips), some scrub pines (they don't grow tall) and a sweet-gum tree (the leaves remind me of dancing stars).

Returning to the inn on that warm day in late August, we passed a holly tree. I was surprised to find the berries already turning red.

That night, matching leaf samples to the corresponding drawings inside my century-old book, I thought about all the trees still at work in the dark woods; the yellow poplar trying to hold its own against the honeysuckle, the chestnut fighting against blight, the holly coloring its berries. Each had its own concerns, its own struggles—just like people, just like me.

Drifting off to sleep, I remembered a letter from a Columbus reader:

"Maybe some time," she wrote, "you could drive to our home . . . and enjoy our beech woods—small, but pretty."

When I get back to Columbus, I thought, I'll make Friday another "someday."

A Journal

*T*hough I graduated long ago, the start of each school year feels more like the new year than January does. Things begin—football, clubs, classes. Autumn brings to mind sharp pencils, white paper, a clean slate.

Embarking on this new year, I again resolve to keep a journal. I want to chart my voyage like a captain writing in his log—mapping out goals, marking destinations. Most of all, I'd like to reel in my darting thoughts.

My adult daughter has been faithfully filling journal after journal since fifth grade, reflecting on her life.

My desk drawer, though, is deep in half-finished or barely begun attempts. I received a book of blank pages as a gift in 1979 but didn't write in it until March 5, 1986—and then, only once. Still, in the midst of all the white, that one ink-marked page tells me what I did, thought and felt on that one day eight years ago.

Sifting through other journals, I find more fragments kept from washing downstream—such as the one written on Aug. 29, 1977: "Tonight I returned from visiting Mom and Dad . . . . I love the orderliness of their home, making me feel free and serene . . . . The rose on my dresser . . . . The roses on the table. The three yellow candles that glowed through our talking . . . . Dilly bread at every meal and making some yesterday with Mother. She sent the two loaves home with me."

Why didn't I capture more moments? All that stands between a journal and writing in it is oneself. Why not treat ourselves and the people we love with the same care that novelists treat their characters? Are not real lives worthy of such attention?

Little by little, however, I had become distracted—polishing baby shoes, planning a graduation party. But, if I had filled up each book, little by little, like a savings account, it would have accrued great value over time.

And a lot of interest—like the kind my son showed in the slim volume I gave him on his 26th birthday.

I had begun it two months after his birth but wrote in it for only a couple of years.

Suddenly, all this time later, I thought of it and found it in the attic.

Lingering a moment—not far from the old cradle—I read my hand-written inscription: "September 26, 1968, 3208 Raleigh Drive, Toledo." How I remembered that glorious fall day when I headed to the drugstore to buy a journal, pushing my firstborn in his buggy.

"Quite a lot has happened to Tyler during the first eight weeks of his life," the opening sentence began. In a later entry, I told of the trip to Elyria, Ohio, where he met his great-grandparents.

On Nov. 14, I described their visit to Toledo: "How your great-grandparents loved seeing their cradle put to such good use . . . . Your great-grandfather asked how old you were, exactly—and I answered, '3 1/2 months.' Such a short life you've lived compared to his long one."

After Aug. 30, 1970, the entries stop. Time swallowed them.

"I want to give this to you now," I told my son on the afternoon of his birthday, "instead of tonight with your presents."

As I sat in a rocker across from him, he opened the journal and read aloud—transfixed at learning the details of his young life. When he began reading about his seventh month, I was struck by what I had written: "Your favorite books are *Pat the Bunny* and *Goodnight Moon*. And you recognize their titles. When I ask, you're able to grab them out of a pile of your other books."

It wasn't a boat that crossed time. A journal, newly found, had turned back the pages of our years.

In the same way I used to read to him, my son was now reading to me. But the story being read today was his—and mine.

Ours.

Maybe

A hammock between two trees, *maybe*—yes and no, no and yes—swings so easily.

It sounds indecisive, but *maybe* is powerful, indicating that the world—neither black nor white—is full of possibilities.

Maybe is an in-between word, a neither-here-nor-there word, a no-thumbs-up-or-down word, that dares to make a difference.

Will a human someday walk on the moon? "Maybe," the answer once went. And one did.

Will Rhett return to Scarlett? Maybe. And why not? Only yesterday is gone with the wind; tomorrow awaits.

"Will we marry?"

"Maybe" mollifies both, buying time for the one who is asked and keeping hope alive for the one who questions.

Any child, moreover, knows when "Maybe someday" means no, as when it follows "May I have a pony?"

Some people consider the word wishy-washy; others deem it prophetic.

A tribal chief, as the legend goes, possessed a prized stallion.

One day, the horse ran away.

"Gone?" cried the people in his village. "How sad."

"Maybe," the chief replied.

The next morning, lo and behold, the horse returned, with 20 wild steeds in his wake.

"Now you have your horse back—and many more," the people rejoiced. "How wonderful."

"Maybe," their chief said.

In a few days, his beloved son, a strong young brave and an only child, began to tame the wildest of the lot. Thrown from the horse, he was trampled, his leg shattered.

"How unfortunate, how sad," grieved the villagers.

"Maybe," their leader said, "maybe." Shortly afterward, a neighboring tribe declared war upon the villagers.

All the braves went off to fight. All were killed in an ambush except the chief's son, who was at home with a broken leg.

Daily life spins legends, too.

A beloved son is elected president of the United States, then assassinated. His brother triumphs in California; then, taking a shortcut through a kitchen corridor, similarly gets in harm's way.

A mother loses her daughter to a drunken driver, then copes with her tragedy by creating Mothers Against Drunk Drivers, saving countless lives and raising awareness.

Curses can be blessings; blessings can be curses.

Success can hold the seeds of defeat, defeat the seeds of success.

Maybe.

"Only a man who knows what it is like to be defeated," Muhammad Ali once said, "can reach down to the bottom of his soul and come up with the extra ounce of power it takes to win when the match is even."

Walt Disney had a more succinct philosophy: "I think it's important to have a good, hard failure when you're young."

He attributed his astounding success to many failures, especially the hard one at age 26.

After seven years of trying to make it in the animation business, he had rung the bell with his creation of Oswald, a cartoon bunny: Stencil sets, candy bars and buttons were popping up everywhere. (Children even wrote asking for an Oswald autograph.)

Disney traveled to New York to borrow more money for his cartoons from distributor Charles Mintz, who wanted Disney to work for him. Having hired away all but one Disney animator, Mintz informed Disney that Oswald belonged to Universal Pictures.

A disheartened Disney still controlled his own future, at least.

On the train back to California, he began to doodle. When he finished, he looked at his sketch, smiled and asked his wife what she thought of the name "Mortimer Mouse."

"How about 'Mickey'?" she asked.

Maybe.

Two Dads

This is a tale of two fathers, one internationally revered and the other beloved by his family, friends and patients.

I couldn't help thinking of the unknown one, my dad, when I toured the Mark Twain House a few weeks ago in Hartford, Conn.

After all, he "introduced" me to the literary legend—the one about whom Ernest Hemingway wrote, "All modern American literature comes from one book by Mark Twain called *Huckleberry Finn.*"

Dad first told me about the gilded manse.

From 1874 to 1891, in the home he shared with his wife, Olivia, and their children, the father of modern American literature wrote many of his famous works—including *The Adventures of Huckleberry Finn, The Adventures of Tom Sawyer* and *The Prince and the Pauper.*

My father had reached only his third birthday when Twain, at 75, went out with Halley's comet.

Yet, growing up, I often merged their two boyhoods, making them not only contemporaries but also "friends."

Each was born into hardscrabble circumstances; each lost his father at an early age—Twain at 12, my dad at 6.

How curious, then, that Twain wrote and Dad liked to repeat:

"When I was a boy of 14, my father was so ignorant I could hardly stand to have the old man around. But when I got to be 21, I was astonished at how much he had learned in seven years."

Though young, both labored hard.

Twain ended his formal education at age 12, first going to work as a printer's apprentice.

My dad, although he continued in school, delivered newspapers and groceries, pulling his weight at Auntie Karen's.

Neither forgot his roots, as books and recountings prove.

The author grew up on the banks of the Mississippi in Hannibal, Mo.

Living in Eau Claire, Wis., Dad knew the mighty river, too, some 45 miles away: Eager for adventure, he would raft with his friends on a nearby tributary, the Chippewa River—catching fish and frying them over an open fire.

Twain led an itinerant life until he married Olivia Langdon.

My father, for his part, felt like a boarder at his aunt's—before becoming a boarder elsewhere while working his way through college and medical school.

As a result, I think, both men delighted all the more in their own homes and families.

Dad adored his modest residence, with its fireplace and screened porch, much as Twain loved his 19-room mansion.

"To us," Twain wrote, "our house was not unsentient matter—it had a heart, and a soul, and eyes to see us with. . . . We never came home from an absence that its face did not light up and speak out its eloquent welcome—and we could not enter it unmoved."

Olivia affectionately called her husband "Youth."

Why? Because he took his childhood, which had been cut short, into adulthood, enshrining it in his books, celebrating it in daily life?

Besides making up bedtime stories, he reveled in family plays for friends.

"Just his walk was funny," Katy Leary, a servant at the Hartford house, once recalled of his part in *The Prince and the Pauper*. "Then he rang the bell for me to bring the pitcher of water in, and he poured it out the wrong way—by the handle and not the nose—and, of course, that took down the house!"

"Father also taught us to skate," wrote Clara, his middle daughter, "on the little river that flowed through the meadow behind the house."

And my dad helped all four of his children learn to skate.

He took up horseback riding at 40, went to Vietnam at 60.

Friends as well as the fortuneteller at the fair always guessed that he was younger.

Until he had his stroke at 74, he might have said what Twain observed at that age: "I am just as young now as I was 40 years ago."

Both knew, too, what Twain put so aptly: "The heart is the real fountain of youth."

My father introduced me to Tom Sawyer and Huck Finn as if they were his boyhood pals.

Mark Twain, therefore, introduced me not only to his boyhood but also to that of my dad.

Their parenting styles had to do with serving something greater than themselves—finishing a book, curing the ill, supporting a family.

Although both are gone, what they stood for remains.

I cannot, as the author said of his Hartford house, think of either father "unmoved."

I cannot think of one without love.

Visit to the Hospital

"Where are we going?" I asked.

I was young—young enough that, when my dad swooped me up on his shoulders, he made the sky seem closer.

That morning, however, he bundled me in a blanket and carried me to the car.

"Where are we going?" I asked again, as he turned the key.

"To the hospital," he answered.

Something was up, I knew, even though I had often accompanied my father, a doctor, when he left to make rounds. Not once before had I worn my pajamas when I waited for him in the lobby.

"But I'm not dressed," I reasoned as I saw other kids heading for school.

"That's OK," he said, gently diverting my attention.

As soon as the hospital came into view, my mood turned festive, less apprehensive, because of the people who usually fluttered about.

Picking me up, Dad carried me from the parking lot, through the entrance and into the lobby.

145

"This is my daughter," he said again and again to colleagues and friends until, as daughter No. 3, I felt giddy from the unaccustomed attention.

Best of all, still holding me, he let me flip a switch on the wall next to his name.

A little light, round as a button, popped on.

"How come?" I wanted to know.

"So the staff can tell which doctors are in," he said, making a game of showing me all the other lights.

I remember his triumphant entry more than my later awakening with a raw and tonsil-less throat (thanks to his partner)—or my first night in a hospital bed.

More than any ether, his manner conveyed that everything would be all right.

"Where are you going?" I asked Mom some four decades later as she and my father got into the car during one of my visits home.

"To the hospital," she answered. "Your dad has an appointment."

"I'll take him," I volunteered, for I hoped to be of help.

I drove the old route etched in his memory for more than half a century, but I had trouble remembering.

Though unable to speak because of a stroke, he pointed the way whenever he sensed that I was about to take a wrong turn.

My 80-year-old father, who had recently relearned how to walk, shuffled next to me. Arm in arm, we inched toward the hospital doors.

Entering the lobby, Dad expectantly veered toward the old roster on the wall.

I wished I could turn on the light where his name used to be. He didn't seem bothered, however, as he scrutinized the list.

Whenever he spotted a friend, he said, "Nice"—the only word he could say.

Through the long corridor, I looked into each passing face.

A few people nodded or even said hello, responding to my hopeful glance, yet none stopped in recognition. Fifty years of service, I thought, and now my father had become a stranger.

Once, after I married, Mother wrote that Dad had asked her to buy a ring to give to a little girl, a patient of his, who had to spend Christmas in the hospital. And I recalled the long-ago dad who delivered me for a tonsillectomy.

As we made our way down the hall, I avoided his eyes, fearing that I might see the sadness I was feeling.

If only I could do for him as he had done for me.

Then, when he stopped and pointed to the right, as I was heading left, I couldn't help noticing the joy.

Although he didn't receive a triumphant welcome as he had in his prime, Dad looked triumphant—neither resentful nor sad, just glad to be who he was and where he was: home.

The light still burns, I realized as the sky suddenly drew closer.

When we finally reached the doctor's door, I stood before the receptionist's desk and said what I felt proud to say:

"This is my father, Dr. Lokvam."

Retirement

*T*ime plays tricks.

Only yesterday, I was startled—even though my father was almost 73—to learn of his impending retirement.

The newspaper announcement jolted me, too. Black-bordered and blunt, it closed the curtain:

"Leif H. Lokvam, M.D., announces his retirement Jan. 15, 1980. With appreciation to patients, colleagues, hospitals, staffs and community."

Recently, I came across the clipping—and wondered how two decades could have disappeared along with my worry: Would Dad, who thought he would practice "forever," become restless and bored?

From all appearances, he adjusted well as he gave up his hard-driving pace to work in the yard ("The trees and the garden are my patients now").

"Read all you can," he used to say when I was growing up. "Learn to play golf. . . . When you're my age, you'll be too busy earning a living. There won't be time."

Suddenly, he had all the time in the world. And so he read—as if his life depended on it—and, perhaps, it did.

What I didn't know then was that after he put down his scalpel he picked up a pen.

I recently discovered a story—"A Mid-Winter's Day Dream"—in which a doctor, obviously Dad, muses about his new status, "brought about not by illness or anything as specific as death, not yet anyway. That would be a much more proper and acceptable excuse."

For the first time, I sensed guilt, as if his half-century of work hadn't seemed enough; and—on his vacation in California, where the story takes place—disorientation.

Not only didn't he practice medicine anymore, but he no longer had his old, scuffed doctor's bag.

In a new place for an extended stay, and without his bag, he began to develop the concerns that so many patients had expressed: "What will I do if I become ill? How can I find a good doctor?"

Back home, at least, the people and places were familiar. In his new setting, "no doors were opened, no pathways smoothed."

That "longed-for paradise of retirement" had turned him into a stranger to others and to himself.

One day, after lunch, he settled into a large easy chair, promising himself that the next day he would look for a physician.

Something—the ratatouille or more likely the James Thurber book he was reading, "replete with wild fantasy and implausible tales about a unicorn in the garden eating the roses"—contributed to some strange happenings:

He saw himself waiting in the surgical department at his old hospital. More startling, he observed himself lying on the operating table, "abdomen and chest bared and ready to accept the bite of the gleaming scalpel."

He was talking, not showing the effects of the anesthetic, "as any other self-respecting patient would do."

At the onset of the operation, all went well.

Soon, however, the surgeon, "whose subspecialty didn't fit the occasion, called out for a general surgeon to take over."

What else could he, the recently retired general surgeon, do but assist in his own operation? He seized the scalpel, told the operating surgeon to step aside and took the plunge.

Becoming more and more tense, he awoke to find himself sitting in the chair and "the unicorn peering up at him from the pages."

The experience sent him back home to the good doctors, nurses and hospitals he knew; to a community where he wouldn't have to carry "a pocket full of credit cards and his Social Security number, and his identity would be restored."

Today, I awakened to the realization that in five years I'll turn 62; in eight, 65—and at least think about Social Security, as any other self-respecting senior citizen would do.

Time does play tricks.

Do I see a unicorn in the garden?

Thelma Lien

*I*n 1948, Dinah Shore filled the air with *Buttons and Bows*, Citation became the eighth horse in racing history to win the Triple Crown and Harry S. Truman was re-elected president.

That spring, 36-year-old Thelma Lien boarded a bus in her Wisconsin hometown of Beloit and headed for Kenosha 2¹/₂ hours away.

"A friend had mentioned that somebody needed a bookkeeping-machine operator, so I took a chance," she recalled recently.

The job had fallen through when she learned that a Kenosha doctor needed a secretary. Fortunately, she knew shorthand.

"I was scared stiff," she said, remembering the day she climbed the white marble steps of the old Kenosha Clinic for her interview.

Yet she found my father, 41 at the time, "congenial and easy to talk to. The next thing I knew, I was hired," she said.

"I was a jack-of-all-trades; anything that concerned the office, I took care of."

She not only filled the role of the receptionist but also balanced the books, did the banking and kept the files. She was known even to wash the windows and scrub the floors.

One time, during dictation, the building janitor appeared suddenly, so scared he was stuttering.

After calming him down, Dad and Thelma discovered what had frightened him: An arm from the clinic skeleton had dropped from the rafters onto his shoulder while he was cleaning the basement.

They thought they'd have to conduct a funeral to dispose of the deteriorating bones.

150

"But Dr. Swift, who taught radiology classes at the hospital, took them off our hands."

Thelma, who doesn't drive, lived close enough to walk to work. Conveniently, she had an apartment overlooking Library Park—for, as she said, "My nose is always in a book."

Sometimes she had us kids over for dinner. On one occasion, she whipped up orange juice "cocktails" and lobster tails to make us feel grown-up.

And she and my mother shared a mutual admiration, each one helping the other.

Thelma first baby-sat for us right after my brother, the fourth and youngest, was born. When she stayed a week or two, she asked in the morning what we wanted for dinner.

Excitement waited to happen until she came to visit: Once, the water heater broke and flooded the basement.

Another time, down in the basement, my toddler brother looked up and asked, "Why is that man coming through the window?"

Thelma, unintimidated, scared him off. The police found only his tools.

Many years later, the 85-year-old woman who served my father for more than three decades continues to be a fountain of information.

"Whatever happened to that old X-ray machine that Dad used to have in his office?" I wondered.

"He sold it to another doctor for a dollar."

"Why did he keep anise candy in his top right desk drawer?"

"Frank Christiansen knew he liked it; he always brought him some whenever he had an appointment."

Of her 32 years with Dad, she said: "The time went so fast, it seemed as though it stood still. My job was enjoyable. I was a member of your family. It was a perfect way."

Dad was never Leif, always "Dr. Lokvam."

"No one could ever say anything against Dr. Lokvam in front of me."

After the national observance of a day to honor secretaries began in 1952, Dad ("when he wasn't in surgery") would take her to lunch.

"We might just go and get a hamburger, but it was entertainment," she said.

In her apartment, Thelma still displays a picture of my father, a photograph taken in his prime, when together they saved the world.

"He was like a brother to me," she said.

Although he has been gone for seven years, she still sees him daily.

I can't imagine a more loyal secretary. Or a luckier boss.

Dad, Age 7

Gone almost eight years, my father rested in the palm of my hand—in a wallet-size photograph, a gift from my cousin.

"Leif / Summer 1914 / Putnam Road," I read in pencil on the back.

Still, on the front, I could barely discern the half-inch figure fading into the forest.

Eventually, a restorer enlarged the print to a 5-by-7—far from the mythic proportions with which an offspring knights a parent but large enough for a glimpse.

The face of my father, at age 7, suddenly stared back at me.

Before, I'd seen only one other childhood photo of Dad—a shot taken a year or two earlier, before his parents died: Facing the photographer, his little jaw determined and his glance confident, he was grouped with his three older siblings.

The look fit the face of the father I knew.

Only once had I observed his countenance quavering outside the family circle.

Even then I did not see, could only imagine, as he embraced a colleague at my sister's funeral.

So much of his life, as a doctor, had been spent comforting others; finally, he needed comfort.

Growing up, I often wanted to reach through the folds of descended decades and pull his younger self into the present. I longed to talk to him; ask him, not as my father but as a friend, what he had felt losing both parents by the time he was 6, only to be saved by an aunt and uncle.

His rescuing relatives were long gone when I entered the world, a world in which I couldn't read the map of memory in any baby picture or childhood scrapbook.

I finally saw the portrait of Dad and his siblings when I was well into my 30s. Until then, like someone born before the birth of the camera, I could only envision what my father looked like as a young child.

Now, coinciding with my 50s, the second snapshot has come into my keeping.

"How cute," I thought at first when I saw the enlarged version of a boy holding two hand-picked bouquets—one for him and one, no doubt, belonging to his sister, the photographer.

His little wool cap, coat and knickers belie the summer reference on the back. (Most likely, a spring day had felt like summer.)

On closer examination, the jaunty wildflower in his lapel doesn't offset the tentative, almost-worried look on his face. His chin is tilted slightly downward; even his stance seems shy, shrinking.

The dust of Putnam Road covers the toes of his high-top shoes, protecting feet that had already traveled a more harrowing journey: The son of immigrant parents, he was born in a homesteading cabin with a dirt floor—to which the family returned when a new home went up in flames.

A few years later, his mother took ill and died; within 12 months, his father died, too. The children were scattered.

The picture that captured him after his move to another new home survived longer than he did to answer my musings.

He didn't know then that in August 1914, on a farm in the same state, his future bride would be born.

Someday she would help him create a home, giving him a sense of place, of belonging.

For years, he had a newspaper route. He later worked at his uncle's market after school and on Saturdays. Before marriage, he put himself through medical school and college.

Such experiences taught him to tip generously any hardworking youngster—and not to forget folks who had done so for him.

Decades later, as I view my father as a little boy, I want to pluck him out of the picture or somehow enter it myself. I want to see him sitting at the kitchen table. I want to fuss over him the way I would a grandchild—serve him his favorite angel food cake, tell him a funny story to brighten his face.

I'd like to be there when he bursts through the back door, so that I might be the one to whom he hands his bouquet. Most of all, I'd like to give him a hug.

"A Child's Garden of Verses"

I rarely saw my father cry, even after a stroke had left him unable to speak.

Once, though, the tears flowed.

I had bought him a present, a copy of *A Child's Garden of Verses* by Robert Louis Stevenson.

The illustrations alone, I thought, would comfort him, remind him of his boyhood love of the poems—which he later recited to his children and grandchildren.

Anticipating his pleasure, my family and I watched him unwrap the gift.

He held the open book in both hands for a moment. Then a sob surfaced—a sound so startling that we all fluttered at once, helping him to his feet.

Out of his presence, we shared our surprise: What had unleashed his tears? For a long time afterward, I couldn't read Stevenson's verses.

But recently, I "was sick and lay abed" in the "land of counterpane."

Like the child of *Bed in Summer*, I missed the old poems—when I saw "the birds still hopping on the tree" and heard the "people's feet / Still going past me in the street."

So I found the *Verses* volume given to my daughter on her eighth birthday.

"May these poems carry you lands and dreams away as you sit reading *The Wind, The Land of Counterpane* or *Looking Forward*," a family friend had written.

On the shelves were other works, such as *Madeline's Rescue*—with Miss Clavel chanting, "Something is not right."

Among other books I had read to my children, I came across Max from *Where the Wild Things Are*; *Curious George*, up to his old tricks; and the bunny in *Good Night Moon*, with the bowl of mush and the red balloon.

Little Orphan Annie, still brushing the crumbs away and shooing the chickens off the porch, stood next to *The Hungry Caterpillar* and *Whatever Happens to Baby Horses?*—the book my daughter so often hugged when I said, "You choose."

The Big Golden Book of Poetry, I'm afraid, has lost its spine and back but not its *Jill Who Came From the Fair*, nor the *General Store* with its "tinkly bell hung over the door."

Have the children who once begged me to read to them run off with *The Runaway Bunny*? They have "grown up and gone away"—even while the stories endure.

The books hold power enough.

If I were to sit in the rocker where the reading began, I would find the memories too strong.

I would recall inhabiting story land with my son, who held his lamb's ear with one hand and turned the pages with the other; and my daughter, who slid off my lap with a finished book and ran to get another.

Whatever happens to baby horses? Whatever happens to little children?

"As from the house your mother sees / You playing through the garden trees," Stevenson writes in the last poem of *A Child's Garden of Verses*, "So you may see, if you will look, / Through the windows of this book.

"He does not hear; he will not look, / Nor yet be lured out of this book. / For, long ago, the truth to say, / He has grown up and gone away, / And it is but a child of air / That lingers in the garden there."

Returning to the long-ago image of my father, I fight back the same tears.

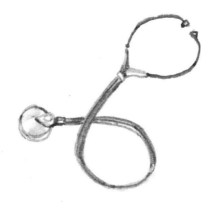

Hospital Rounds

"The great thing in life," Carmen Agra Deedy writes in *The Last Dance*, "is not so much to dance well but whether one is willing to dance at all. ... To sing, even if you sing off-key. The crow has as much right to a voice as the nightingale."

Rising from breakfast to head for the hospital, my father, a doctor, greeted the day with enthusiasm.

He often said, quoting Longfellow's *A Psalm of Life*: "Let us, then, be up and doing, / with a heart for any fate; / Still achieving, still pursuing, / Learn to labor and to wait."

Then, with a wave and a smile, he was off.

Certainly he encountered times when he would have preferred not to go—holidays when he might have wanted to linger with the family.

Yet I have only the one memory of his departure to see patients on his daily rounds.

I found no photographs of such leave-takings among the brittle negatives unburied last year in my parents' attic—nor any of his homecomings late each evening through the back door.

His leaving and returning—seven times a week, year in and year out—became bookends that bracketed his days and those of his family, too.

I found plenty of other pictures, however, just waiting to be discovered for more than a half-century: the boy flanking the aunt and uncle who raised him, the intern posing before Ravenswood Hospital in Chicago and the young father holding his firstborn.

So many other moments, except by the shutter of memory, were never photographed: Dad at the back door or along Lake Michigan.

Recently I took some 200 negatives to a photographic restorer, who put them on a disc.

All I have to do is click a computer key to zoom in on the images, many of them previously unfamiliar.

Suddenly, my parents' first house is being built in 1936.

Then, 10 years later, Dad is leaving on a fishing trip.

Thanks to technology, the restorer, as if by magic, could even add me and other family members to either scene.

So, too, might an image burned into one's consciousness be altered by the mind's eye.

One night, long after my father had suffered a stroke and lost his speech, Mother awoke to find him not only dressed but heading downstairs.

Hurriedly, she followed and tried to coax him back to the bedroom.

He resisted.

Soon, his hand was reaching for the back door.

She could only guess his reason for wanting to leave.

"Are you trying to tell me you're going to the hospital to make rounds?" she asked.

He nodded affirmatively again and again, relieved to be understood.

"Maybe you should eat first," she said gently. "You'll need your strength."

And so, at 3 in the morning, they had breakfast.

Afterward, she distracted him by suggesting a nap, then guided him back upstairs.

He fell asleep and later awakened anew, the urge to leave having vanished.

The story has always saddened me—until now.

I edit the scene and find a picture of duty and dedication: Dad was only "up and doing / with a heart for any fate."

No longer able to speak, he could still sing with his heart.

He just wanted to join the dance.

My Father's Voice

*M*y father's voice is with me still. Deep and resonant, filling the hills and valleys of my childhood, his voice lulled me to sleep at night with *Little House in the Big Woods*.

His sonorous tones—and even just the sound of them from down the corridor—made his patients feel better. And me, too.

Like Dr. Oliver Wendell Holmes, the original "autocrat of the breakfast table," Dad must have liked the sound of his voice. His old scrapbook offers confirmation:

"Leif. We are with you. Talk, talk and win," urges a 1926 telegram from fellow college students before a statewide, extemporaneous speaking contest.

My mother delighted in telling how, after being introduced to him, her mother confided in amazement, "Why, he talks even more than you do."

And so began their 57-year conversation.

Not just the expressions, such as "Save some for a rainy day" or "You've got it pretty good in America," but also the content and enthusiasm remain.

Around the breakfast table he'd sometimes recite a beloved poem by Holmes. He liked everything that the good doctor wrote, from *Old Ironsides* to *The Chambered Nautilus*.

Yet he especially favored *The Last Leaf*, about an aged major who had participated in the Boston Tea Party: "But the old three-cornered hat, / And the breeches, and all that, / Are so queer! / And if I should live to be / The last leaf upon the tree / In the spring,— / Let them smile, as I do now, / At the old forsaken bough / Where I cling."

My father's thoughts remain, too, lingering in letters:

"Mother wants to know if you girls are keeping a menagerie (zoo) in your cabin—are you?" he teased in a note to camp. "Why don't you let the poor mouse and bees go?"

And, in 1982, as my husband and children and I were about to move to our new home, he was consoling: "You are quite right about the pangs of change. I remember the bittersweet feelings of our moving from 7th Avenue to 3rd to this day."

On Father's Day 1986, when a life-changing stroke suddenly struck him, his golden voice was silenced. Six years later, when his three sugar maples had turned wine-red, "the last leaf upon the tree" slipped away.

I had no idea, more than a decade ago, that the pain of missing Dad would eventually be replaced with the joy of having had him in my life, and, with it, the realization that my father is with me still. Before he was bound by time and space. Now he is everywhere.

"It's the kind of day that makes you want to live forever," he would say when the sun thawed us into spring or the sky showed us the right amount of blue. And he does, whenever I spy the blue peeking through or feel the sun's warmth.

Trees remind me of the ones he planted—especially the four for each of his children.

Sifting through old family slides, I discover images—an oak in a yellow headdress, the lake in an icy shroud—captured by Dad on his early-morning route to the hospital. Little did I know, sliding into my school desk, that he was preserving a moment as transient as our lives.

Even a cardinal carries news of him. When my daughter masters his whistle to answer the bird, I recall how her grandfather taught her the skill.

One Saturday my son called from Boston. From his office window, he could see the USS Constitution, Old Ironsides, being towed from the harbor into open water.

He found Holmes' poem written in 1830 on the Internet, and over the phone I listened to the words that had rallied a nation to demand the government preserve the ancient frigate rather than scrap it:

"Oh, better that her shattered hulk / Should sink beneath the wave; / . . . . And give her to the God of storms— / The lightning and the gale!"

As my son read aloud, I heard another voice. Sailing into my mind came my father's recitation at the long-ago breakfast table. Neither stroke nor death has stopped Dad:

He is speaking still.

Paternal grandparents, John and Gunvor Lokvam,
wedding day, Lillehammer, Norway, 1898

A Sense
of Home

*Who am I? Like you, I am more than
myself, more than where I live. I am
a line, part of all who have gone
before and are yet to come.*

Civil War Letter

*K*uwait City, the Tet Offensive, Inchon, Guadalcanal, Verdun, Antietam. Before battles, on lonely Sundays, what do homesick soldiers think?

Here in my son's bedroom, I hold a letter dated July 27, 1862. A paper-thin link to a vanished era, the document brings the writer to life whenever it's read. As I pause, sitting on the bed, Degrass Chapman, my children's great-great-great-uncle, speaks again, just as he did 129 years ago from "Camp Green Meadows, Werster, Va."

"Dear Brother. One year ago today we made our first march into this state, and in that time we have seen some country and some beautiful scenery, but not a single place as beautiful as home."

Home for Chapman was North Eaton in northeastern Ohio's Lorain County. He belonged to the 23rd Ohio Volunteer Infantry Regiment's Company K, known as "Howard's Rifles," which had been formed at Elyria early in the Civil War.

Writing on a Sunday, he explains the Sabbath is usually a very lonesome day in camp, "as we have no drilling to do and the day is long." Like other soldiers in other wars, thoughts turn homeward and are preserved on paper. On this particular Sunday, "most of our boys are outside the line picking berries, of which there is any amount of different kinds."

He mentions mutual friends, adding that William, a fellow volunteer, "is sick again and looks very bad. Medicine does not seem to do him any good, and I sometimes fear he will not live to see Ohio again."

War, a sobering rite of passage, turns young to old, the inexperienced to seasoned soldier. Chapman senses the change within himself, confiding, "I am fast growing old. None but men of iron constitution can stand what we have. The last year has plainly aged me. Two years more will make quite an old man of me in feelings, if not in appearance."

He has his opinions regarding the war's progress: "Tell me all how they get along enlisting more soldiers in Lorain. I see by the papers large meetings are being held all over the Union to see what can be done. A good deal like setting a trap for a fox after he has stole all the chickens."

From this one letter—hearing his heart, sighting his soul, taking his political pulse—I know more about the man than many a neighbor down the street. Lifelike, he looms before me. I imagine him still there, encamped at Green Meadows, where the weather is fine and "the cool nights just right for sleeping."

Yet history tells me different. By September 1862, the 23rd Regiment's Company K of the Ohio Volunteer Infantry has engaged in three battles. Its third encounter, fought at South Mountain, Md., preceded the great battle of Antietam.

Awarded the sad distinction of having been the single bloodiest day of fighting in the entire Civil War, Antietam took place Sept. 17. More than 12,000 Union soldiers died, and the Confederate loss was almost as great.

Chapman, now a sergeant, has enjoyed the dry weather at Camp Green Meadows. Yet, during the night of Sept. 16, a light rain fell steadily, covering him and his Union comrades, as well as the Confederate Army on the opposite side of Maryland's Antietam Creek. By dawn, a gray fog filled the hollows in and around Sharpsburg, Farmer Miller's cornfield and the woods.

When Ohio's 23rd Regiment clashed with the Confederates on the field that day, Degrass Chapman was struck by rifle fire. For 36 hours, as day dissolved into night, night into day, he lay wounded and dying. Thirty-six hours to think of his wife and child, his mother and brothers. Thirty-six hours to think of his life and pain and approaching death.

Finally, a Rebel soldier, coming upon him in the cornfield and finding him still alive, offered him a sip of water. At 24, the young Yankee had tasted war, the cup of human kindness and death.

"Two years more will make an old man of me," he writes from Camp Green Meadows. Two months, and he was dead.

Yet, whenever his words are read, he lives again. He's probably off picking berries, I think, folding the letter. "Of which there's any amount of different kinds."

Letters Home

*F*rom the start of the Civil War 135 springs ago to the computer age, the hunger for home and connection remains the same.

"The boys from Eaton are all in my tent writing to friends," Degrass Chapman, 23, wrote to his brother Harlan on a Sunday in 1861. "They get a good many letters more than I do . . . . Tell Mother I would like to see her. She must write to her soldier boy. Tell the neighbors to write me a line . . . . Do not forget to write me."

A native of North Eaton, Ohio, Chapman, my children's ancestor, was encamped with his infantry unit in western Virginia—far from his wife and son, his childhood family and friends.

A year before his death at the battle of Antietam, Md., in September 1862, Chapman wrote in another letter to Harlan:

"I should like to be with you today to sit and chat with you and Mother, wife and child and brother George . . . . Write and tell me how much wheat and oats we had. Have you threshed yet? What did you do with my rifle, if anything?"

To George, he noted that he had "such a big washing to do. The river is our washtub."

"Write soon. Received one letter from you and answered it immediately."

"Ever kind Mother, / I received your letter," he began on Dec. 29, 1861. "This is the day which, when at home, we called the day of rest but not so here. The continual rattle of wagons and the noise of loading and unloading . . . are carried on the same as on other days . . . . It would suit us much better if we could have now and then a day of rest for reading and writing."

Half a year later, war weariness had increased.

"Dear Mother, / I believe you owe me one letter yet, but I can't wait any longer for an answer to my last," he wrote on June 18, 1862, from Camp Jones on Flat Top Mountain in western Virginia. "It is raining hard outside, and we have all crawled into our tents for protection. We have nothing to read in the newspaper line, so while the boys are joking and cutting up with their pranks I will try to think of something to write. I am afraid my letter will be dull and stupid, for I feel that way myself. We have been drilling all this forenoon, but the rain will keep us from performing this unpleasant duty.

"Our camp is said to be on the highest mountain in this part of the state . . . . Off to the south, a person can see the distance of 30 miles. It looks beautiful in the morning when the sun is rising. So often I think of you and wife . . . and wish you were with me long enough to see the sight, but I have seen too much of all Virginia to want to see any more of this country.

"What has become of brother Harlan? I have had no letter from him in a long while . . . . It is getting dark, and I must close."

In the same file as the Civil War letters are notes typed six decades later by Harlan's grandson—my father-in-law—to his mother in Elyria.

On Oct. 19, 1924, from Akron, he urged her to tell his brother and sister-in-law to write: "For outside of you and Max (his younger brother), I have received no letters from any of the family."

"Mother, dear," he wrote five days later, "you will be careful, won't you, for if anything happened to you I know I could never go on with college work, or anything for that matter . . . . I am counting the days until Thanksgiving . . . . You will find me out in the kitchen with one hand in the cookie drawer and the other in the icebox. But that won't prevent me from giving you a GOOD hug and about 6 tons of kisses."

April 19, 1925: "Tell Max to write if he finds the time."

In a stack of e-mail printouts, I find word from my son, a law student—13½ decades after his ancestor died in the Civil War, seven after his grandfather attended college.

Yet, in some ways, the three voices are one voice, calling to connect.

"Thanks for your e-mails and real, live letters," my son wrote on April 5, 1995. "I don't know when I will be able to come home again soon. I hope you can visit me out here."

June 2, 1995: "It's hard to believe how little we see each other . . . . I like how you closed your letter with 'My always friend and son.' . . . Best wishes, my always friend and mom. Write soon."

Erie D. Chapman Jr.

$\mathcal{T}$he call arrived early—earlier than usual.

For as long as I can remember, my father-in-law in Toledo placed a phone call every Saturday to each of his four children—Ann, Chip, Martha and John.

The calls showed his caring—as did the individual, thrice-weekly letters he wrote to them and their families, and the presents he gave to everyone on his birthday.

"He died in his sleep," Martha told my husband by telephone that Saturday before an August dawn.

Erie Chapman Jr.—born 90 years ago on a kitchen table in Elyria, Ohio—loved living.

When he wasn't busy serving others or accomplishing his goals, he documented his family's life and his own through home movies, slides and photographs—and in more than 120 scrapbooks.

In 1986 he wrote an autobiography and the family history: "How I wish I had asked my mother and father more questions," he said. "Now there's no one left for me to ask."

Still, he managed to fill more than 150 pages with his memories—among them, his marriage to Molly Murbach, a boyhood spent playing along the Black River, championships in welterweight boxing and freestyle swimming at Western Reserve University in Cleveland.

Growing up, "I was the skinny kid everybody picked on," he once said. "The YMCA gave me health and life."

Having served the Y for 48 years, he was inducted into its Hall of Fame.

He also was named to the U.S. Volleyball Leaders Hall of Fame for initiating what is known as "power volleyball"—the lightning-speed type seen in Olympic competition.

His teams won six straight national championships while he directed the Hollywood YMCA from 1945 to '54.

There he became a lifelong friend of fellow handball player Art Linkletter and once cautioned Tarzan—Johnny Weissmuller—not to swear.

Earlier this month, despite acute pain from cancer, he managed to type still more goals: "Eager to continue Saturday family phone visits" was one.

The last on his list: "Sand is running low in my hourglass, so try to be positive."

"Our children," he liked to quote, "are the living messages we send into a time we shall not see."

On the first Tuesday he did not live to see, his four children and a grandchild spoke at his memorial service.

Martha told of the time her father asked the head of a car dealership: "Which salesperson is really down on sales and needs to sell a car? I would like you to introduce him to me so I can give him a sale."

And she remembered his rescuing two struggling swimmers, who "are alive today, thanks to my dad."

"When I decided to quit my legal career two years ago, I knew you worried about me," John read in a letter to his father. "Rather than question my decision, you told me you were going to buy the first 50 copies of my novel . . . . How kind of you, especially considering that my novel is a contemporary romantic comedy and all you ever read were westerns."

Ann reminded the mourners that "many of you were with my family in 1959 when I was married . . . . As Dad and I walked down the aisle, I was filled with the emotion of his letting me go. Now, 36 years later, I'm letting him go."

"He had the best life of anyone I could imagine—filled with energy, suffused with success, blessed by length, lived in complete love," said his namesake, Chip. "The dominant characteristic of my dad . . . is suggested in a single word: integrity."

Tyler remembered his grandfather's teaching him to build a fire even in rain by whittling wood chips from the undersides of logs:

"Couldn't we take just / One more trip to Michigan," he asks him in a poem, "Where the sky will make us rich / With the gold it drips down?

/ At night, we could prepare / Our camp among the pines / And talk about the days / We thought would number / More than the quiet stars / Huddled around the moon."

Now, the hourglass stands empty.

Too late to tell him that the donation of his body to the Medical College of Ohio was so like him: a life of service, a death of service. Too late to mention Art's call: "I wanted to tell him goodbye," he told Molly.

Although his family can no longer store up news to tell him on Saturday, something tells me that the conversation with him will never end.

Martha Chapman

$\mathcal{M}$y father-in-law, like many other dads, liked to record the heights of his children.

He'd measure his older daughter, then his older son.

Then, with his third child, he'd always say: "We don't have to measure Martha. We know she's 10 feet tall."

Thanks to positive parenting and her own winning spirit, Martha's height is the last thing on anyone's mind.

Textbooks define her form of dwarfism as achondroplastic.

"She's the most normal, well-balanced person I know. She can cope with every situation," her older brother said. "There's really nothing 'wrong' with her. She never has seemed unusual or abnormal, just shorter. She's about 4 feet, a little over."

Neither he nor I can say exactly how tall she is—because what makes her Martha isn't her height.

She doesn't have any problem with herself, only with the way people sometimes treat her.

"Such comments are part of my life," she said on the eve of her 50th birthday. "I try to tune out adults who laugh and tease. I'd rather have the kids come up and ask me questions.

"The best comment I ever heard was when a little girl saw me walking down a hospital hallway and said, 'Mommy, look at the little doctor.'"

Another favorite incident occurred during her 19-year stint as a nursery-school teacher.

One fall, after the first day of school, a 4-year-old preschooler told her mother: "Everybody got taller over the summer except Miss Chapman. She didn't grow at all."

Martha, who for the past 15 years has worked as a hospital receptionist, drives a car with the help of pedal extenders, has her own apartment, volunteers, plays bridge and serves as a soul mate to her family and countless friends.

Recently, she was asked to counsel couples whose children have her physical limitations.

"When I visited one newborn's mother," Martha said, "she was hesitant to hold her daughter because she was different. The father, who started to cry, could not accept the child at all. They were thinking of putting her up for adoption. I told them that whatever decision they made would be the right one. If they chose not to keep the baby, then that was right for the baby, who shouldn't grow up in a negative setting.

" 'This has never happened before in our family,' " she said they told her. "I said we'd never had this happen before in our family, either.

"I never said 'normal' because that connotes that their baby and I are different. My parents always had me do tasks just like the rest of the family; they never treated me any differently. In fact, there wasn't anything my siblings could do that I couldn't.

"When kids would tease me about my height, my sister, brothers and parents always defended me."

Martha had the following advice for the troubled parents:

"If you decide to raise her, treat her as you treat your other children. Accept her condition and be positive about it in front of her.

"If your daughter feels that she's different or that she's not accepted in society, that will really give her a feeling of inferiority."

Later that day, the mother was holding her infant. Within a few days, the father was doing much better.

"Now, he just dotes on his daughter."

Martha has a gift for bringing out the best in people.

"I can't think of anyone else who's so comfortable with herself," a nephew said, "and who makes others feel so comfortable, not just with her but with themselves."

My father-in-law was right: Martha's stature is beyond measure.

Molly Chapman

*W*hat my 87-year-old mother-in-law wanted for her recent birthday, I never would have guessed.

On her 85th, Molly had asked for "18 holes of golf with the family." On her 86th, she had made the same request.

This year, she thought of something different.

The oldest playing member of her country club still manages a round of golf a week, of course.

She also plays bridge and goes bowling, and walks 3 miles a day—regardless of the weather. (One icy morning, after falling and breaking her wrist, she brushed herself off, walked home and drove herself to the hospital.)

"Molly's so fit," an acquaintance marveled, "that she bounds up the stairs like someone half her age."

Besides regularly attending church, she volunteers every Friday afternoon—as she has done for 32 years—at the Toledo Hospital information desk.

She makes a mean potato salad, too.

Members of her family eagerly sampled her specialty again—along with ham, sweet corn, salad and dessert—when we arrived for her recent weekend celebration.

I don't know many women her age or any age who would serve such a spread instead of allowing herself to be treated.

So what did the mother of four, grandmother of four and great-grandmother of four really want?

Well, Molly entered the world on Aug. 21, 1912, when the "century of electricity" had barely begun.

From her father, she inherited an appreciation of music and nature.

They whistled *Scheherazade* from one room to another while getting dressed in the morning and played Tchaikovsky's *Fourth* on big, thick Edison records.

"His winter hikes took me sometimes to a stream to pick watercress or in spring to Ely woods to spot the first skunk cabbage or hepatica," she said. "My love of birds grew out of these walks as well. My golf games are always more enjoyable if I hear an oriole or pheasant, or spot a scarlet tanager."

From her mother, who "loved everyone and was always kind and friendly," she "learned to respect others and to try to forget myself."

Molly, a widow after 60 years of marriage, adapts to change by staying current. Each day, for instance, she reads *The Wall Street Journal*.

Maybe her daily reading gave her the idea of what to request on her birthday.

Born in the year of the first successful parachute jump, she hoped to leap into cyberspace so that she might send e-mail to her children and grandchildren.

So, on the morning of her birthday, our party of nine visited several stores in search of a personal computer.

"You learn fast," the saleswoman said as Molly, a Northwestern University journalism graduate (class of 1934), began to type on her laptop of choice.

When we returned to our homes after the weekend, we could almost hear a collective cheer from six states as her first message lighted up our screens.

"What a thrill to hear from you on my very own PC," she wrote. "Thank you all for making it possible."

In addition to sending e-mail, she'll get to take "walks" on the Internet, learning even more about birds and flowers, music and bridge.

"E-mail is just a miracle to me . . . like TV," she said when we spoke by telephone. "To think it goes out into the airwaves and ends up in the right place is amazing. We can't let it completely cancel letters, though. I like to write, so I probably will."

Should I be lucky, and healthy, enough to reach 87, I want to be like Molly.

On second thought, I wish to be like her right now.

Letter to Washington Irving

July 1995

To: Washington Irving,
    the Squire of Sunnyside

Dear Sir:

 $\mathcal{N}$ ow that you are in that sleepiest of hollows, I hope that this will arrive in the next post—for as you once wrote,"One of the great blessings we shall enjoy in heaven will be to receive letters by every post and never be obliged to reply to them."

I just spent an enchanted weekend along your Hudson River.

No wonder you thanked God you were born on its banks.

Mark Twain—who, after you, celebrated another river—could have written your words:

"I think it is an invaluable advantage to be born and brought up in the neighborhood of some grand and noble object of nature: a river, a lake or a mountain. We make a friendship with it . . . for life. It remains an object of our pride and affections, a rallying point, to call us home again after all our wanderings."

In a strange way, the yellow-fever epidemic was a blessing: It forced you to spend some childhood summers outside New York City in the more healthful countryside around Tarrytown, N.Y.

174

To your heart's home on the banks of the Hudson, you returned at age 52—after wandering Europe and achieving fame as a writer.

Your river and woods and Catskill Mountains called to me, too.

I fell in love with them as a child by reading *Rip Van Winkle* and *The Legend of Sleepy Hollow.*

And so, coincidentally, at 52, I set foot on the property that you bought at the same age in 1835, creating your beloved home of Sunnyside.

You should be happy to know that the wisteria, which you ordered from China and planted in the late 1840s, still frames the front door.

Your description from *Wolfert's Roost* best explains what I saw when viewing the house: a "little old-fashioned stone mansion, all made up of gable ends, and as full of angles and corners as an old cocked hat."

I felt as if I had come home.

No wonder Dr. Oliver Wendell Holmes, your friend, called Sunnyside "the best-known and most cherished of all the dwellings in our land."

From every room on the west side of the house, the river still sparkles, inviting the eye to wander out the windows.

I followed the view, landing on the piazza, or side porch. Lingering there, I felt as you did when you wrote, "I have several charming views of the Tappan Zee and the hills beyond, all set as it were in verdant frames, and I am never tired of sitting there . . . on a long summer morning . . . sometimes dozing . . . in a pleasant dream."

On a recent Sunday, I couldn't tell whether I had been dreaming like you—or Rip.

I felt as if I had dozed for a decade since I had last seen my son's friend Steve, who is suddenly 27—a year older than you were when your fiancée died of tuberculosis.

Did you never marry, never share your home with a wife, because of a lifelong devotion to Matilda Hoffman's memory?

More fortunate than you, Steve had married Dawn, as comely as Katrina Van Tassel, the day before at a village church.

While my son ushered wedding guests down the aisle, I recalled that Steve and other boys once had run away from him.

"Why did they get mad and stop playing?" I had asked.

"Because I told them what you said: that, even though we hate girls now, someday we'll like them."

My prediction had come true in the twinkling of an eye: Before me stood Dawn, in a bridal veil and gown; Steve, the groom; and his brother, the best man, married with two children.

Twenty years ago, we assembled parents had been calling in our children from neighborhood play for supper; now, we were sitting down to a wedding dinner.

Afterward, watching the revelers dance and twirl, noticing how it had rained everywhere but there, I sensed the continuing magic of the Catskills.

That wedding was every wedding.

So your stories, Mr. Irving, are our stories; your Hudson River is our river.

I could spend all morning writing to you, just as I could have tarried all day on the piazza.

Yet, at my desk, unanswered letters and paperwork also "lie hissing at me."

So I shall close and remain respectfully yours.

The Headless Horseman

Childhood was scary enough without Halloween.

Huddled under the covers, I'd watch night mask the day, shadows slide across walls, trees tap at my window.

Daytime brought terrors, too: worms unearthed under a rock, a dog that bit instead of barked.

Even without costumes, some people were spooky.

"Pete the Bottle," a town drunk who roamed the cemetery, wouldn't hurt a flea, some kids said—but he'd grab a child and throw her into an empty grave, said others.

Taking the shortcut through the cemetery called for courage.

Instead, I always went around.

A spindly "Moth Man" darted about the woods, killing whatever he would catch. He had a box, fastened between his handlebars, in which pins poked through wings no longer free. Instead of peddling ice cream, he sold moths and butterflies frozen in flight.

Stories that Dad told frightened me, too. Still, I begged to hear *The Legend of Sleepy Hollow* once more.

"The Headless Horseman rides again," he'd say when fall gusts stirred up leaves and dust.

Like Ichabod Crane, I savored ghostly tales in front of a fire. Yet at night, walking the short distance home or shivering in bed, I wished I'd never heard such stories. Little did I know that one day the phantom would ride—or roll—into my life.

Halloween, the spookiest occasion of all, was a night when real ghosts roamed Earth, haunting country roads and city streets.

The promise of treats, the downfall of every child, lured us to other houses—where eerie sounds escaped the windows, gremlins jumped from shrubs and candles guttered inside pumpkin skulls.

To make matters worse, or better, we went trick-or-treating twice each year, on Halloween and the evening before. The tradition made twice as much sense to us: We got double the loot.

Of course, not everyone took kindly to the custom. Some doors were shut in our faces; some ladies told us we ought to be ashamed.

Other neighbors couldn't wait to open their doors, chuckling good-heartedly as they parted with homemade popcorn balls, cookies or—what none of us wanted that night—apples.

One year, friends and I mapped our strategy and ran from house to house, groaning bags rapping against our legs, as we grabbed all that we could.

Then we spread our spoils on Mary's carpet, organizing and swapping Tootsie Rolls and suckers, Milk Duds and Good & Plenty boxes.

I soon headed for home. Spotting the front-porch light, catching a whiff of smoke from the chimney, I began to run the rest of the way toward safety.

Dropping to my knees in a living room illuminated only by firelight, I examined my hoard. I scooped up candy with both hands, letting it sift through my fingers. I cackled to myself like a miser.

Something out of the corner of my eye suddenly interrupted the reverie.

Near the coffee table, on the floor, did I see our cocker spaniel?

"Here, Nippy—come here, girl."

Yet she already would have greeted me.

What, then, was the dark shape over by the couch? Probably nothing, I thought as I began counting my candy.

"One, two, three . . ."

Wind rattled the porch door. The clock on the mantel ticked.

My heart stopped, then started to pound.

No longer curious, but frightened, I stood, backing away.

An ember shot up, lighting the room even more.

Then I saw it—a human head, a man's severed head, lying on the floor.

I shrieked all the way upstairs to my startled parents.

Finally, grasping what I was saying, they laughed, relieved. My sisters, they said, must have planted a joke.

Dad, in fact, had borrowed a mannequin's head from a store and brought it home that night. He planned to carry the head at a party: With Mom dressed as Ichabod Crane, he would go as the Headless Horseman.

Full moon or not, when fall gusts stir up leaves and dust, I recall how Washington Irving inspired one of my scariest Halloweens.

Thanksgiving's Portal

Gone are the geese and the dazzling leaves. On farmhouse porches, jack-o'-lanterns sag, forgotten. Fields are empty now. The table is full. So move inside, follow the aroma of turkey and yams, cranberry and pumpkin pie, and gather round.

Just as Plymouth Rock signaled arrival in the New World, Thanksgiving Day marks the end of our yearly voyage. Sailing into harbor, we find family and friends.

The table anchors us and ties us together.

Imagine an empty stage, bare except for a dining-room table and chairs. Imagine two doorways: one for entrances, the birth portal; one for exits, the death portal.

Thornton Wilder conceived such a set for his remarkable one-act play, *The Long Christmas Dinner*, which traces a family's history through nine decades. Showing the generations during a continuous meal of individual Christmas dinners, the play celebrates the cycles of life. Births and deaths are represented as relatives appear at and disappear from the table:

"I never told her how wonderful she was," says Genevieve, a girl of the middle generation, after her mother's death. "We all treated her as though she were just a friend in the house. I thought she'd be here forever."

Why did Wilder, that most American of writers, not call his work *The Long Thanksgiving Dinner*? Christmas, Hanukkah and Kwanzaa, for instance, emphasize our differences; Thanksgiving draws us together. This is one of America's most unifying holidays and can be celebrated by all races and religions. Observed on the altar of all our tables, the ritual of Thanksgiving emphasizes family and continuity.

Patty Wetherbee of Worthington, Ohio, remembers traveling as a child from Columbus to her grandmother's house in Orient. Pumpkin and mincemeat pies made a tantalizing impression, yet the table gave her the most lasting:

"It stretched from one corner of the room to the opposite. Everybody would be there—us, my mother's two married sisters and their husbands, plus Aunt Blanche, who never married, and all the cousins. Grandmother sat at the head. She and Aunt Blanche did all the cooking.

"We ate and talked and laughed and argued politics.

"My uncle, who was a farmer in Pickaway County, was the Democratic Party chairman down there. And my father was a Republican.

"And Grandmother," remembers Wetherbee, laughing, "would get political arguments started on purpose."

It was at the Thanksgiving table that Wetherbee also filled up on huge helpings of family lore, learning, for instance, about her grandfather, a watchman for the B&O Railroad, who died before her birth but who shared the love of gardening that she has now.

Today she and her husband carry on the Thanksgiving tradition: This year, three of their six children, along with spouses, and three of their nine grandchildren will gather around their Worthington table.

Since 1910, a table has been in my husband's family. For most of that time—spanning both World Wars, the Depression, the Korean War and Vietnam—it resided in Elyria, Ohio.

My mother-in-law, her sisters and her brother dangled their childhood feet against its clawed feet and around its circular pedestal, scuffing memory into wood. On its broad surface in 1935, my parents-in-law held their wedding dinner. Through the years, the bride and groom returned to the table with their children and grandchildren.

The original owners, our children's great-grandparents, were married for 73 years. Before they died, they gave us their table. Around its generous surface, we've celebrated more Thanksgivings—remembering those no longer present and recalling other feasts, like the one served on a card table in a first apartment.

Most memories, however, blur into one long Thanksgiving dinner. Usually, only when a portal opens—or closes—does a year stand out from the rest.

181

In 1987, our friend Jeff Kaplan's sister died. When Karen, at 39, lost her five-year battle with cancer, her brother, in remembrance, placed a black band around his wrist.

In November 1994 on the anniversary of Karen's death, Kaplan and his wife, Darcy, became parents of a daughter. The black badge of mourning was removed. The baby girl took her place at Thanksgiving's table. But first, during an 8 a.m. service at Agudas Achim Synagogue, she received her given name: Karen.

A portal closes. A portal opens.

November—a Fitting Month

To jot down a Thanksgiving grocery list is one thing; to sift through the pieces of family—and a nation's—history is another.

Yet we do both, don't we? We live in the present, enjoying the holiday. At the same time, we drift along on a stream of memories.

With everyone gathered at the table, the glint from a goblet reminds somebody of the polished gleam on the Vietnam Veterans Memorial. Another family member, lost in thought, recalls paper turkeys parading across the windows of a grammar school.

"Did you know," a youngster pipes up, "that 216 years ago today—on Nov. 25, 1783—the last redcoats evacuated New York City?"

"Well," says another small historian, not to be outdone, "one day and six years later, George Washington proclaimed a national day of thanks."

November—as gray as Plymouth Rock, or as a West Point uniform— is a fitting month to cradle both Thanksgiving and Veterans Day.

Does the family remember that on an earlier Thanksgiving—Nov. 25, 1863—Union soldier Harlan P. Chapman was wounded in the battle of Armstrong Hill in eastern Tennessee? The Ohio native, born in Lorain County, carried a musket ball embedded in his hip for the rest of his life.

Gone, too, is the grandson who, as a youngster, worried that the long-lodged ammunition might explode at any moment.

The father of the Civil War soldier, Thurot Chapman, served in the War of 1812. His grandfather, Constant, fought under the command of Gen. George Washington in the Revolution, experienced the hardships of

Valley Forge and the battles at Germantown and Princeton—not to mention the surrender of Cornwallis.

One of Harlan's grandsons served in World War I; another, in World War II. A great-grandson, his namesake, fought in the Vietnam War, was captured in 1965 and spent the next seven Novembers as a prisoner of the Viet Cong.

Thankfully, we have arrived at another Thanksgiving—a holiday that sails on even as we come and go.

It plies its way this year through peace—like a peace that once returned to the country after the Civil War.

Harlan P. Chapman married and eventually settled on a farm he called "the Hedges," named for the rows of Osage orange trees he planted.

A Currier and Ives homestead, which he built in 1884, stayed in the family for more than 100 years and hosted many a holiday dinner.

Chapman descendant Connie Riedel, 75, of Colorado calls to mind when Monopoly was introduced during the Depression: She played the game with her relatives, again and again, during a Thanksgiving visit at the Hedges.

Above the parlor fireplace, keeping watch over all, was a picture of the Civil War veteran (her great-grandfather) who died in 1920.

It still hangs there, even though the home belongs to someone unrelated to the Chapman family.

When Ron Dennis bought the house in 1994 with his wife, Kathy, little did he realize how much he had in common with the original owner: Dennis was wounded in a war on the same date—Nov. 25, again a Thanksgiving—during 1969 in Vietnam.

On this Thanksgiving—whether at the Hedges or in our homes—all of us, too, share at least one bit of history, involving a rock and a first step onto a new land.

Mother-in-Law Restores Order

*T*he *giving* in Thanksgiving, she creates our homecoming and makes it hum.

She lets us descend for the day, or days, by opening her door, arms, heart—and hearth.

My mother-in-law, a great-grandmother, is hosting Thanksgiving again.

Instead of our welcoming her, she is rescuing us.

She picks up the pieces of lives chaotically lived as we and her grandchildren career into Toledo from Columbus, Boston and south Florida.

Does she brace herself for the onslaught or welcome the chaos?

We arrive with baggage, cluttering her front hall and neatly kept bedrooms. We linger at the table, telling our tales.

She listens serenely.

Do we notice the cornucopia, each piece of fruit thoughtfully selected and arranged? The green candles? The music?

Tonight, will we wonder how freshly scented sheets and towels found their way to our rooms?

On Friday, when she returns from a daily 3-mile walk, will we sense her tiptoeing, preparing breakfast, while those who watched too much television still sleep?

"She's the essence of graciousness, always making sure that everybody else is fine," one of her sons said. "She creates an environment in a magical, quiet way by never calling attention to herself. If someone tried to compliment her, she would deny that she had anything to do with creating the magic."

He remembers growing up to "classical music playing on the radio, the grace of a person watching birds out the window as she quietly worked in the kitchen . . . . Even today, when you come into view, she wants to know if you need something to eat, something to drink. It ends up being more a spiritual nourishment than a physical one."

A friend has said for years that she takes notes on my mother-in-law so she can act similarly toward her sons' future wives.

One morning, when I was (impatiently) overdue with our first child, I looked out the bedroom window and saw impatiens in the garden below. My mother-in-law had planted them at dawn.

On our fifth wedding anniversary, when we took our second baby home from the hospital, she had prepared dinner for two with champagne.

Today, packed inside moving boxes are the Christmas stockings she knitted, her needlepoint, cards and letters.

Her example, however, is the lasting gift: volunteerism and a love of music, nurtured in my husband and children; and a love of nature's music.

This visit, rather than speak of herself, she draws us out again.

Yet recently I found a letter she wrote, describing her father, that gives a glimpse of her:

"He was gentle and fair, and never showed any partiality. His mother read him Grimm's Fairy Tales and Greek mythology, and to his dear Swiss father he would ascribe fair business practices. He was a Christian gentleman with fine Christian principles."

As we gather, I'll share her letter with some of her father's grandchildren and great-grandchildren.

Generations continue to convene in the ever-changing configuration called family.

Yet the holiday doesn't just happen.

Who knows what the hostess thinks when the day is done?

Or on Friday, at breakfast, when she serves the bagels that a granddaughter loves? Or on Monday, when she mails a pair of forgotten glasses?

May we be the *thanks* in Thanksgiving.

The Unopened Gift

*A*lmost a year later, there's still one Christmas present left to open. Wrapped in gold foil, tied in green ribbon, it sits day after day on the desk.

The rectangular box is feather-light and doesn't make a sound when I shake it. Someday I'll open it. Maybe this Christmas but not now.

The gift is from my friend June. It arrived after her death last December 17. As long as it remains unopened, it's something she has yet to give me. The experience hovers in the future, waiting to happen, as if she were still alive.

Her package reminds me that life itself is a gift, not to be wasted but to be opened and lived and appreciated.

The wrapped present also represents inner gifts that all too often are left undiscovered and unexplored. Whenever I say, "I don't have time," "Not now," "Someday," I'm choosing to leave certain abilities, certain opportunities unrealized, both in myself and in others. As a teacher once cautioned my class, "Don't stand in the way of your own becoming."

Lillian Hellman said of her play *The Autumn Garden*, "I suppose the point I had in mind is this: You come to a place in your life when what you've been is going to determine what you will be. If you've wasted what you have in you, it's too late to do much about it. If you've invested yourself in life, you're pretty certain to get a return."

I'm told that on the day my friend died, after losing her long, courageous battle with cancer, a nurse in her hospital room broke into tears.

"For the rest of my life," she vowed, "I'm going to try to be as good and kind as June."

Of course, that was June's greatest gift. The person she was and the life she led inspired all who knew her. Showing amazing grace under pressure, smiling through pain, she always focused outward, on others.

Her crowded memorial service, the outpouring of love, the moving tributes all proved that in her 62 years of life June had not wasted what had been hers. She had invested herself in life, all of her life.

Toward the end, as sick and uncomfortable as she was, she remembered family and friends. Her daughter-in-law, I later learned, went Christmas shopping for her, then spread the presents on the hospital bed. After June decided what each person would receive, the gifts were carefully wrapped and tagged.

The day after her memorial service, I was told that one of the presents was for me. A few days later, a friend dropped it off. How remarkable, I remember thinking—a final, stunning gesture reaching across the transcendent chasm.

For having known June, my life has more resonance. But, oh, how it would sing had I taken more time to discover all there was within. I knew her but not well enough. So much more I could have done, should have done.

That's why I'll leave her present wrapped, for a while longer, at least. A daily symbol, it reminds me to slow down, to savor life, to explore my gifts and those of others.

After all, it isn't so much what she gave in the midst of dying but that she gave me anything. The fact that she remembered transforms this package, wrapped in gold foil, into a gift more priceless than gold.

A Feeling as Old as the Flag

$\mathcal{A}$s I slid the pan of lasagna from the oven, I felt myself sliding to the floor. Sue Van Dyke slowed me, then caught the pasta before she led me upstairs—where, for the rest of the evening, I could hear her offering seconds, quieting revelers, washing dishes.

The next morning, still weak from the flu, I discovered her healing note on a clean counter.

Sue is the kind of friend who can pull everything out of my closet, throw it on the bed and mix—until I'm dumbfounded to discover so many new outfits from "nothing to wear."

In the 13 years since I came to Columbus from Toledo, she has always known when to phone.

Recently, she offered to help me move. I get too frantic during December to help myself, let alone someone else, yet she insisted.

"I checked my calendar for Monday and Tuesday, and it's OK with Don," she said. "Your helper will be there. Start making my list."

Sue showed up early—on a Sunday—with her 76-year-old mother, Mimi Tomlinson. Daughter and mother wore matching "Celebrate" T-shirts.

(When Mimi, who lives in Columbus, used to visit Toledo, she and Sue would wait up until after children and husbands had gone to bed; then they'd pull out the sewing machine and whip up a pair of curtains, or build a bookcase or paint a room.)

"We thought we should get your kitchen set up before tomorrow," Sue said from behind the wheel of her son's pickup. "You've heard of Two Men and a Truck? We're two women and a truck."

Mimi and I handed up box after box, along with chairs, while Sue stacked everything, Rubik's Cube-like, on board. After a short drive down the street, we unloaded and unpacked—and went back for more.

The next morning, before the moving van arrived, my helpers pulled up, handing me a cup of coffee.

"You need more shelf paper and some other things," Sue said. "We'll run to the store and meet you at the new house."

When I got there, they had the coffeepot going and were unloading groceries, making sandwiches and even chilling champagne for a future toast.

When the van delivered the first load, Sue crisscrossed the house to direct the movers—"Set it there, a little more to the right"—and Mimi lost herself in dish barrels.

I opened a kitchen cupboard to find the spices all lined up. In the living room, pictures hung on walls; plants rested on tables.

None of us sat down until 5 p.m., and only for a moment, when Sue insisted that we gather in the living room for tea.

Already, the little place felt like home.

Late that night, Sue and I crawled back to the old house, full of echoes, where beds still stood.

Waking with a start, I wondered whether I'd locked up. Tiptoeing past her room, I found Sue wide awake, making lists for the next day.

"My feet have blisters," she said after another day of moving.

On Wednesday, Sue pressed on until she had to head back to Toledo. She wanted me to feel "settled." She kept apologizing for leaving—after already giving up four days.

I watched her and Mimi drive off at dusk.

"Wait," I wanted to say. "We forgot to make a toast."

In the 27 years I've known her, nothing has stymied Sue—a woman who could have served as a midwife; tamed the West; or led troops into battle.

Days later a letter arrived with pictures, one showing Sue by the front door.

"Just realized you have a bracket for Old Glory," she had written on the back.

When Sue, Mimi and other friends rallied round, I felt a feeling as old as the flag—with visions of prairie grass, barn raisings, spring planting and the air, full of dust, at threshing time.

That spirit lingers. Like a wagon wheel, it still crosses our path.

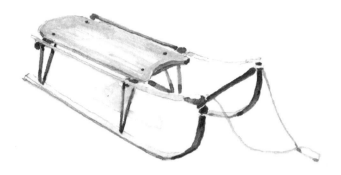

Here I Stand

*H*ere I stand, on a hill between two generations.

I can slide down one side to reach the past—or down the other, pushing off toward the future.

I'm visiting my son at his new apartment in Boston. While he's asleep on the living-room sofa, I'm awake in the bedroom.

Back home in Columbus, a small sled rests near the fireplace—far from the hills of Eau Claire, Wis., where the boyhood relic belonged to Dad.

My brother recently discovered it, carefully wrapped in an old blanket, in our parents' Kenosha garage.

Sometimes, passing the green wooden sled with its metal runners, I picture a boy belly-flopping onto it and zooming down a slope. The rope, brown and frayed, turns new in his young hand as he races back up the hill, shouting.

How little I know of the man I thought I knew so well.

Who gave him the sled? Was it a present or a hand-me-down? Who went sledding with him?

I do know, when he headed home each dusk, he entered the loving kitchen of his Auntie Karen—who, along with Uncle Allen, reared him from age 6. His parents had died in 1913, several months apart.

I know he put himself through college and medical school. And I know he liked to take his children sledding and tobogganing.

On those heady afternoons, we flew faster than the wind. Always, whenever the movie *Citizen Kane* was mentioned, I'd hear him whisper, "Rosebud, Rosebud."

What do I know of my 27-year-old son? Looking about his room, I see the dresser we found together and a mirror I sent from Columbus. I note the picture of his father delivering a speech during college; the framed *Harper's Weekly* from March 16, 1861, depicting Lincoln's inaugural procession; and the *Good Night Moon* poster.

Yet when and where did he acquire a copy of the 1936 Dorothea Lange photograph *Drought Refugees From Abilene . . .*? Or the poster of a Matisse painting?

I long ago kept track of our every moment—but what do I know of his days and friends, his law school and leisure? He doesn't cook, I've discovered, for his kitchen cupboards hold books.

When he was young, he liked to go sledding, too—on a Flexible Flyer down a hill behind the high school. Earlier, on visits to my parents', I pulled him in a little blue sled that Dad had made for my sisters and brother and me.

I didn't know then about my father's sled. I learned of it three years after his death when my brother gave it to me.

Our dad, on a trip back to Eau Claire, had found his old sled in the stable behind Auntie's house, my brother told me. By then, we were already grown—as my children would be when, unbeknownst to me, I did exactly what Dad had done and carried my "Rosebud" home.

Strange that a sled remains but a father doesn't—nor the childhoods of our children.

Eras and roles—daughter, wife and mother or son, husband and father—overlap one another like books on a shelf.

In Boston, picking up *The Golden Treasury of the Best Songs and Lyrical Poems in the English Language* and *The Poetical Works of John Keats*, I'm startled to find inside each my father's signature from 1926.

He was 19 and living at "2127 Van Hise Ave., Madison, Wis."

I feel parentlike and proud to see his young hand, knowing he earned the money for each book he ever bought, for every course he took.

Earlier, my son and I saw *Sense and Sensibility.*

Emerging from the theater into falling snow, we scurried to meet the streetcar. I wanted to tell him that, even though he had taken my arm, I felt unsteady, dizzy and suddenly older—as if I were my own ancestor.

I was my father pulling a sled; I was Auntie Karen in her kitchen; I was John Lokvam, my father's father, reading a map by lamplight in Norway.

The hill on which I stood kept rising.

I was Gunvor, my dying grandmother, leaving behind four children in a new land.

Looking over the fresh snow, free of any footsteps or the markings of a sled's runners, I thought of generations before and of new kids, my kids, shouting down the slopes a hundred winters from now.

The Music Plays More Softly

On Jan. 9, 1977, I thought the hours, let alone days, would never pass.

Suddenly, 22 years have gone by.

Grief, I once heard, is like the volume knob on a radio: When a loved one dies, the loudness reaches its peak. Over time, the intensity eases; at last, the sound drops below hearing range.

Then, one day, something—a photograph or a melody—appears out of the blue and increases the volume again.

Up and down, down and up. Grief may fade, but it never goes away.

That first February without my sister Sonja, my sister Karen wrote a poem to honor what would have been her 37th birthday.

The verse was the first of many, as we—Karen and, eventually, Mother and I—poured our grief into poetry.

Yet the vessel was not large enough to hold the pain.

From the moment my father's call came, forever dividing time in two ("before Sonja died" and "after Sonja died"), I fell into a barren land. Plucked from my life, I plummeted downward, like Alice, into another.

I talked mainly of Sonja, and thought about her even more, during the first year and longer. I felt different, the sharp pains in my chest sending me to the doctor.

As gently as he could, he said: "Grief is painful, physically and emotionally painful."

I even wore her sweater to feel closer to her, her coat to button up my hurt. My friend Marge, marveling at my obsession, took the opposite route.

Her mother died of cancer the same day Sonja left the world, but Marge had mourned the impending death for so long, said her sad good-byes for so long, that after the funeral she tried putting grief in its place. She gave away most of her mother's possessions and got on with her life.

With Sonja, we hadn't had time for a farewell, hadn't talked of her being ill—much less close to death.

So I set about giving a long goodbye, not just to her but to the part of me that went with her.

I read book after book on death and dying. I slept in her old room whenever I returned home and rummaged through the relics of her childhood in the attic.

A couple of times, when I knew that my brother-in-law would have left for work, I called the apartment he had shared with Sonja. In an era long before answering machines, I just wanted the telephone to ring where she had laughed, cooked, lived.

A part of me hoped that all of a sudden she'd answer—and I'd awaken from a horrible dream.

I cannot say when I took the first step back, nor how long the trip lasted. I know only that I had to pass through grief's wintry door.

Death had slammed shut the one to Sonja, refusing to open it.

Eventually, the dirge quieted; the hours quickened.

Now, more than two decades have disappeared.

Hard to imagine that Sonja would have turned 59 on Feb. 11, which came and went without a poem—although I did send a "Sonia" rose to Mom. Hard to believe that Karen just paid me a visit and, instead of talking nonstop about our sister, we discussed her only twice.

Yet, even when the volume and frequency subside, grief still hurts.

I once railed against the last lines in *Out, Out*: "And they, since they / Were not the one dead, turned to their affairs."

How could poet Robert Frost write such cold words? How could "they"—a boy's parents and sister—possibly turn to their affairs?

The years have answered the questions and taught me something else: Sonja was waiting right there inside me all the time.

As the music—lovely, grateful tunes of everything we'd shared—started to play more softly, I could finally hear her.

The other day, as Karen was leaving, I asked her to let me know when she got to Peru. Checking e-mail, I found her missive.

Then, out of habit, without a computer or a second thought, I sent a message even farther.

"Sonja: Karen arrived safely."

"April Is the Cruelest Month"

$\mathcal{A}$s night's lid closes on the jar of day, I see the last rim of light.

From the window, all is dark below—save for the daffodil faces reflecting white.

I recall T.S. Eliot's words "April is the cruelest month"—not just because snow, rain, sleet and hail have pounded the planet.

April was the fourth month after my sister's death—and, in some ways, the cruelest: Numbing shock gave way as grief grew choking weeds.

That spring, visiting her grave, I asked my brother-in-law whether his despair had deepened, too. His face answered.

There's an ache to April whether a heart be empty or full.

Longing for life, Earth continues in labor. Some days are stillborn; others, promising.

April, most of all, is a messy, slippery, howling time when rain and lightning, thunder and wind deliver the season.

Yet, turning the soil, our hands are surprised to loosen autumn's scent as much as spring's. They uncover a chrysanthemum's decaying roots, which enrich the ground—or bump one of the daffodil bulbs planted in the fall.

Seeds of birth and death, we keep relearning, sleep inside one another.

Alone in the house, like a night gardener, I tend a bed—or, rather, what is buried beneath mine. On hands and knees, in a spurt of nocturnal spring-cleaning, I unearth a box.

I resolve to weed the trove quickly—pluck out the treasures and discard the rest.

Yet the time capsule keeps me mired in reflection.

I dig up an unfinished, undated letter to my daughter on the eve of one of her birthdays:

"I remember the day I called the doctor's office," I began, "and learned about your existence.

"Yours was an easy pregnancy . . . . I had a sense of your determined personality as you moved about and made yourself comfortable.

"Yours was an easy birth, too—and early, by a week. We came home together from the hospital on your due date."

Next I open a copy of Richard Sewall's *The Life of Emily Dickinson* with a marker on Page 355. I see "The Lilac is an ancient shrub / but ancienter than that / The Firmamental Lilac Upon the Hill tonight."

I don't remember reading her sunset metaphor before or underlining the words. Did I do it during a lost May of lilacs or a May in which I was lost?

In a stash of photographs, I find my son—as a college freshman—with his first significant girlfriend.

The 18-year-old self of my 27-year-old no longer exists, nor does the relationship.

The pictures were taken on a weekend visit to his college, where he seemed so grown-up.

Now, from the vantage of this future spring, I am struck by how young he appears.

Back then, his paternal grandfather still had a decade to live.

Tonight, I find a copy of a newsletter mentioning that my in-laws had become great-grandparents for the fourth time.

"Many thanks for your helpful and encouraging calls," he wrote on the enclosed note. "No. 12 radiation treatment this morning after a bad night."

When his father died of cancer in August, my husband received daffodil bulbs as a memorial.

Their blooms reflect light even in a growing darkness.

By 11:30 p.m., I feel exhausted from the emotional dig. I throw out a few magazines; mainly, I put everything back for a future sorting and fall asleep on a bed of tangled memories.

As night turns, the lid loosens.

A friend is dying, her family by her side.

The next morning, countless others and I will learn the news. Sheila Feinknopf, 57, died at the start of a new day.

Recounting her bone-marrow transplant in 1994, she once said: "When you've been in a hospital room for a month and a half, it's your world."

She hesitated to be taken for a walk, she recalled—yet her husband insisted.

"He wheeled me into a small courtyard. It was a warm spring day; the pansies were in bloom, I had forgotten how beautiful it could be, and I started to cry. 'This is why I'm here,' I thought: 'to live.'"

In the midst of our dying, so are we all.

A Sense of Home

I walk strange halls, see neighbors I do not know and find a small cup—bent during the move—from my daughter's childhood.

Here I am, uprooted again.

How can I feel planted when I missed May at Dawes Arboretum, with its littleleaf lilacs and tricolor beeches, and its bluebird battalions?

No matter that pear trees stand in my new yard: Next year, dressed in white, they'll remind me of a German Village spring. In turn, I'll recall my favorite restaurant and mourn how far I must travel just to share lunch with friends.

I regard with awe anyone who moves willingly, who thinks nothing of starting over in a different community, who doesn't lose oneself trying to find footing in a new land.

While my husband and I recently had a house in Columbus and, because of his work, an apartment in Nashville, we now have a house in Nashville and an anchoring apartment in Columbus.

Towers of unpacked boxes soar inside the rooms in Tennessee; the contents of a pack rat's storage locker are stacked in the garage.

One day years ago, while pushing my firstborn in a stroller, I passed the home of an older neighbor.

Suddenly, her garage door sprang up to reveal mounds of house-hold goods.

The sight unsettled me. Instead, it should have warned me of what was to come: the curator's duties of middle age.

With each move, my hands touch more relics of a growing past—a son's beer-can collection, a daughter's toy stable and herd of horses, a grandfather's cradle in which both children slept as newborns.

All these artifacts and more have traveled with me.

Why do so many of us fail to sift and winnow? How do our possessions come to possess us? We store them forever in attics and basements, lugging them on move after move.

Someday, we promise ourselves, we'll try to eliminate the chaff. Fortunately, pressed as we are by the present, we often don't.

And so a pair of Hans Brinker-like skates from a vanished Norway, a bootjack from an 1880s Ohio homestead and letters written by Union soldiers during the Civil War all survived to reside in the South, along with report cards and countless other mementos.

Resting, too, under our new roof is a courier's leather packet made to slip onto a belt.

Worn a century ago by my father's father, it contains several letters of introduction—references—handwritten in Norwegian and carried with him to the United States of America.

"Mr. John Lokvam has been my neighbor and acquaintance for many years, and I am glad of an opportunity to recommend him to any position to which he is capable of filling as an honest young man of exceptional, good character," O.F. Tiliebo of Lillehammer, Norway, wrote on Feb. 26, 1901.

O. Borgen took pen in hand on June 25 a year later.

"Mr. John Lokvam has been in my employ as a clerk and bookkeeper for seven years, and has always proved himself honest, loyal and satisfactory to me in my business, and now, when he has decided to emigrate to the United States, I wish him luck, and it is a pleasure to endorse him to the best of my ability."

What the letters must have meant to my dad, who lost his father at age 6.

They ground even me as I complain about a move from one state to another—nearly a century after my grandfather crossed an ocean.

Who am I? Like you, I am more than myself, more than where I live. I am a line, part of all who have gone before and are yet to come.

That's why we save tangible links—old letters, photographs and other keepsakes.

They provide a sense of home, wherever the house.

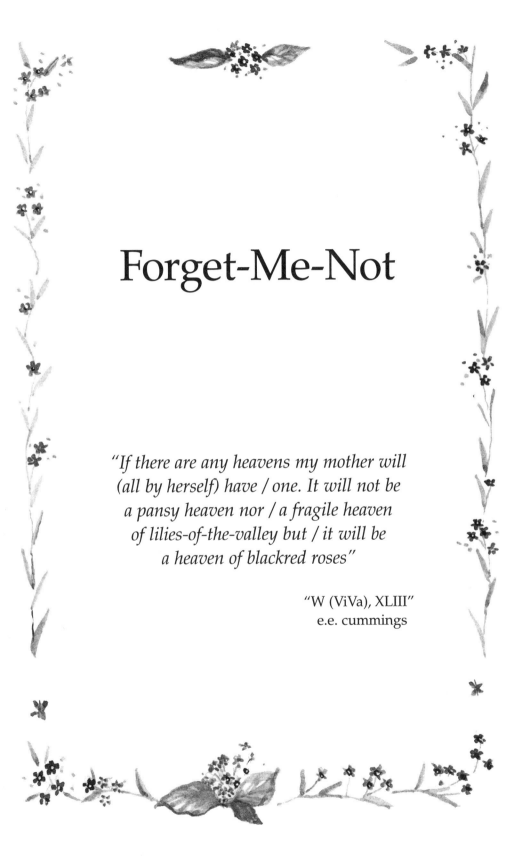

Forget-Me-Not

"If there are any heavens my mother will
(all by herself) have / one. It will not be
a pansy heaven nor / a fragile heaven
of lilies-of-the-valley but / it will be
a heaven of blackred roses"

"W (ViVa), XLIII"
e.e. cummings

Karen and Mother, Easter 1939

The Night Air

The night air was humid, yet a soothing coolness flowed from Lake Michigan. The combined fragrances, distilled during 18 summers and filling me with a sense of place, are still the best. Four decades later, I breathe them in and I know I'm home.

I remember leaving my friend Mary's house on such an evening, the streetlights swimming through a canopy of trees. Although I was only 14 or 15, I have never felt as wise or knowing or good as I did at that moment, when, over the lake, the stars and the future hung in infinite space.

Like a bird darting from branch to branch, I recently returned to attend Mary's daughter's wedding. As my brother helped me lift the suitcase from the car trunk, Mom searched for her key. Is home still home, I wondered, when all the other houses on the block have changed hands in the past 50 years?

I re-entered the same back door I first knew at age 7. Though my daily role in that scene ended ages ago, the long-running play called "Family" continues. Now a guest performer on the stage, I have lived long enough to see characters come and others go—and to know what playwrights mean when they say the second act is the hardest to write.

At the close of Act I, my friends and I left for school and marriage. In 1970, Mary wed her groom in the chapel of Kemper Hall, the school she and I had attended. Each morning, from sixth grade through 12th, we had stood side by side, sharing a hymnal. Our pews had held her mother 30 years before, as well as other girls since the school's founding in 1870.

The aged institution gave us a sense of place; we knew that if it had endured that long, it would still be a school long after we graduated. And so one Oct. 31, after lunch, Mary, Ginny, Sue and I signed a slip of paper stating that on every Halloween, we would revisit that spot. We solemnly placed the note beneath a sundial's green copper face.

We never fulfilled the vow. One June, Mary and I checked to see whether our note had survived. It hadn't any more than our promise— nor the school, which closed its doors 25 years ago, becoming a community center.

At least the buildings and chapel still stand. At the century's turn, Mary's daughter was married before the same altar that her parents were.

Former classmates and I examined each other in the hope the name would come as we crossed our old hockey field, this time in heels, to attend the reception at the art center. When it was still Mr. and Mrs. Anderson's mansion, we'd ice-skate on the lawn's rink.

"Remember how they'd let us come inside to get warm?" Joan recalled. "We used to stand right here."

A chapel, a hockey field, a lawn—all were hallowed because they'd once held us, imprinting themselves on us, and we, them. Strangers became acquaintances when we discovered we'd grown up in the same town. When does home or a hometown become more memory than matter?

Because everything is ephemeral—people, jobs, centuries (even the Great Lake lapping close to the reception's white tent hadn't existed before the ice age)—we found ourselves congratulating not only the wedding couple, but also ourselves.

Somehow, we'd been allowed not only to survive but also to return. One minute I was a schoolgirl, sharing a hymnal with Mary; the next, I was watching her daughter dance at her reception. Even Mary's mother, who now uses a cane, strutted to *New York, New York*.

By the end of Act II, I realize that weddings are as much for the families and friends as they are for the couple. This is what they're about, too, I thought, sitting next to Mother, who, despite Alzheimer's, seemed appreciative as some of her former students approached our table in greeting. It was as though she, a past teacher of drama, were receiving her own curtain call and applause.

That night, with my old bedroom window flung open so I could inhale the best air anywhere, I thought of the sundial. The next morning, I'd hear the cardinals stirring in the pine tree. The same cardinals, only different ones, just like me.

Wisdom Compensates

$\mathcal{A}$ snapshot I recently uncovered shows my mother, as a young woman, waiting for a ferry. Years, however, carried her to the present, delivering her 83-year-old self to my door.

My brother steadied her elbow as the two of them stepped over the threshold for the first time.

After our hug, she looked about my new, empty nest and declared, "How nice."

I welcomed the motherly approval, just as I had as a child when each fall, on back-to-school night, she'd sit at my desk and assess a new classroom.

Watching her move about the house, though, I viewed her more as if I were the parent.

Would she, recently recovered from a broken leg, slip in her new surroundings? Or would something slip in her conversation, revealing her short-term memory loss?

Alzheimer's is her constant companion.

At dinner she fell into the repetition of a story, forgetting each time that she'd just told it.

Sitting at my table must have reminded her of a table from her childhood, the one her parents took along when they lost their farm during the Depression.

"Why do we have to leave?" she asked her father as they piled into a truck loaded with their belongings.

"We're going to Madison," he told her, "so you kids can attend the University of Wisconsin."

And they did, working their way through school.

"Imagine: Instead of bemoaning his loss," she said with admiration, "he made it sound like an adventure.

"'Get all the education you can,' he always told us. 'No one can take it from you. It won't rust or decay, or go out of fashion.'"

After the family settled in a rented, second-floor duplex, my grandmother—knowing all about bread lines—urged her children to invite their college friends home for meals.

"I don't want anybody hungry on that campus," she would say.

"So we'd always have a big table full. It was an education in itself."

Again and again, Mother relived the Depression, her goodbye to farm and field, her parents' sharing what little they had.

Why such repetition? Was she feeling a new sense of loss? Or was she merely reminded of the camaraderie in a cramped duplex?

During her visit we had scones and macaroons at a friend's table, where tea and conversation flowed.

What if her memory loss, I thought, made her forget such an exceptional party? I would have to prompt her, I realized, before she wrote her thank-you.

How limiting are labels and assumptions.

When I asked her the next day what she remembered, she mentioned nearly everything—from the six people sitting around a table of plenty to the blue-and-white dishes decorating the walls.

When she had finished writing, I checked her note. She should have checked mine, for she had remembered to thank the hostess for something I forgot: the nosegay favors.

"During the Depression," said Mother, looking up from the breakfast table on the morning of her departure, "I thought we had nothing. In reality, I had everything—my health, family, friends and school."

While many facts or memories elude her—such as the month and, sometimes, the year—her wisdom stays intact.

Still, as she rose to leave, I felt a childhood panic, a homesickness for the way she used to be.

"Oh, Mom," I sighed, wishing I could transport her from now to then.

She stood for a moment. Then, sensing my sadness, she hugged me.

"I'll be back," she promised.

The Scorched Diploma

$\mathcal{T}$hings happen in threes, they say.

That year was no exception: Dad's stroke, Mother's cancer and, as if those weren't enough, the fire.

The house remained, but much of the inside was either burned or ruined by smoke and water damage.

Sifting through debris, I came across Mom's framed diploma, scorched, from the University of Wisconsin.

Long before the fields turned fickle and failed, long before the Great Depression claimed the farm and family pride, she fell in love with learning and with Miss Learn—her only teacher for all eight grades in the one-room Carpenter School. It was there she discovered that an education "could take you to places you had not yet dreamed."

She later attended high school in a nearby town. After her junior year, her family sold the farm and moved to Madison, Wis.; she tried hard at her new school, earning the highest average in the senior class.

She wasn't named valedictorian, as she'd been enrolled for only a year. Still, she was allowed to give the "senior farewell."

Living at home during college, she typed graduate theses to pay for tuition.

Nothing deterred Mother from her goal—not even a proposal from a doctor, eight years her senior, who wanted to "take her away from all this."

"I will marry you," she told him that September, "but only after I graduate in June."

The day after she received her degree, the "simple ceremony" took place.

"While in school," the newspaper said, "the bride was a member of the Wisconsin Players and took important roles in university dramatic productions. She also is a member of National Collegiate Players."

After rearing four children and serving her community, Mom taught drama for 15 years.

"Since 1958," a former student, now a college professor, recently wrote, "you have guided my theater views from suggesting plays to read, productions to work on, to the insight that theater is constantly changing and should never be locked into one stereotype. My (higher) education showed me how valuable the theater education you gave me was, for so many other students were less prepared and certainly less read than I—all because of you."

These days, at times, Mother cannot recall the beloved student's name—or even who I am.

Back home for her birthday, I took a walk with my brother and sister.

"There's Chris with two women," she told my husband, watching out the window. "I don't know who they are. And I don't ask."

Alzheimer's disease takes her to places she never dreamed, locking her into a new role. Each day resembles a "farewell speech," as parts of her memory, parts of her life, fade forever.

Even we, her family, cannot say when or how the illness started.

We had signs, to be sure: her increasingly repeating "I don't know; I can't remember; I forget," said as one sentence—or her driving a well-known route and suddenly becoming disoriented and lost.

Did six years spent caring for a stroke victim defeat her? Or the stress of her cancer? Or the fire that swept through the house?

What sweeps through Mom destroys her connections. Her diploma can be reordered, but not her mind.

When memory goes, do we become a stranger not only to other people but also to ourselves?

"Get all the education you can," Mother, like her father before her, always said. "It's the one thing people can't take away from you."

Yet Alzheimer's can.

The Faintest Graphite

*W*hy was a nearly empty folder of old typewriter paper hidden in a box of photographs? I almost tossed it out before something made me pause to open it.

My mother's handwriting—a treasure unburied—filled 11 pages.

"The faintest ink," my father-in-law liked to say, "lasts longer than the strongest memory."

Her penciled notes prove that even graphite endures longer than a mind afflicted with Alzheimer's disease.

Written at least a decade ago, the pages look like a rough draft but contain nothing sketchy.

The thoughts, vivid and clear, hang together within the framework of a lucid mind.

"The Koshkonong prairie had rich, black loam," she recalled of her Wisconsin upbringing—when tobacco was the cash crop.

She and her sister, I discovered, were given the profits from 1 acre to finance their room and board so they could attend the high school in town and return home on weekends.

"The frustrating part of raising tobacco was knowing when to sell," she said. "Different buyers offered different prices on different days, and it was maddening to sell at one price when another buyer appeared the next day offering you much more.

"Tobacco was a hazard, from the time you steamed the beds to be rid of weeds to the planting, the tobacco worms, the rust, the hail and, if you successfully reached harvest, the frost! Every stage had its threat or terror."

Even without the "threat or terror" of Alzheimer's, don't all of us, to some degree, become fragments of our former selves? A name, a face, a few measures of a melody—so much slips away as we let go of the past with one hand and grasp the future with the other.

Yet, because she spent some moments gathering memories on paper, I have a clearer understanding of my mother then and now.

Her favorite childhood retreat in the front yard was a large maple tree that grew close to Rt. 83.

"One or two cars a day came down that road, and I wanted to see them and report on them. I spent whole days up there, my sister and brothers bringing my lunch to me."

She also waited for the Watkins man to stop by in his wagon with needles, thread, scissors and vanilla. She especially lived for the arrival of the traveling grocery truck so she "could buy a real ice-cream cone."

"Black Hawk's trail once crossed our lawn (a large depression in the yard hinted at a well), and Grandmother's hill across the road gave up many Indian artifacts . . . . But the best were thousands of windflowers that we picked each spring."

She loved walking the stone fence from her farm all the way to a neighboring property—"until one day," she said, "I saw a huge snake coming out from between the rocks and noticed a nest of squirming newborns. I didn't enjoy the fence after that."

Instead, she traipsed along the gravel road to visit the Lentvedt girls.

"Mrs. Lentvedt always invited me to stay for supper. I loved her fried potatoes."

The one-room school was named for a Yankee—Orlow Carpenter—who used to say, "When I die, just bury me out in my orchard."

"Do you remember what Mr. Carpenter used to say?" I asked after reading her recollections.

"No," she answered, so I reminded her.

I also told her of how she often went fishing at Lake Koshkonong, catching bullheads and carp, and how Lake Ripley had "bass and better-tasting smaller catch" and how she even fished the Rockdale creek where watercress grew.

"You wrote of taking the cream to Deerfield, and you mentioned Waterloo and the Fourth of July, Cambridge and its harvest festival.

"Remember how you were afraid that vagabonds would appear at any minute? Your mother told you they had lived in a wagon at the four corners you passed on your way to school and that one day they had stolen her wedding ring."

"Yes," she said, remembering.

She then recalled lying on her back between rows of corn to watch the clouds winging by and to witness glorious sunsets.

The frost on the crops was "beautiful" and, at the same time, "ugly."

Whatever direction her life took or whatever horizon lay ahead, she'd once said, it would have its origin in home and the Koshkonong prairie.

My beautiful, 84-year-old mother encompassing ugly Alzheimer's? How?

Yet, as she wrote of the growing season, every stage has its threat or terror.

Hiding Shoes

*W*e have taken to hiding my mother's shoes.

Not all her shoes—just the high-heeled ones, like those she had on when she fell down the basement steps.

Now and then, despite Alzheimer's disease, she finds them.

Recently, on a day we were heading for a reception, she emerged from her bedroom ready to go—ready, that is, except for her feet.

"What's wrong?" she asked, sensing our disapproval.

"You look fine," my brother, my sister and I rushed to explain. "It's just your shoes."

Alzheimer's had erased not only the months of mending, the trip to the hospital and the fall but also the cause of her accident.

"You wore those the day you broke your leg," we again reminded her.

"I did?" she asked, amazed to learn of her injury.

"You have to wear your other ones," we explained. "Do you want help tying them?"

"No, thank you. I'll do it," she said, returning to her bedroom.

The roles have reversed as we have become more parentlike and she more dependent.

Yet Alzheimer's has not destroyed all her patterns: Our mother still adheres to the notion that certain occasions require dressier clothes—and shoes.

We follow patterns of our own. We don't want to show disrespect by giving away or throwing out her offending shoes, in case "she just might need them."

Are we fooling ourselves that someday she will return to the person she used to be?

Often we catch a glimmer—as when we watched *Wheel of Fortune* and she guessed "coupon" before anyone else did. Or when she heard us talk about someone behind his back and cautioned, "You never know."

Or, at the end of my visit, when she said, "It comes around in a flash, doesn't it?"

Still, my siblings and I are learning as we go—the way a parent does in rearing a child.

I don't alert Mom weeks, or even days, before I plan to visit.

I once thought I was giving her something to look forward to. I was—and creating problems for my brother, her caregiver.

Besides her other repetitive questions, he had to answer, again and again, the constant "When will she get here?" Not only Mother, at 84, has changed in the 49 years she has lived in her house.

A storm recently felled the cherry tree; a maple strangled on its own roots—and, on Mom's birthday last year, her close friend Everetta, who began singing in the choir with her in 1935, died.

Mother no longer sings in the choir, nor does she paint or call friends to initiate a get-together.

"The hardest thing about being a caregiver," says my 48-year-old-brother, who returned home to look after her, "is when the person you care for no longer cares."

He finds solace in rides on his motorcycle; as always, she finds comfort in her garden.

"I spot some yellow," she said at the kitchen window, forgetting the name *crocus*.

We went outside to inspect.

"I'm glad you're wearing those shoes," I said.

"They're my walking ones. I suppose they're safer," she sighed, as if we hadn't spoken of shoes before.

In her sigh, I was transported back to a time in childhood when I hid my sturdy brown oxfords under my bureau at lunchtime.

Why did I have to wear such clunky shoes when Joan got to wear patent-leather Mary Janes?

"A gravel playground will chew up a pair of dress shoes in a second," Dad would proclaim.

And so, after lunch, I wailed for all the walls to hear:

"I can't find my shoes!"

We looked everywhere, of course, except under the bureau.

"You'll just have to wear your good ones," said Mom, giving up.

"They'll get ruined," I cried, pretending to care.

"We have no choice," she urged, quickly helping me into them.

All afternoon I felt guilty, and at recess I couldn't bring myself to play. I never again hid my shoes. Now we hide hers.

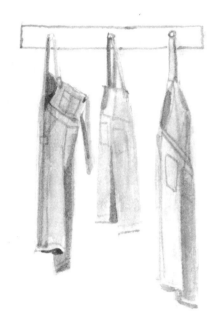

A Skirt Versus Pants

$\mathcal{D}$ad wore the pants, not figuratively but literally.

Although she shared in a democratic union, Mother preferred not to wear what was long considered male clothing.

She never made a meal in slacks, never taught school in a pantsuit, never wore a pair of comfortable jeans.

She was born in 1914, during the reign of the hobble skirt—a long garment so narrow below the knees that it hobbled the stride. She married in 1935, during the decade of stylish trousers—donned by Marlene Dietrich, Greta Garbo and Katharine Hepburn.

Yet pants, and especially bluejeans, were anathema to her.

Growing up, she and her sister wore bib overalls to labor in the tobacco fields. Ashamed of being seen in their work clothes, they hid whenever friends from town made an impromptu visit; the girls did whatever they could to escape what denim represented.

Jeans may have gained acceptance by the American fashion scene in the 1970s—but not by Mother.

Just the way she said the word—not so much with a sneer but certainly with a dollop of disapproval—revealed what she thought.

Her fair-mindedness was frayed at the cuff:

"Look at those jeans," she would often say. "Why would young women, at the most attractive time in their lives, go out of their way to look so unattractive?"

"Mom," I'd say, "your three daughters wear jeans."

Absent-minded responses—"Really?" or "That's nice, dear"—told me that she saw only what she wanted to see.

Watching sweat suits jog past in the '80s, Mom called them "sloppy joes"—because they made people look so, well, sloppy.

Her inner scanner (which everyone, even somebody who claims not to pay attention to fashion, has) informed her during the '90s that she had joined the minority.

"I had my hair done today, and I was the only woman wearing a skirt," she noted.

Or she'd turn to me in an airport and say, "See if you can find one woman besides me who isn't dressed in pants."

Her skirts stood out almost as much as the once-controversial pantsuit had.

Remember when—even though trousers had won approval from Bill Blass, Oscar de la Renta and others in the late '60s and early '70s—women called restaurants to ask whether pants were allowed?

When that hurdle was finally cleared, jeans became the next bar of discrimination: Twice, my denim-clad daughter was refused admittance to an eating establishment.

Mother never had to worry about being denied.

I realize now, however, that she must have felt left out in the cold—or just plain out of it, like a modern Miss Havisham:

"I must be the only woman in town," she sometimes said, "who doesn't own a pair of pants."

She was proud, I assumed.

Then, last winter, wishing to keep her warm, I sent her some navy slacks on a whim. When I visited soon after, I asked whether she had tried them on.

"I haven't, but I will," she promised as we sat around the kitchen table with my sister and brother.

I figured she never would.

Later, after leaving the room for a minute, Mom reappeared in the doorway. Glancing at her, I looked away, then looked back again before I let out a scream. Startled, my brother and sister turned, too, and screamed.

Then we stared in disbelief: For the first time, our mother was wearing pants.

Did children, grown or otherwise, feel the same way during the 1890s when their mothers first donned divided skirts to ride bicycles? Or during the 1920s, when they tried on slacks and even shorts to play sports?

Mom looked great—and youthful, much younger than her 85 years, and happy.

"Now that the weather has turned cool again," my brother recently told me by phone, "Mom wears your pants all the time."

"They're not hers; they're mine," she teased in the background. "She gave them to me.

"It feels so good to be with-it," she said when she got on the line.

Ladies in their 80s have minds of their own.

Dec. 31, 1999

"*I* was looking and looking, and not finding you," said Mother, smiling as she arrived at the breakfast table on the first day of her visit.

"Who used to say that?"

"Karen did when she was little," I reminded her.

During my childhood, Mom often repeated my sister's plaintive plea and the story of her getting lost.

Alzheimer's disease, however, has erased the details.

"I feel like I'm in a dream," she said. "Am I the first one up?"

"No, Mom, everyone is up."

"This is like being in heaven. Is Chris already up?"

"Yes," I told her, assuring her that my brother, her full-time caregiver, would appear downstairs soon.

"What kind of cereal is it?" she asked, looking at her bowl.

Her favorite, I reminded her—the kind my brother gives her each day in Wisconsin.

She sampled a spoonful.

"This cereal is good," she said. "I'll have to buy some when I get home."

After a second spoonful, she announced: "Even your cereal is better than I have at home. I must be dreaming."

Then, with all the interest of a new inquiry, she asked, "Is Chris still sleeping?"

The evening before, Mom had suggested that she "better start for home."

"You just got here today," I explained. "Besides, your flight doesn't leave for two weeks."

"Well, silly old me—I thought we drove. That's the only thing that I don't like about getting older: forgetting things. My mind isn't what it used to be."

Still, now and then, insights bubble to the surface.

That evening, when we glimpsed the moon, I reminded her about Dec. 22, the shortest day of the year.

"That means the night will be the longest," she said.

After expressing her pleasure at being on "vacation," she observed: "Having Chris at home is like having a vacation, too. He shops and cooks and cleans; he does everything. It's like I'm spoiled."

The hardest part for my brother, I'm beginning to understand, involves not caring for Mother but seeing someone he loves become diminished, acting more parental while she turns more childlike—and practicing a patience he didn't know he possessed.

Each time we'd get in the car, if more than two of us were going, she'd ask, "Shouldn't I sit in the back?"

Each time I'd open the door on her side and say:

"No, Mom, sit here in the front. It's easier for you to get in. Grab the handle above you with your left hand as I help you in. If you face your palm this way, it's easier to get a better grip. That's right. One, two, three—there you go. Now we'll fasten your seat belt."

She and I took a drive to watch the last sunset of 1999 spill its colors.

In her 85^1/$_2$ years, she has witnessed many sunsets—especially those on the prairie of her Wisconsin youth.

"A sunrise and sunset there were spectacular," she once wrote. "In the pastures there were meadowlarks, bluebirds, cowbirds to hear and see. We picked windflowers and shooting stars, explored the holes of ground animals, wondered about small Indian mounds. . . . Space was satisfying, looking to the horizons or across fields . . . or lying on my back between tobacco rows, watching sailing clouds."

Did her mind also travel back to her long-ago prairie?

Suddenly, in the quiet of the car, she confided, "I had a sister, but I can't remember where she is now."

"Oh, Mom," I thought, "why has Alzheimer's taken the person I once knew so far away? I'm looking and looking, and not finding you."

Yet, before I could tell her again that Florence had died, she added: "But why should I be so upset if I can't remember? That was then; this is now. I'm grateful to be here, happy in this moment."

Good words to pack for the next 1,000 years.

Before it disappeared, the sun found my mother in its light.

Changes

*W*aiting at the bus stop on a Memorial Day visit home, I couldn't help noticing the street sign "Pershing Boulevard"—commemorating the World War I U.S. general.

The patriotic holiday and a birthday—my brother's 50th—had occasioned my trip to Kenosha, Wis.

A flood of memories came to mind when Chris and I, along with Mom, reached the old house—her home for half a century.

That night, on a knoll just south of town, a Civil War statue kept watch. Bearing a soldier's likeness, it guarded men such as George Hale (a volunteer with the 33rd Regiment who fought at Vicksburg, Miss.) and Frederick S. Lovell (his commanding officer)—who later became the town postmaster.

Throughout the cemetery rest the graves of soldiers from other wars—such as Pfc. Ricky J. Whitehead, who died at age 20 in Vietnam.

And near the tombstone for Coach Ingle, who taught at the high school, are buried my father and sister.

The past determines the present—freedom or its absence, the birth of a sibling—and changes what "was" to what "is," layering not only a country's history but also a family's.

Even a house provides an archaeological dig.

At the back door, I half-expected our cocker spaniel—Nippy, a childhood pet—to greet us.

Fifty years ago, when my parents moved into the house, electricity had reached their town only 50 years earlier. Eventually, we acquired a television and, later, a dishwasher. Through the years, we added a microwave oven, fax machine, computer, cell phone and garage-door opener.

What would soldiers who laid down their lives think of the at-ease way in which we live ours?

Smithsonian-like, the basement stores a mangle (once used for ironing sheets), an empty freezer (once used for storing a garden's fruits and vegetables) and even the stove from the original 1928 kitchen.

The attic holds faded newspaper clippings, some of them having to do with an uncle who helped restore order to Norway after World War II and another who died in a plane crash.

In five decades, layers of wallpaper and wishes, dreams and dust appeared and disappeared in the various rooms.

Outside the window on the landing, a flag with 48 stars—then one with 50—often flew from the balcony.

I recalled how Dad, perched on a ladder, secured Old Glory and how he sat on the screen porch, listening to a ballgame. I remembered, too, how he gave up such ease to go to Vietnam, offering medical aid to civilian casualties.

The porch is enclosed now; the country is at peace.

On Memorial Day, President Clinton urged Americans to observe a minute of silence at 3 p.m.

What a scant amount of time, I thought. Then I realized all that could happen in a second: a life lost or won, a war begun.

A minute is better than none.

In the sunlit Kenosha cemetery, whose original land was donated by Charles Durkee, the 2000 ceremony honoring the war dead drew only about 75 people.

They fought so that we might have the freedom to forget.

"I clearly see a dark cloud is fast gathering over our beloved land," a prophetic U.S. Sen. Durkee wrote to his brother in 1860. "This country . . . is about to pass through such a terrible, such a scorching and devastating ordeal as history nowhere has furnished a parallel."

To bring something back to mind, one must keep memory alive, both collective and otherwise.

Yet its flame can be snuffed out through ignorance, indifference or disease—for Mother, a "devastating ordeal" in the guise of Alzheimer's.

On the first night of my recent visit, I noticed a note she'd left for Chris: "Were we supposed to pick up someone?"

Blue Forget-Me-Nots

$\mathcal{A}$s a child, I coveted the silver heart bearing blue forget-me-nots on one side and, on the other, my name and birth date.

It dangled from a bracelet along with three other charms commemorating the births of my sisters and brother.

Mine delighted me most, for what child wants to be forgotten by her mother?

I can't remember when she stopped fastening the silver bracelet, just as I can't recall when she stopped wearing certain outfits.

Last weekend, in any case, I was helping her wade through her closet, finding out what still fits.

Suddenly, in the midst of her tugging off tops over her head and struggling out of skirts, she sat on the bed and said: "Oh, Kirsten, let me tell you: You can't imagine what it's like to be your old self trapped inside an older body."

She laughed good-naturedly, but she wanted me to hear something that I, instinctively afraid, didn't want to steer the conversation toward.

"I know what you mean: How did you get to be 86? How did I get to be 57?" I said offhandedly, glancing at her for only a second before reaching for another outfit.

How could I—29 years younger and yet unaffected by Alzheimer's disease—possibly know what she meant?

For a moment, like the dresses and skirts puddled at her feet, she had lowered her guard.

Was she trying to warn me—a daughter who can still walk easily and run; bound up a flight of stairs; and hop in a car to drive here, there and everywhere—not to take anything for granted, not even my aging body?

Instead, trying to divert her attention, I took down some old hatboxes.

"Who did I think I was?" she said, reading names such as Lord & Taylor and Blums of Evanston, and chuckling at her youthful vanity as much as at the feathered green hat, the berets and the forget-me-not creation she wore in the '50s.

On her dresser stands the little framed quotation, courtesy of Minnie Aumonier, she has had for years: "When the world wearies and society ceases to satisfy, there is always the Garden."

What happens when the gardener wearies? I wondered the next morning as she sat near the garden and I made a stab at pulling up tall brown grass that choked the blossoms.

I can't remember when she gave up her flower beds, when the task of caring for them became too much work.

Many a morning, daylight barely outlining the garden, I awoke to see her planting, weeding, keeping the grass at bay.

She did the mulching, spraying and pruning, and even the tending of the Concord grapevines, without complaint.

Working the soil must have reminded her of growing up on her farm, where she fell in love with the windflowers on Grandmother's hill.

Last week I saw her pink and white phlox and her rosebushes in bloom.

Drivers once slowed to get a better view. Strangers were known to take a few cautious steps off the sidewalk for a closer peek when, spring through fall, her flowers reigned.

These days, tending her, my brother hasn't time to tend the garden.

Recently, a new garage replaced three of the six beds—including the grapevines, the old vegetable garden and a few limbs from the pear tree.

Some of the rosebushes, even the one she moved from our old house 50 years ago, temporarily reside at a neighbor's.

"Sit down; you're working too hard," said the woman who worked harder than anyone I've known, wobbling to her feet.

"No, Mom—sit, please," I said, filling bags with weeds as I thought of the day before, when I'd given away the part of her past that no longer fit.

My sister and I have discussed converting all but one of her beds into grass.

"There is always the Garden."

Is there?

"Aren't you hungry?" Mom asked as I plucked some tiny flowers nudging the fence.

"Oh, how darling!" she said as I held them out to her. "What's their name?"

"Forget-me-not."

Turning Points

*T*he masks of comedy and tragedy represent not so much the double aspects of theater as different expressions of the human face.

A former drama teacher, Mother once wore a pin bearing the twin specters—and I find myself caught between them.

The "subject" lines in e-mail missives bear witness to the dichotomy "The wedding" vs. "Mom's changing condition."

"You have to balance between death and life—they are two aspects of the same thing, which is being, becoming," Joseph Campbell writes in *The Power of Myth.*

Mom intuitively knew.

"You are always becoming," she wrote at the end of one of her poems. "Fly free of your cocoon / Use the wings you have."

Sixty-six Junes ago, at age 20, she looked forward to her wedding.

Thirty-four years later, she celebrated the birth of a grandson—the grandson who, these days, is preparing to celebrate his June wedding.

Today, she is receiving hospice help to cope with her Alzheimer's disease and cancer.

Her recent descent was razor-sharp: One day, with assistance, she walked into her doctor's office. By the next week, she needed a wheelchair.

In her dining room, where a hospital bed looms, a mother who gave birth to four children labors to stay alive—or not?

"She speaks in gibberish now, very nonsensical," my brother said. "And she never stops talking when she is awake. She's starting to have trouble swallowing—which is not a good sign . . . . I have to spoon-feed her now and put the straw in her mouth. Sometimes she can't suck through the straw, so then I give her liquid one teaspoon at a time.

"This truly is the long goodbye."

With dual emotions dueling, I fear the prospect of a mother's passing and anticipate the joy of a son's marrying.

A funeral and a wedding, though strikingly different, share remarkable similarities: Both honor the surrender of one way of being for another. Both inspire a ceremony and, afterward, a reception with a communion of fellowship and food. Finally, both bid farewell to a life once known.

"Have you found a mother-of-the-groom outfit?" a concerned friend asked last week.

"I haven't," I said and remembered that I had to pack a black dress for Wisconsin just in case.

A few days ago, making arrangements for the rehearsal dinner, I conferred with the Boston caterer and florist.

"I'm glad that you are coming," my brother said the same day, "to help me plan Mom's final arrangements."

"To everything there is a season. A time to weep, and a time to laugh; a time to mourn, and a time to dance."

What happens when two seasons collide?

The two masks hide behind each other.

How do I endure? I take comfort in recalling how, after the deaths of my sister and father, Mother showed such strength, focusing more on others than herself.

Once upon a March, she could hear creeks roaring into spring.

Will she listen to spring again? Or live beyond the wedding?

I don't want her to suffer any longer. Still, I can't imagine waking up one morning and not finding her in the world.

"Dying's part of the wheel, right there next to being born," Tuck assures Winnie in *Tuck Everlasting*. "You can't pick out the pieces you like and leave the rest.

"Everywhere around us, things is moving and growing and changing. You, for instance. A child now, but someday a woman. And after that, moving on to make room for the new children."

Fly free of your cocoon, Mom.

Use the wings you have.

Free as the Wind

*I*n the weeks before my mother died, the winds conspired.

They started on one side of the world and moved across it, planning to snatch her in their wake. It was as if she were a flower—one of the little shooting stars she used to pick on Grandmother's hill—about to be plucked out of the universe.

When the winds passed, they pruned. My mother was no more.

I had sensed the gathering gusts even before hearing her labored breath.

Nothing, however—not her years of Alzheimer's disease, nor cancer, nor even hospice—prepared me for the loss.

Yet how much more can an 86-year-old mother be expected to give? When is enough enough? Though the flower has vanished, some of her final gifts, like found petals along the path, remain.

The day before her funeral, as we prepared to go to the visitation, we noticed a change in Mother's yard. The first blossoms—her purple, white and yellow crocuses—had opened. She had planted her garden more than 50 years ago, so we had seen it burst into bloom again and again. Yet never had it cheered us more.

"Don't be sad," she seemed to say in spring's rebirth. "I am with you still."

We were used to interpreting what she might be telling us because in her last days, we did just that. Perhaps it was the morphine that hospice prescribed, perhaps it was the advanced stage of her diseases, but, toward the end, she spoke mainly gibberish. Whatever the cause, we couldn't understand her words.

Sometimes, in the midst of her ramblings, I'd hear "Philip" or "Bob" or "Florence," the names of her deceased brothers and sister.

After my last visit with Mother, my brother Chris, who had cared for her for six years, said in a note, "Her muttering has increased immeasurably. What a strange odyssey this is becoming."

That day, however, she had surprised him:

"I just have to tell you what happened a little while ago as I was giving Mom some water. As she kept up her constant chatter, I was lamenting to her that I felt badly because I couldn't understand what she was saying. All of a sudden, out of the blue, she said as clear as a bell, 'I love you, Chris,' and then went right back to muttering unintelligibly."

Though they were the last clear words Mother spoke, they were not her final gift.

A few days later, my sister, Karen, who'd spent the night, was about to leave. She entered the room where Mother was sleeping.

"'Bye, Mom," whispered Karen, who stood on one side of the bed while Chris stood on the other. "I'll be back tonight."

Mother took a quick breath, yet didn't exhale. As Karen tried to find a pulse, Chris watched for the breath that never came.

Though her hands were cold, he later said, Mother's face was the hottest he'd ever felt it. The air above her head shimmered the way it does above a road on a sweltering summer day. In a rush, the quivering waves streamed to the ceiling and departed through it.

"I never saw anything move so fast in my life," my brother told me the next day as he and I stood in the same spot.

A few years ago, a friend had shown me a book of Renaissance-type drawings of human figures. In one, long lines clustered about the top of the head. People used to believe, she told me, that the soul exited there.

Some will say that what my brother saw didn't happen. Others will offer a scientific explanation. I believe he witnessed Mother's spirit leaving her body.

Now, the three of us have the gift of knowing that she is not so much dead as she is free.

Free as the wind.

Like Mom

*T*he first Mother's Day without Mom represents a rite of passage.

So does the first day without her.

"As long as they are around," Jane Howard says of parents in *A Different Woman*, "we can still be innocent children. When a parent goes, half of that innocence goes, too. It gets ripped away."

On the telephone, as I shared the news of her death with my children, I recalled how Mom had informed me when Dad died.

Suddenly I realized I was telling them the way she might have.

In the slow, strange dance of her Alzheimer's disease, her offspring had already learned to lead—as Mom, ever more childlike, followed.

Yet, with Mother gone, I found myself taking small steps in a new direction—odd transitions and adjustments so little they almost went unnoticed.

Packing to leave for the funeral, I put a pair of slippers into the suitcase.

I don't wear slippers; Mom did. Leaving my old room on the day of the service, I made sure I left it serene and orderly—the way she kept hers.

And, for the first time, I slipped a handkerchief into my purse just as she would have.

That morning, I managed to get ready for church first instead of last, calmly waiting in the front hall—again, just as Mother used to do.

I not only felt like her; I felt her—and some of her strength.

"I remember, when my mother died, it hit me that now I was the 'matriarch' and had to set an example," a friend wrote.

"Trying to fill enormous shoes is overwhelming, and I find it hard to believe my daughters call me for comfort and advice. That was Mother's job and responsibility. But somehow the words I speak come from my mother's heart and wisdom."

"How fortunate we are," another friend noted, "to carry the love of a good mother in our hearts forever. I know the grief of loss, the eagerness to pick up the phone to call Mom, the shock of feeling like a motherless child, even at our age. It comes and goes in waves—like the tides.

"One thing, however, is a constant. The love and faith of a good mother stays in your heart forever and gives comfort over time."

"I am no longer anybody's child," Madeleine L'Engle, author of *A Wrinkle in Time*, said after losing her mother. "The rhythm of the fugue alters; the themes cross and recross. The melody seems unfamiliar to me, but I will learn it."

What I'm learning to accept is that I won't be getting any more letters—for I had a mother who wrote to me.

Who doesn't want to arrive home to find such a letter waiting to lift the mood?

Although I no longer have her, I have her correspondence collected in bureau drawers and attic boxes.

Like Howard, I, too, feel "like a deck of cards being shuffled by giant, unseen hands."

Knowing that I've saved her letters is saving me.

Whenever I reread one, I experience her again—as with the note she wrote consoling me when my son left home for college:

"I understand the tug of sadness you are experiencing and sympathize completely. We do think the new babies are ours forever. And they are. It's just that they have to go where they can be taught more than we can teach them, in college and in the world. But you said it right when you said, 'Letting go is getting back.'

"You are ours now more than ever! How we treasure each letter, each visit . . . . And, by the way, I should have thanked you for the lovely pictures of Ty and Tia—see, you have even given us them!

"When you keep love at the center, everything is added—especially peace. In the Gospel of John, chapters 13 to 17, you will find the last words of Jesus to his disciples. They are the best words for all of us for all time: Keep love at the center."

On Sunday, the old letter will comfort me anew.

We do think our mothers are ours forever. And they are. It's just that they have to go where they can be taught more than the world can teach them.

Gardening Takes Root

*W*hen I go in search of her, I often picture my mother at first light, in the garden, on bended knee.

She would weed and plant in a race to beat the heat. When the sun shone overhead, she would rise as well—to go indoors and fix breakfast.

Her summer garden held a large bouquet: roses and peonies, phlox and daisies, bleeding hearts and forget-me-nots, pansies and snapdragons.

She claimed to love them all.

What she favored, if truth be told, was the rose.

Just as she overlooked the prickly behavior of her children, she didn't dwell on the thorns.

She nurtured the plants without complaint; preparing and fertilizing the soil, dusting and spraying the bushes.

"Tell me their names," I'd sometimes say when I wandered outside, angling for permission to go somewhere.

"This is Peace, my favorite," she'd explain, pointing out the pale yellow petals edged in pink.

I liked the Queen Elizabeth pink blooms even more.

As I grew older, I was introduced to each new rose: Chicago Peace, Tropicana, John F. Kennedy.

I've long since forgotten the other names.

Books and nurseries might remind me of the difference between a floribunda and a grandiflora.

229

Yet I wouldn't be learning from her hand how to cut above a five-leaf branch or when to spray—or, for that matter, which spray to use.

Snipping flowers, she'd carry her clippings into the house—where bowls and metal frogs crouched on the kitchen counter, awaiting her arrangements.

Bouquets blessed the family home from the drop-leaf table in the front hall to bureaus in the bedrooms.

In the self-absorption of youth, I never paused long enough to learn the mysteries of growing roses.

Last June, the first without Mom, I had my first rose, New Dawn, planted below a trellis.

This year, my sister sent our mother's favorite.

The hybrid tea Peace, according to the All-America Rose Selections, is "one of the popular roses of all time . . . and was smuggled to the United States from occupied France in 1945."

When I think of Mom, I think of peace: She valued harmony above all else, not only in the world but also in her family. On long car trips, while her children bickered in the back seat, she was known to hum a chorus of *Beautiful Savior*.

Fussing over my new Peace rose, delighting in each bloom, I was determined to provide company.

So I've added a hybrid tea called Chicago Peace, a deeper-toned version discovered in a Chicago garden in 1962; the white John F. Kennedy, another hybrid tea; and Queen Elizabeth, a grandiflora.

As I cut and clip, I begin to see my mother in a new way.

It wasn't work, I suspect, that drew her to the garden.

Each garden has its roots in the love of flowers—but also in the love for another person, someone who has made the world more beautiful.

Mom, perhaps, remembered her own mother, who was raised on the Koshkonong Prairie of Wisconsin at the farm built by Norwegian ancestors.

Or maybe she thought of her grandmother Anna, known as "the Rose of the Prairie" because she visited the sick and took baskets of food to the poor in her horse and buggy.

On the summer mornings of my childhood, Mother probably thought of that prairie—the rich loam of home.

Each time I carry flowers into the house, each time I try to fashion a bouquet, I sense an extra pair of hands.

Most of all, I feel a certain peace.

Roses Ever Bloom

$\mathcal{M}$y mother had reached the prime of her life when I first heard the words of e.e. cummings:

"If there are any heavens my mother will (all by herself) have / one."

Still, on that spring day in college, my eyes blinked back tears.

I sensed the poet's voice, although an English professor was reading the lines from *W (ViVa), XLIII*.

No longer a curiosity because of his lack of capitalization, cummings became a reality to me when I heard of our shared admiration for mothers.

"It will not be a pansy heaven nor / a fragile heaven of lilies-of-the valley but / it will be a heaven of blackred roses."

Strange that a poem can stay with us for a lifetime.

As a child, I perceived my father as stronger than Mom—before I saw her nurse him back from tuberculosis.

Then, I was sure, she had just as much vigor.

The image of blackred roses struck me again when I recently read a letter she had written to a granddaughter in 1978, a year after my sister Sonja died of complications from diabetes:

"Papa and I feel very sad and lonely for (your) Aunt Sonja, as I know you do. I like to think of her spirit still being with us. And I often say, 'What would Aunt Sonja do, say, feel or think?' . . . I think she would like the good things in her to live on in us."

Marriage to a doctor, my mother once told me, gave her a feeling of security about health problems she might encounter.

Yet she "doctored" Dad, especially during the six years after his stroke from which he forever lost the ability to speak.

Near the end of his life, Mom endured breast cancer without the benefit of his spoken counsel but with the warmth and support of his eyes and heart. They seemed to fulfill the cummings poem: "My father will be (deep like a rose / tall like a rose) / standing near my / (swaying over her silent)."

Later, in 1992, a vase of blackred roses overwhelmed me at his funeral.

Moments of grief wash ashore many fragments, including the sound of my mother's voice at the visitation.

Spotting the sagging shoulders of her five grandchildren, she embraced each one.

"It's sad to know that we won't see Papa anymore," she said. "What would be really sad is if he had led a terrible life or been a mean person or had never loved you. Instead, we're able to . . . give thanks for the good man that he was."

Eight years later, after she lost her fight with Alzheimer's disease, I noticed the strong shoulders of all her grandchildren, her pallbearers.

And, today, I imagine her heaven filled with blackred roses but also the pale yellow ones edged in pink called Peace and many of her other favorites—peonies and delphiniums and phlox, pansies and lilies of the valley.

And, most of all, forget-me-nots.

Still true to the poem, my father will "whisper / This is my beloved my / (suddenly in sunlight / he will bow, / & the whole garden will bow)."

Legacy of Love

*H*ow lucky to have had parents who lived so long.

And how lucky to learn still more about them as we sort their belongings.

My brother, my sister and I have three months in which to take apart what Mom and Dad spent half a century creating: home.

Their residence, in the family for 51 years, recently sold.

Pulling out a desk drawer in my old bedroom, we found the key to their safe-deposit box on the very day my sister had paid to have it drilled open.

Beneath the key rested an envelope—lying in wait since 1977—with the notation "Copies of signed listings of distribution of personal property."

Three typewritten sheets—one each for my brother, my sister and me—tell what our parents wanted each of us to have, in addition to "personal effects from attic and storerooms, all family pictures to be divided equitably and all paintings and ceramics not mentioned to be divided equitably."

Everything from the "Wisconsin" chair to the old pewter pitcher is earmarked.

For two days I've helped go through bureaus, cabinets and closets.

My brother, who vows not to save anything from now on, shreds old medical records and canceled checks.

The attic and basement await the arrival of our sister.

I feel like an archaeologist, uncovering layers of family history.

A box in my father's closet holds, among other memorabilia, his 1928 commencement program from the University of Wisconsin.

Yet a small white envelope with the handwritten words "My Darling" catches my eye first: The card inside bears a red poinsettia; the date, Christmas 1949; and words from my mother.

"Dearest Leif, / How can I thank you for another lovely year? You are to me so wonderful that any goodness you may see in me is only your reflection. I love you, and I'm so very happy."

Among her papers I find a Christmas card from him.

On the front, Dad inscribed "Marian Jessica"—affectionately including her middle name. Inside, after the printed inscription ("Bright Christmas Wishes"), he added:

"Now and always! And to remind you that we'll take that trip to the jeweler for the ring or what strikes your fancy (when all the pressure is off) and also to remind you that I love you very much!"

In another closet I take down the box bearing a label in my handwriting: "Mom's wedding dress."

I first saw the street-length gown just a decade ago, while helping to salvage my parents' possessions after a fire.

On this trip, for the first time, I read not only her description of the dress worn on June 25, 1935, but much more in a copy of a letter.

"Today, Papa and I have been married 44 years," she wrote in 1979 to a granddaughter in Madison, Wis. "How happy we were then and are now.

"Go to the First Congregational Church on the corner of Breeze Terrace and University Avenue and walk from the back of the chapel to the front, following the center aisle. I walked there on your great-grandfather's arm, wearing a chiffon dress with a jacket that had turned-back, knife-pleated cuffs, peplum and collar, a purple velvet belt and an orchid on my shoulder. As I reached the altar I saw Papa wearing a smile.

"After cake and kisses and best wishes, we were off in his old Chevrolet. It was hot as we traveled dirt roads south and east. Roses were climbing over every fence, and dust and rice were in every crevice and seam.

"It is very exciting to live with him, and wonderful, and I love him more now than 44 years ago!"

How lucky to have had parents who loved so long—their children and each other.

How do we divide love "equitably"? Or keep it in a safe-deposit box?

We don't have to: For the rest of our lives, each of us gets it all.

"The Razor Edge of Danger"

*T*he airline stub for Sept. 10, the day before America changed forever, reads: "Retain for your records."

Tucking the ticket scrap into my wallet, I headed for Wisconsin to visit my parents' home for the last time.

"Have a good trip," my son said by e-mail. "As sad as it will be to see everything . . . go, imagine how happy your dad would have been if someone had told him in 1950 that the place he was buying . . . would serve as a family home for the next 51 years—a sheltering setting for countless Thanksgivings, Christmases, birthdays . . . and for three weddings.

"The purchase of 7115 worked out very well, indeed."

My sister, arriving the next day, and I descended on Kenosha to help our brother move family possessions.

In the basement, we found a notebook that Mother had kept.

"Theater should continue to produce plays having the merit of Wilder's *Skin of Our Teeth*," she wrote. "Time may change, but man does not."

On Sept. 11, we watched horror unfold.

My sister tried frantically to reach her elder daughter, who was scheduled to attend a meeting at the World Trade Center. She also hoped to track down her younger daughter, who lives in Manhattan.

So much can depend on taking a wrong turn, or a right one—or forgetting a purse.

My firstborn niece, fortunately, had left her purse at home and caught a later train.

Nearing the towers shortly before their collapse, she had joined the throng running north.

The second daughter, also safe, was donating blood.

Back in Wisconsin, we were glad that our parents did not have to see us disassembling their house—and more grateful that they didn't witness the attack on their homeland.

So much reverberates against the backdrop of the national tragedy.

The attic yielded photographs of a uniformed uncle who fought at the Battle of the Bulge and of another who, because he spoke Norwegian, was dropped behind enemy lines in occupied Norway. Uncovered nearby was the war diary that Father kept after he volunteered as a physician to treat civilians in Vietnam.

In the attic, too, stood stacks of *Time* and *Life* magazines—rising monuments to history that three siblings carried, decade by decade, down to the dining-room table.

Old newspapers also surfaced.

"Extra! Extra!" proclaims the one from May 7, 1945. "Germany Quits!"

Throughout the day, I couldn't help thinking of *The Skin of Our Teeth*—asking my brother to save a copy if he found one.

We said goodbye to one another on Sunday, expressing gratitude not only to the house but also to our parents, who had made it a home. We remarked on Mom's bread from the oven, Dad's bushels of apples kept crisp in the cold attic—and the balcony above the front door where the flag flew.

"You've got it pretty good in America," our father, an orphan of immigrant parents, used to tell us.

And he was right.

Act 3 of *The Skin of Our Teeth* begins after a war, showing the Antrobus family's home in disarray.

"It's getting light," Mrs. Antrobus says. "There's still something burning over there—Newark or Jersey City."

Later, she asserts:

"Just to have known this house is to have seen the idea of what this world can do someday. So we'll go on putting this house to rights."

"When you're at war," her husband observes, "you think about a better life; when you're at peace, you think about a more comfortable one.

"I've never forgotten," he continued, "that living is struggle. I know that every good and excellent thing . . . stands moment by moment on the razor edge of danger and must be fought for—whether it's a field or a home or a country."

The Little Bank

The heart of the kitchen, at the heart of my childhood home, was the "little bank."

The object lent a feeling of security: Whatever came our way, we knew we had the square pewter box blackened with age, resting on a windowsill—to keep us safe.

With a scene like the one on the Blue Willow china pattern, the bank showed a footbridge and a pagoda.

The exotic design fed my imagination: A genie, I thought, must have presented the piece as a gift.

A wish was granted, at least, whenever the box was opened—3 cents for a bus ride, a nickel for a Popsicle, a quarter for an afternoon of cartoons.

As the Sept. 11 anniversary drew closer, I found myself thinking about the family relic.

Then my sister reminded me that our mother had once played the lead in *I Remember Mama*.

To keep them from worrying, the character tells her children that she has a bank account for family emergencies.

"It's not good for little ones to be afraid," Mama reasons.

In our house, Mother dubbed the blackened box the "little bank" to assure us we'd never be strapped for bus fare—or sweet extras.

We were urged to live within our allowances, yet we were sometimes allowed to dip inside the container for bonuses.

By the time my younger brother could push a chair to the sink, stand on the seat and peek inside the box, he discovered dimes and quarters—instead of the plentiful pennies of my day.

Today, as a truck driver, he often makes the road his home.

"What was it about the little bank?" I asked him as he drove from Kansas City, Mo., to Dallas.

"It was cozy," he said, "like Mom."

Kind and considerate, loving and consistent, she let us bank on her again and again—and never came up short.

"Even if you got in trouble," my brother said, "you always knew she'd never fly off the handle.

"In the real world, a lot of people don't take time to be nice, let alone care . . . . For some people, anything is better than home. For me, home was better than anything."

We three siblings remember what she wrote about the Depression, especially about the closed banks.

"Many friends of mine (at college) couldn't access money for food," Mom recalled. "When I told my mother, she said, 'Bring them home . . . for meals.'

"When her own mother had died, she had to drop out of school at age 16 to care for six younger sisters. Eventually they received university degrees—all except my mother. Now here she was . . . (cooking) for other students.

"One day I asked, 'Where are you getting the money to buy all these groceries?'

"'Since we lost the farm,' she said, 'I don't trust banks anymore. I have been putting Dad's wages under the rug.'"

Through the years, the magic of the little bank disappeared.

It held not coins but paper clips, buttons and other odds and ends.

Yet the love of our mother, for us and for others, was undiminished.

A year and a day ago, when the World Trade Center was attacked, people called their love ones.

Many were rescued because of the love of friends, co-workers and strangers.

"There is no security on this Earth; there is only opportunity," Gen. Douglas MacArthur once said.

All the "little banks" of the world aside, the opportunity for love may well remain the only security.

Saved Letters

Crossing time and space, my mother and I meet again on a bridge of words.

Her letters from the past two decades lingered until recently in a chest of drawers.

Her notes from the 1960s and '70s still nestle in boxes buried somewhere in the attic.

Over time, a few have been lost. Yet I've never knowingly thrown out any.

After acquiring the bureau, I'd open a drawer—in much the way one opens a mail slot—and drop a just-read note inside for posterity.

The saved letters saved me during the years she was afflicted with Alzheimer's disease: Even when mail from her slowed, and eventually stopped, I knew I had evidence of her once-lucid mind.

So I've begun to organize the correspondence.

The volume of her writings staggers me: I've already filled seven oversize three-ring binders.

She wrote not just to me, of course, but individually to her three other children, too. A diligent homemaker and devoted friend, she also taught, gardened and volunteered.

How did she find the time? Mother never saw herself as too busy.

On July 10, 1984, she vowed: "I promise to be better about letter writing."

The first binder alone, however, contains 108 missives from the years 1981 to '84—marking a steady stream of about 36 a year.

Only the seventh volume, for 1994 to '98, is slimmer, because of the onset of her disease.

"My desk looks like a disordered mind, though every day I make inroads . . . . All these letters need answering," she confessed on March 4, 1983.

Bills and checkbook balances left her uninspired.

What made her "leap for joy" were her family and "your coming home—all of you—for Thanksgiving! . . . I will be like a squirrel putting away nuts as I prepare" (Nov. 3, 1982).

"Yellow, yellow everywhere," she wrote on May 5, 1982. "American goldfinch—five and six at a time at our feeder. Daffodils and hyacinths. Buds of tulips and fruit blossoms. Two vegetable gardens ready for Dad to plant the seeds. The paths all straightened in the flower garden.

"It is the feeling you have when you get your home all beautiful and in order."

Rereading family letters is like exploring a diary, one that spans the generations.

She greeted my family during the summer of 1983 with "This is the first letter to Columbus, so I feel moved to say, 'Welcome to your new home, your new city, your new lives.' We'll be thinking of you all new."

At some point, I must have conveyed a sense of homesickness.

"Tuck . . . childhood inside yourself, as well as your parents," she advised on Oct. 11, 1982, "and then, whether we are here or there or even gone, you've got us.

"Now I should confess that we do not follow all this advice too well, for I am always very sad at leaving. I clean cupboards, I do a lot of thinking and missing, but I try to keep partings cheerful . . . . Think back to your childhood, and keep the things that made life seem all right to you and keep those things as an adult. You'll know what they are."

Such kept letters have become priceless—even in the salutation "Dear Kirsten," from when she still knew my name.

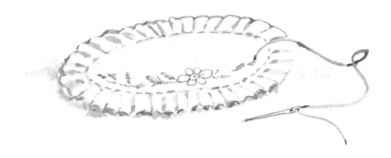

The Line From Mother
to Daughter

"*D*o you often think of your mother?" I once asked Mom.

"Oh, yes—every day," she said.

"After all these years?" I wondered, for my 67-year-old grand-mother—while reading a newspaper on a farmhouse porch—had died of a heart attack in June 1949.

I retain few memories of her, having known her for only my first six years.

Yet I ached for her whenever I saw friends in the arms of their grand-mothers.

Now that my mother is gone, I understand the answer she gave me long ago: I think about Mom, in one way or another, every day.

How strange what time might shake loose, as well as what might still be revealed about a person—whether she left Earth two years ago or more than 50.

This year, just in time for Mother's Day, Mom gave me something years in the making.

I discovered it while mining a mountain of memorabilia.

The items, most of them musty, that she once stored in the attic remind me of other scents: chalk dust in a one-room schoolhouse, freshly mown grass on graduation day, wedding peonies on the altar.

Among the keepsakes I inherited is a doily, embroidered by the young hand of my mother some 80 years ago, and a Mother's Day greeting made by an equally small hand, that of my sister Sonja, about 50 years ago.

Tucked inside Mom's high-school commencement program (which lists her as giving the senior farewell) is a small clipping from 1931: "Marion Owens gets typewriting award: Central High senior given silver pin for record in accuracy and speed."

The skill became her lifeline: She typed her way through the University of Wisconsin, earning 25 cents an hour to pay for books and tuition.

Also while attending college, and living at home, she was encouraged by my grandmother—who had dropped out of high school to care for younger siblings—to invite hungry friends for a home-cooked meal.

One day, the dean of women handed my mother a knotted handkerchief filled with change and crumpled bills.

A cleaning woman had saved the money to send her daughter to college—until the child died suddenly.

"Give it to someone who needs it," the mother told the dean, apologizing that she didn't have more.

To my mother, though, it meant everything.

Along with another program—from June 24, 1935—and a newspaper photograph showing 1,500 seniors at her college commencement, I found a letter dated Feb. 27, 1945:

"I couldn't believe my eyes when I saw that big check coming out of your letter," wrote a new dean of women to my mother, then 30. "I assure you it can be put to good use, and if you prefer to remain anonymous I shall respect your wish. Are you sure it was through my office that you were lent money? I have no record of it . . . . And won't you tell me something of yourself?"

The gesture tells me all I need to know—as does the way she saved my father's notes, including one written on a prescription pad in June 1935:

"Dearest, / I was under the impression that only myself need to apply for the license. However, it requires both parties. Thursday is the last day for filing in order to be married Tuesday. Therefore, take this to the county clerk in Madison . . . . It's still raining here, so we should have good weather on our trip. All my love, / Leif."

A letter dated June 6, 1949—in handwriting I don't recognize—held the biggest surprise:

"Dear Marian, / While the chicken gets done, will write a few words to thank you for the wonderful days I spent with you . . . . My bus rolled into Madison at 6:20, so I had plenty of time to get dinner. There was fresh catfish in the refrigerator. I had sort of a sinking spell when I came home . . . . I promised the girls some candy so will (mail it) . . . or wait

until you come the 19th. Hope Kirsten keeps up her eating spree . . . .
Hello, Sonja, thanks for being my bed partner, and to Karen for giving up
her privacy. Most love to you, Marian dear. / Grandma."

In search of Mother, I found my grandmother.

"If you find someone who is hungry," as she often told her daughter,
"bring her home."

A Tablecloth of Thanksgiving

A tablecloth of Thanksgiving, fashioned from the fabric of our country, stitches past to present in a patchwork pattern, from the Mayflower to the moon landing—and beyond.

Other designs—such as a first apartment and a first job, and the marriage responsible for gathered generations—reflect family lore.

This year, new panels woven into the priceless cloth symbolize the courage of firefighters, police officers and postal workers.

All of us making our way to the table search for new footing in the new world. Instead of Plymouth Rock, we seek a bedrock of safety.

Gratefulness grows from seeds of deprivation, as the first Thanksgiving sprang from hardship.

Out of the depths of the Depression came a congressional ruling that after 1941 the fourth Thursday in November would be observed as Thanksgiving Day and be designated a federal holiday.

Year after year, that "monument" calls us home.

Only since I lost my mother do I appreciate what she did to create Thanksgiving.

What made her arise before everyone else and tiptoe down to a dark kitchen to stuff and bake the turkey? Or to prepare breakfast (with homemade cinnamon rolls) and, later, to mash the potatoes, make the gravy and serve her pies?

Most of all, how did she accomplish everything so serenely?

"The family of man is made up of little families, just like yours and ours—and yours grew out of ours," she once wrote to one of my nieces.

"We ought all to love our homes, for it takes all the family members working together to make a happy one. When I come to your house and get hugs at the door and hear you playing the . . . violin, watch your brother lay a beautiful fire, experience your dad's kind welcome as he settles me into a cozy chair, see your mom making a good dinner and watch your sister sewing, I feel loved."

Mother explained that somewhere behind her granddaughter's family life stood a grandfather and grandmother who "taught your dad about kindness, music teachers who taught your parents to enjoy music, a great-grandfather who enjoyed violins, a great-grandmother who enjoyed cooking and baking.

"Meaning for me has been our family. I love Papa and all our children. I like cleaning, baking, cooking, knitting, watching fires, smelling bread baking, entertaining all of you at Thanksgiving. . . . Years ago, people called this 'keeping the home fires burning.'

"Some people are poor, some rich, some die young, some live to be old—but this does not give meaning to their lives. What makes the real difference is the quality of life they live through love. The family of man needs love to have peace in the world."

After Sept. 11, Mount Vernon reader Dolores E. Fogle, 77, decided to "do something if there was just something I could do."

"I found my answer when I thought of volunteering in the local hospital auxiliary and in a free clinic for the uninsured/underinsured which . . . started up recently," she wrote me. "In trying to decide which I wondered why I had to make a choice—so I applied to both and was accepted by both, despite my age.

"My health is good. Soon, grass-cutting will cease; garden no longer needs tending . . . . I felt the need to give something of myself, and I feel wonderfully good about my decision. In a way, I'm waving my own little flag.

"I love the love and caring and compassion, and the unity and the patriotism. It is always there for us. Too bad it sometimes takes a catastrophe to bring it to the surface—something terrorists could never understand."

Thanksgiving, reaching the four corners of our country, is folded and put away when the day is done. Yet its fiber remains.

The Perfect Thanksgiving

The old house still stands, yet Mom didn't hang the curtains.

Smoke rises from the chimney, but Dad didn't build the fire.

For half a century, whenever geese and leaves took flight, Thanksgiving always knew where to thump on the door.

The holiday blew into town each November, making us button our coats as much as count our blessings.

We no longer gather inside 7115 3rd Ave., where Mother once labored for our benefit, buying provisions and baking pies all in preparation for the big day.

In the dining room, the shy Bridal Rose china tiptoed out of the corner cupboard to make a rare appearance with the Rose Point flatware. The water goblets, with their etched designs, waited patiently—until we children restlessly made the crystal sing by clinking our spoons.

I still see Mom at the oven door, basting the turkey: at the kitchen sink, endlessly peeling potatoes; and at the stove, stirring the gravy.

Returning home after long absences in different locales, my two sisters and I couldn't wait to greet one another.

"Where did you get that outfit?" we'd squeal, becoming lost in conversation.

Eventually, the aroma wafting up to our rooms made at least one of us ask, "Shouldn't we be helping Mom?"

She wasn't worried; instead, she probably was grateful that her squabbling daughters had grown up to delight in one another's company.

Not yet parents of grown children, how could we have imagined such thanksgiving on her part, thinking that, for a mother, the holiday meant only work?

She gave her offering graciously, without complaint.

She realized, and so did Dad, that everyone becomes a pilgrim from home to home, traveling from one stage of life to another, making the way from one Thanksgiving guidepost to the next.

For anyone who lives long enough, the day ultimately resembles a lengthy game of musical chairs.

Each of us progresses from being the youngest at our parents' table to being a parental host at our own—and even to being a guest at the feast of our grandchildren.

The places change, and so do the people.

And yet, somehow, the holiday remains constant through all such wanderings.

I still hear the crackling flames in the fireplace, my brother-in-law's rendition of Scott Joplin on the piano and the shouts from the den that accompany a touchdown.

I remember playing charades and watching old family slides before falling asleep on sweetly scented sheets, all in a house of readiness where I always felt welcome, never in the way.

True, the place with a curving path to the door won't greet me on another Thanksgiving. Nor will the mother and father who once made it a home.

Still, today, I give thanks that they once did and, even more, that they were mine.

Thanksgiving just happened, I used to think.

Now I realize that Mom—perfect in my eyes—created the perfect Thanksgiving because of how she made her family feel.

When the day crossed the threshold, she was there.

Angels

$\mathcal{A}$ngels appeared each December, some with the first snowfall. Mom would help me into my red snowsuit, leggings and all—tying the cap under my chin and adjusting my boots, whose buckles had minds of their own. From then on, I needed no assistance as I plunged myself into a world of white.

Falling (deliberately) on my back, I'd catch my breath—then huffing, watch my puffs rise like chimney smoke.

The universe fell mute, until I shattered the silence, yelling skyward for my sister Sonja.

Our arms and legs swiping the snow like windshield wipers, we fashioned a host of angels and archangels. With each one, not wanting to break the outline, we executed an odd dance: We painstakingly rose to a squat, then stood to hop as far from the imprint as possible. Then we twisted around to see whether, despite our efforts, we had marred our heavenly creations.

Still, the angel hovering atop our Christmas tree outshone all the others. Her halo, golden hair and glimmering gown made her the most exquisite creature I'd ever seen. That she was so unreachable—her wings brushed the ceiling—is perhaps what made her my favorite decoration.

249

Her beauty triumphed at night, especially when the lights were off—except for those on the tree. Imbuing her with fairy-godmother qualities, I confessed to her what I was hoping Santa would bring.

In January, when the tree came down, Mom let me play make-believe with my "queen of the living room"—without a doubt, eventually wearing her out.

Each year on Christmas Eve, closing the door behind her, we crunched past the sleeping snow angels that bedecked our yard and entered the cold cave of our car. On one of the earliest holidays I remember, I found myself sandwiched in the back between my two older sisters. I scrunched low, scanning the black dome of night for signs of a sleigh.

After we arrived at church, the pitch of meeting and greeting grew dizzying. Mothers snagged the collars of running boys and hushed squealing girls. I lost sight of my sisters and soon found myself wedged between my parents in a pew. Swinging my boots, I fidgeted, looking about at the tree and wreaths, the boughs and bows—and, most of all, breathed in the woodland scent mingling with the fragrance of burning tapers.

The organ boomed forth with *Hark the Herald Angels Sing*. With everyone standing, Dad held me in the crook of his arm so I could see the choir enter.

A hush fell over the congregation, and Mother whispered to point out the crescent-shaped arch high above the altar. Suddenly, the mahogany doors opened to reveal angels—their sweet voices singing *Away in a Manger*.

The real, live cherubs were attired in dazzling robes, silver halos and white wings. I was as dumbstruck as the youngest shepherd on the first Christmas. Only after the angels moved on to *Silent Night* could I focus on Mom, who said my sisters were singing among them.

Yet how could they have grown such halos and wings, I wondered. Later, when I saw Sonja and Karen crowding into our car in the same outfits they had worn to church, I figured Mom was mistaken.

Recently I came across an old photograph, with my 4-year-old self, taken by Dad on Christmas morning. My sisters and I are seated among our presents with Mom. I scanned to the top of the tree, hoping to see my long-lost angel. Unfortunately, she had escaped the camera's lens.

My eyes returned to our little faces, Mother smiling down on us. Only then did I realize the miracle: An angel had lived in our midst all along.

A Time of Thanksgiving

"You who have stood at the bedposts and seen a mother on her high harvest day, the day of the most golden of harvest moons for her. You who have seen the new, wet child, dried behind the ears, swaddled in soft, fresh garments, pursing its lips . . . you know being born is important. You know nothing else was ever so important to you."

"Being Born Is Important"
Carl Sandburg

Miles and Tyler, 2004
© 2004 Tia Chapman

Grandchildren

$\mathcal{W}$ith Thanksgiving in the wings and Christmas around the corner, I have enough to worry about without inventing more.

Yet, at 55, I fret over "grandchildren."

When will I meet them?

Both my 30-year-old son and my 27-year-old daughter are unmarried; neither hears wedding bells in the near future.

So, for now, I'm able to share my wish.

If they had spouses, I couldn't even address the issue. I'd be considered—and rightly so—a meddling mother-in-law.

I am blessed, of course, to have two children, but I yearn for grandchildren—and have for some time.

Five years ago or maybe 10, I recall, I was up in the attic with my son and daughter. They were horsing around, pulling some of their childhood toys from a box.

"Be careful," I admonished them in a tone that surprised even me. "I'm saving those for my grandchildren."

They were taken aback at my siding with someone other than them.

Until that moment, I wasn't aware that I'd been thinking about grandchildren. Yet, on a deeper, subconscious level, I must have been. Why else would I have intervened, protecting their interests instinctively?

Poised at evening's threshold, I knew I'd grown old.

How many more Thanksgivings will pass without highchairs? We can't choose to have grandchildren as we once did children.

Would-be grandparents simply have to wait and wait, all the while realizing that we, too, have biological clocks that are winding down.

I would have made a better grandmother at 48 or 52 than I would make today or in a few years.

Not only do I tire more easily, but with each passing year I put that much more distance between me and a grandchild.

What was most difficult about a recent move from the home where our family had lived for 13 years was packing items from the attic—those leftovers I'd often pictured in the hands of a future granddaughter and grandson: my children's books and toys, some of their clothes and costumes.

Up there, too, were a dollhouse, a small table and chairs, a little fort and even an old saddle from my husband's childhood. The sum of it all? A grandmother's hope chest.

More than once I envisioned myself playing with my children's offspring in the attic. Now I've buried the playthings deep inside a storage locker.

Even with no grandchildren on the horizon, I find myself losing sleep over the thought of them. Will I be ready to drop everything at a moment's notice and help? Or will I see my grandchildren only during the holidays and on vacations?

We think we make those choices once and for all with our children. Little do we realize we'll confront them again a generation later.

While waiting, at least I get to observe those who've gone before—and learn from them.

I know that my children are hoping to find the right partners. I also understand that people are marrying later than they did before.

Still, others keep telling me that they are experiencing one of the greatest joys in life.

"We're so sorry you don't have grandchildren," they say. "We wish you did, so you'd know the happiness we feel."

I wish I did, too.

At this rate, I probably won't meet my great-grandchildren; but, hopefully, I'll see a grandchild or two come into the world.

Now that will be a time of thanksgiving.

Dining Out With Children

$\mathcal{F}$or 14 days, while Dad was out of town, Mom had us children all to herself.

On the seventh day, she rested—or at least she intended to relax.

She taught Sunday school and attended church, then treated herself—and us—to a meal at Ogie Thompson's.

Why, I used to wonder, would she have taken the three of us, age 7 and younger, into a white-linen restaurant?

When I had children of my own, I understood: Sometimes the "waiter" at home needs to be "waited on."

All went well with my mother and siblings until we were leaving.

Near the cash register, a little bell had "a thin leather strap hanging down from it," recalled Karen, my elder sister.

Our mother had bestowed the privilege of ringing the bell on Karen, who skipped ahead with the money.

Sonja, however, dashed ahead—and rang it first.

Outraged, a shrieking Karen yanked her sister to the floor.

They scuffled and tussled, ignoring the startled stares.

"They had to pry us apart," Karen said. "I'm sure our proper mom, her soul all cleansed from two or three hours at Grace Lutheran church, was mortified."

Both sisters were confined to their rooms until dinner.

During her exile, Karen wrote a letter that began: "Dear Daddy, / Mother is a witch."

The note, which he saved, provoked a round of laughter whenever it was shown.

Every family, I suppose, has a story of "dining out with children" that grows in the retelling.

When our firstborn was a few months old, my husband and I took him along on an overnight trip.

The cafe was closed when we arrived at the inn. The only choice: the formal dining room.

We approached the hostess with our son in an infant seat.

Raising her shoulders and lowering her voice, she delivered a withering shot:

"Children are not allowed."

We pleaded our case: At that late hour, the room was nearly deserted.

Finally, against her better judgment, she relented.

As if by magic, or beginner's luck, our newborn slept through supper.

I haven't forgotten that maiden voyage nor the cold reception: I saw the same look many times through the years.

Often, the concern was justified: the sudden spills, the squeals of anger or delight, the debris beneath a highchair.

So I was grateful whenever a host or maitre d' made us feel welcome.

Recently, as I waited with my two grown children to be seated for a Sunday brunch, a young family came through the door: an impatient dad, a beleaguered mom, three giggling girls and a baby with mismatched bootees.

I recognized a woman in need of being "served."

Later, at the buffet, I noticed the mother surveying the food while balancing the baby on a hip.

I looked up just as the child, dangling, swiped his fingers through the whipped cream.

From where I sat, I had a view, too, of the older children running back and forth.

Just yesterday, I thought, my two were their ages.

That evening at a gourmet restaurant, a youngster erupted in a temper tantrum.

My son interrupted his story: "I'm sorry, but they shouldn't allow little kids into places like this."

"I know what you mean," my daughter said. "Did you see that baby at brunch who was drooling into the buffet food?"

Suddenly I remembered the hostess at the inn and others like her.

My children had become "them."

Rites of Passage

$\mathcal{S}$unrise gives birth to each new day—and to us.

We find our footing in the east, our confidence at high noon, our journey to the west.

The wheel winds along our circular path, the sounding of a day, a year, a life.

On a glorious Sunday one July, our son was born.

The weather didn't matter: Even in a blizzard, each milestone would have seemed as thrilling—the moment of birth, his first cry, our first glimpse.

The next morning, too excited to sleep, I awoke before 5 a.m. Later, I heard the birds begin to sing—first one note, then a melody and finally song after song, each separate from yet connected to the others.

I felt more whole, more connected to the universe—despite being one again instead of two—than I ever had before.

In the growing grayness, as the newborns being wheeled down the hall chirped hungrily, the world turned apple-bright and shiny.

A mother never forgets such feelings.

She remembers lying on her side, the curve of her arm hollowing out a warm nest for her newborn.

Oh, what a movable nest: All it took was the crook of that arm, or breadth of a lap, to create a "home."

The rocking chair became a pendulum, measuring time when hours still moved like hours instead of minutes. Oh, the places it went without leaving the room.

Books since closed were opened there—again and again.

How long did the rocker preside opposite the now-vanished crib? Slowly, other sights faded from the scene: the highchair, the playpen, the buggy, even the baby, then the boy.

A mother often saves vestiges of those times, and so did I: what our son wore on the trip home from the hospital, a favorite blanket, the white knitted sweater with three little kittens, a cup and a spoon, a music box that still plays Brahms' *Lullaby*.

Sometimes, I stumble across them by accident; other times, I seek them out for comfort, perhaps winding the key, hearing the notes nudging me back.

A heightened moment—the first day of first grade, graduation from high school—stirs memories.

Another of those moments arrived with a recent telephone call: As quickly as my husband and I once shared the news of his birth, our son announced his engagement.

Remember one of the first lessons learned as parents? We feel happier when something good happens to our child than if it had happened to us.

Hearing the news, I was too excited to sleep. I was still awake when the wheel of light reached the horizon, when the first birds trilled.

My husband responded with tears of joy, as well as a wish that his father were still alive.

I thought, too, of my father.

He never told us how he proposed to Mother. Couples, he said, should keep some secrets to themselves.

Then, after his death, Mother observed as we drove past the University of Wisconsin campus in Madison: "Oh, there's the park bench where your dad proposed."

I thought of my engagement and marriage, of how bright and shiny the world seemed after the births of our two children—just as it did the morning after my sleepless night.

And I thought of our future daughter-in-law, laughing, with golden hair.

"Birds' song and birds' love, passing with the weather / Men's song and men's love, to love once and forever," wrote Alfred, Lord Tennyson. "And you my wren with a crown of gold . . . you my queen of the wrens! . . . We'll be birds of a feather / I'll be King of the Queen of the wrens, and all in a nest together."

Goodbye, little prince from long ago.

Wedding Presents

*A*fter nearly 35 years, the white blanket, the pewter pitcher and the casserole with the hen-shaped lid are still part of our lives.

Even now I remember who gave us those wedding treasures, each a reminder of that long-ago day.

Bridal gifts can grow on the recipient—or not.

My sister can't stand the china or silver flatware she registered for 41 years ago. Yet she loves the present of a painted, papier-mache rooster that she "hated" at the time.

Sometimes gifts take on a life of their own. When my husband and I moved into our first apartment, we set about unpacking our few possessions. Suddenly, I realized we didn't own a coffeepot.

"I'll run out and get one," he offered. When he returned, my non-coffee-drinking husband triumphantly held out a little aluminum coffeemaker. Not much larger than a fist, the 2-cup pot reminded me of a child's toy.

Yet it actually did make coffee in the months before an upgrade to a larger electric one. Because it shared our first married days, however, I could never bring myself to throw it out.

The unglamorous little pot has become more valuable with each passing year. Though we've never made coffee in it since, it sometimes holds flowers—and always a memory—of an impossibly young, 22-year-old groom bringing his bride a present.

Another favorite gift (because of what happened afterward) is one I gave. On my wedding day, before they awoke, I left a present for my parents on the kitchen table.

"What's this?" they asked at breakfast.

It was fun watching them open a gift instead of the other way around.

Delighting in the new pewter coffee service, Mother placed the circular tray, along with the coffeepot, creamer and sugar bowl, in the center of the round table.

Unlike my wedding gifts, uprooted eight times since that day I left home in 1966, the set has stayed in the same spot. Whenever I open my old back door, it greets me anew: It always the same; me, always changed.

People know from their children, or when they were children themselves, that sometimes the box in which a gift arrives brings as much enjoyment as the present.

Such was the case when our son, who will be married June 23, received a gift.

"Grandma Chapman sent Judith and me a beautiful . . . bowl with our names on it and the date of our wedding," he wrote his father.

"You would appreciate what the bowl arrived in. It is a Harry and David box. It was addressed to your dad at: 10723 LeConte, Los Angeles, Calif.

"The date of the postmark is Dec. 18, '53.

"Sender: R. Murbach. (My son's great-grandfather.)

"I am more amazed when mundane, flimsy objects of everyday life survive than I am when precious ones do," my son continued.

"Think of the *Paddle-to-the-Sea*-like journey this box has endured. Ordered in Ohio by your grandfather, it arrived from Oregon at 10723 LeConte just a week before Christmas 1953. It probably sat in your refrigerator or on a table during the holiday season. Your dad and mom and you and (your sisters) ate the pears it held. Later, it probably sat in a closet in the house.

"It was there on that last day when it went into the moving van along with the rest of your family's possessions. Then, it traveled all the way across the country to Elyria and then to Toledo. . . . So, it was literally 'present' during every event that occurred in your parents' homes for the past 48 years.

"Amazing how much an empty box can hold."

And how far some gifts will travel.

June 23, 2001

$\mathcal{A}$ wedding can make a person do strange things, I thought as I flew to Boston with a security "blanket" that once soothed my son.

Lambie—a stuffed animal both matted and ragged—was stowed in the overhead compartment.

With so much left to do, I remember thinking, too, that I'd feel relieved when the whole event ended.

What I wouldn't give now to relive everything, preparations and all.

Organizing a wedding often takes a year or more. Why not use the same time, I once reflected, in planning a marriage instead?

At last I see the wisdom in ceremony: The details build a bridge between the bride and groom and their families, creating common ground. As a result, I feel close to my daughter-in-law—as if I'd known her for years.

Helping with the rehearsal dinner and some of the other festivities was a gift; sharing a goal, the best way to bond.

"I've never felt enveloped by so much love as when our son got married," a friend said last year.

I knew what she meant when our family and friends arrived.

Earlier, after learning of the engagement, some of them had not only lent wedding-planning books but also offered advice and passed along lore.

"Try to stay in the moment," one said. "The wedding weekend will be over before you know it"

She was right.

"Drawing up the guest lists and the seating arrangements," another offered, "is the hardest of all."

She, too, was right.

"Do as much ahead as you can; no matter how early you start, you'll run out of time."

Right, right, right.

Legend and superstition ride on the back of ritual. So they did for us, even in an enlightened June of 2001: "something borrowed, something blue, a sixpence in her shoe"—and gin.

Gin? Yes, said a friend whose neighbor had mentioned, according to a Scottish legend, that the liquor would ward off rain.

Before an outdoor festival, gin should be poured in vials and placed at the base of trees.

The idea had worked for the neighbor, then for my friend. Maybe it would work for me.

At the hotel, I found gin in one of those tiny bottles from a wet bar. But I didn't have any vials.

So a friend, along with her husband and another friend, released a drop on each of the trees surrounding the reception tent.

Rain tore up and down the Eastern seaboard; the Boston area was to have showers all weekend.

Somehow, though, a magical, dry, circle engulfed the party in Cambridge for three days.

Instead of offering a toast at the rehearsal dinner, I gave one to my son at a family gathering the night before.

I announced first that I'd forgotten to invite an important individual; some of the others looked aghast until I produced the long-ago confidant and constant companion.

A few stories about Lambie made the rounds, including one of the times the toy was lost—then found at a market.

And soon he was forgotten again.

On the wedding day, before the evening ceremony, the bride gave a surprise baby shower for a bridesmaid; and the groom, an impromptu tour of historic sites.

In the end, spontaneity—a child poking the wedding cake, nieces and nephews joining hands and dancing with the bride—makes a wedding memorable. So do the people—from the acquaintance who helped me set up the nursery 33 years ago to my 88-year-old mother-in-law.

And, most of all, the bride and groom: She looked beautiful and jubilant. He never looked happier or more confident.

That's what I thought as I unpacked Lambie and put the stuffed animal back in the bureau drawer of the guest room.

Decades later, I finally understand just what my son saw in him.

Journal of a 90-Year-Old's Birth

$\mathcal{H}$ow miraculous that a journal, kept afloat through nine decades, surfaced for Molly's 90th birthday.

At my mother-in-law's recent party, a relative brought the vessel from the past.

"It's a shame to have these things remain in a closet when they could see the light of day," said her niece, carrying a box of mementos to Toledo from her home in Elyria.

Many of the items had belonged to Molly's father, Ralph.

Family members sorted old photographs and letters, including those that Ralph's wife, Ellen, had written early in their 71-year marriage.

"Sweetheart darling lover," begins the one sent to San Francisco's Hotel Argonaut on Sept. 24, 1914.

"It seems as if my heart would break from lonesomeness. . . . See what there is to see but hurry home, too. Don't ever leave me again for any length of time. Your own, Ellen."

In Molly's eyes, her mother, who lived to be 91, became a young woman again.

A red leather journal that belonged to Molly's father caught my attention.

I was transported back to the groom's wedding day on June 7, 1911.

The 6 o'clock ceremony at Ellen's home in Lorain was about to begin: "With regular, unbroken, unfaltering tread, we approached the bower. Ellen . . . stood there so bravely with her veil and orange blossoms. . . . Rev. Davis started and a hush fell over all."

As 1911 melted into 1912, I was delighted to see that Molly's birthday, Aug. 21, was recorded and asked my son to read aloud:

"A little baby girl has arrived," Ralph, the new father, wrote. The year before, he and his bride had moved into their home.

"Since then we have been as happy as two could be. We thought there was little to make us more happy, but we dreamed of the day when we should be three. One day our hopes were confirmed and we knew we had but to wait. She carried the little one so well that few thought anything was doing till December."

At 8 a.m. Aug. 20, his wife began to "feel pains," his journal continued. "At 8 in the eve, Dr. McClure came and ordered the nurse at once. The nerve was superb. If ever I dreamed of mother love it was but a shadow of the demonstration Ellen gave."

On Aug. 21, "What a pretty little girl. Not red and wrinkly, but clean and clear and good to look at. A girl that will be the companion and joy to her mother who bore so much pain that she might live. Only when (Molly) is a mother will she know."

We drifted back nine decades to her newborn cries, to her mother who "cried because the baby cried," to her proud father thanking Dr. McClure at the door.

That very night a train brought the baby's grandmother from New York, bringing a white silk cap, cape and shawl from London for the little one.

"I've never heard any of this before," said my astonished and moved mother-in-law. "This is the shock of my life."

"Instead of a gift," the invitation to her party had read, "please bring a written memory for Molly."

Little did her young father know that putting pen to paper would lead to the best present.

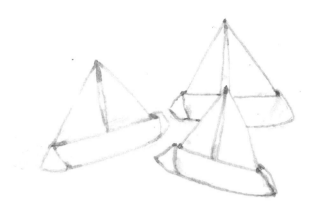

Homecomings

*L*ife, one long visit, is made up of shorter ones.

"Don't hurry. Don't worry," golfer Walter Hagan notes in his 1956 autobiography. "And be sure to smell the flowers along the way."

For as the title of a poem by Maxine Kumin states: *Our Ground Time Here Will Be Brief.*

Throughout their lives, humans venture forth and return again. Our son and daughter didn't grow up in our empty-nest house. Yet it is filled with relics from their childhoods, including ourselves.

How I hope it feels like "home" when they, along with our daughter-in-law, arrive this weekend.

I await their stay just as I did a visit with my parents.

Do offspring ever understand how much their time back home is anticipated? Perhaps they don't—until they become parents themselves.

Then they experience the countdown: the planning, the baking, the cleaning—and the pulling out of keepsakes.

In a stash of old letters I recently uncovered, my sister Sonja expressed delight in trips home from college.

"Dear Mom and Dad," she wrote on Jan. 5, 1962: "Thank you both very much for a wonderful Christmas and good vacation! Our home is the best in the world, and you have made it so."

April 30: "Just a note with a big thank-you for the wonderful vacation I have just had. How I enjoyed the good talks and companionship, yummy food, errands, the garden, rides, etc. I'm rested and ready to work."

May 16: "I've just had breakfast and thought of you all around the table."

Through the years, my three siblings and I looked forward to our many returns home.

The visits took on a different tone, however, after January 1977, when Sonja died suddenly.

"I'll always remember Dad's putting his arm around me Saturday night in the kitchen as dinner was being prepared," I wrote in a journal that August. "He told me how much it meant to Mother and him that the children and I had come for the weekend. But it was I who felt grateful. We all need each other, especially now.

"As if seeing it for the first time, I was struck by the orderliness of our home, the clean surroundings, everything in its space and place.

"And everywhere there was beauty—the roses from Mom's garden on the table, the three yellow candles that glowed through our talking."

During that weekend, my young son and daughter made paper hats in the basement—all because their grandmother, who praised their efforts, had wisely set out the materials.

At night, long after the children had fallen asleep, I spotted hats on all the bedposts.

We ate dilly bread at every meal, even toasting it for breakfast.

The day before I left, Mother helped me make two loaves, then sent them home with me.

I'll bake dilly bread again, although I haven't tried it in years, for the weekend homecoming.

Perhaps my children will remember the old standby and the family meals at which it once reigned.

Only after all these years do I realize how visits from my siblings and me must have reminded my parents of their own homecomings.

Their reunions must have sparked memories, too, in long-ago relatives of whom I know so little.

"And we ourselves shall be loved for a while and forgotten," Thornton Wilder says at the conclusion of *The Bridge of San Luis Rey*. "But the love will have been enough."

Grandmother-To-Be

*M*arital vows usher a couple down the rapid road of decades.

Looking at the photographs from my wedding, I'm startled to see how many of the celebrants are no longer living: my parents and sister, his grandparents and father—and other relatives and friends.

I'm also struck to see missing from the pictures our world as my husband and I know it today: the relatives and friends we had yet to know and, most of all, the children yet to be born.

Thirty-five years ago, a doctor confirmed that we would become parents for the first time.

Just a few words changed our lives forever.

How impatiently I waited nine months—and longer—for the son who was almost four weeks overdue. And, three years later, for the daughter who arrived a week early.

They both fled the nest long ago, leaving behind their childhood books: *Pat the Bunny, Good Night Moon, Where Do Baby Horses Go?*

I know the works by heart, if not by word—the curled pages and the worn covers, even the coverless ones such as *Make Way for Ducklings*.

My hand pulls *Babar and His Children* from the shelf.

How our children used to love hearing the story about the king and queen awaiting the birth of their first child (and ultimately being surprised by triplets).

"Babar is trying to read, but finds it difficult to concentrate; his thoughts are elsewhere. He tries to write, but again his thoughts wander . . . . Oh, how hard it is to wait for one's heart's desire."

At dinner on a recent visit to Boston, words edited our lives again. Our son and daughter-in-law are expecting their first child.

Make way for grandchildren, I thought, hearing the exciting news. And the family mobile shifts again, each member ending up in a new place in the changed configuration.

"There is something very special about your child having a child," a friend wrote upon hearing the news. "It's more than the fact that you are becoming a grandparent."

And I thought back to that swirling moment when I first heard the words: the tug of tide and moon, the shift of generations, the start of a new journey.

I realized that I was not so much me, but part of a family—connected to all that has come before and will arrive afterward.

Youth is consumed with finding one's purpose or goal in life. Yet now, later in life, I realize that just being part of the line was part of my purpose.

As a youngster, I used to wonder what it must feel like to know someone first as a baby, then as an adult. Luckily, as a parent, I got to find out twice. Hopefully, as a grandparent, I'll live long enough to learn again.

Like a kaleidoscope, a life holds a collection of colliding images: an August Saturday and a Bach arioso, a July Sunday and a baby's first cry, and a subsequent July and a memorable dinner. And each time—from "It's a boy" to "We're expecting a baby"—words shape the experience.

How can an unborn child possibly know all who eagerly await its arrival?

Before putting away the old photographs, I see once more white roses and ivy on the mantel, tables in white cloths on the summer lawn, and bridesmaids and others wishing a young couple well.

Even grandchildren, I now realize, were hinted at with the words, "May you live happily ever after." For the first time, I imagine their cherublike reflection that day—hiding in a mirror or in a sparkle on the lake.

Yet we weren't thinking of grandchildren, caught up as we were in the cutting of the cake, the throwing of the bouquet, the ducking under rose petals and rice.

All this while, they've been waiting their turn. I must learn to be patient, too.

Still, as the book says, "Oh, how hard it is to wait for one's heart's desire."

Letter to a Grandson

$\mathcal{D}$ear Miles,

A summer e-mail from your mother described you as being about the size of a small sweet potato.

Your father, she said, "talks" to you "every night and every morning, and puts on classical music. . . . He's going to be such a great dad; he already is."

And to think that tomorrow, Feb. 16, 2004, you already will be four weeks old! In the video of your birth, you seemed to know your parents.

There you were—"clay, touched by God."

Minutes later, a nurse placed you, wailing, beside your mother, with her face and your father's framing you.

You fell silent at the sound of their voices, as if relieved by the togetherness.

"We're so happy to meet you," your mother said. "We're going to know you for a long, long time."

On your first day, the image of you with your parents formed an eternal tableau.

"Being born is important," wrote Carl Sandburg, a poet whom you will someday come to know:

"You who have stood at the bedposts and seen a mother on her high harvest day, the day of the most golden of harvest moons for her. You who have seen the new, wet child, dried behind the ears, swaddled in soft, fresh garments, pursing its lips. . . you know being born is important. You know nothing else was ever so important to you."

Each birth creates us—and our families—anew.

For we, too, are born again—a son into a father, a daughter-in-law into a mother, parents into grandparents.

Even before you were born, I sensed the stirrings of grandparenthood, as I bustled about unearthing your dad's baby clothes and buying new ones. Afterward, watching your father change your diaper or lull you to sleep ("There, there, little Miles, little son, little son"), I was reminded of when my parents visited me after his birth.

"It makes me appreciate all that you and Dad did," he said, echoing what I'd told my mother.

"Don't you feel lucky to have been allowed to live long enough to see your grandchild?" your Aunt Tia asked us, taking picture after picture as your grandfather and I held you. "Not everyone gets the chance."

Nor to see a child become a parent himself.

I remember an August e-mail from reader Kari Inglis of Columbus, who shared her experience of becoming a first-time grandmother about five years ago.

"That was watching my son become an instant father. He spent long times just looking at his son, born a month early, with overwhelming love.

"And when his father-in-law, a retired ob-gyn, went to pick up the baby, my son said, 'Be careful with his head.'"

(Miles, your dad cautioned me in the same way.)

The tenderness I saw as my son gazed at you took my breath away.

So did the love of your mother, who dressed you in one of your father's newborn outfits and handed you to me.

As you napped in my arms, I noticed the traces of my children's infant faces and pondered those of my parents and grandparents and relatives unknown—all the shoulders on which a baby stands, back to the beginning.

"I can see why you called me Sweet Pea when I was a baby," my son said, "because that's the way Miles looks wrapped in his blanket."

And, 35 years later, I held you even tighter, knowing how quickly you will grow up.

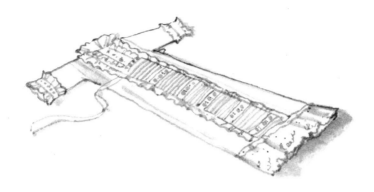

Baptismal Heirloom

*H*ow did everything happen so fast?

One minute, as a bride-to-be, I was selecting a china pattern with my mother.

The next, I was removing the Spode Grey Fleur de Lis from the buffet on my grandson's baptismal day.

I set my plates on the dining-room table next to a similar tower of china that had once belonged to Mom.

Anticipating the evening ceremony, I found myself revisiting my son's long-ago christening.

"If you think you are excited (to be coming home) for Thanksgiving, you ought to know how excited we are," Mother wrote me on Nov. 7, 1968. "The baptism would be fine any day you want . . . so you name it."

Almost 36 years later, I recall not the details—only impressions: my son in the paternal christening dress, worn first in 1887 by his great-grandfather and 55 years later by his father; my family around the font in the chapel of the school I once attended; the reception afterward.

I also remember that I discovered my mother, early in the morning, "touching up" the baptismal gown.

The sight of her skimming the iron over the Victorian tuck work and between intricate rows of lace touched me as much then as it does now.

Today, I wonder what occupied her thoughts.

What the future held for her grandson? Her four babies, finally grown? Or, perhaps, a similar task performed by her mother?

"Here, Mom, I should be doing that," I apologized, knowing I could never do it as deftly.

"I'm happy to. Besides, I'm almost finished," said the woman who was always lending a hand.

The dress, which has circulated through my husband's family with each christening, made its way back after 35 years.

A host of recollections rose as I lifted the heirloom from the box—such as the difficulty of maneuvering tiny arms through the tiny sleeves.

At an open house, grandson Miles was passed from one pair of welcoming hands to another as easily as a day, a decade or a generation slips into another.

Pictures of several ancestors wearing the gown graced a shelf nearby.

The oldest living relative—his 91-year-old paternal great-grand-mother, who had worn the dress in 1912—cradled him with a knowing smile and a telling tear.

One moment, it seems, Mother and I were dressing my son—and the next, I was assisting him as he slid his son into the same outfit.

It isn't so much the crush of years that makes a person feel faint as the weight of memories.

More recently, I studied the photographs showing the different hands of loved ones who helped ready Miles: his father's in the center, his great-aunt's on the right—and, on the far left, a deeply veined set with a knobby bone at the wrist.

For a second, recognizing my mother's, I felt my breath taken away.

Then I realized that it was mine.

A pair of hands can hold an infant son or grandson and even a mom, but it cannot grasp them forever.

What the hands cannot hold, the heart can.

Cradle Song

The oak cradle, like a small crib in size, swings on its two posts when given a gentle push.

The Victorian artifact, dating from 1887, first held my husband's grandfather.

Eighty-one years later, our firstborn slept in it.

Eventually we attached a mobile to one side. Later, heeding an idea from a book, we tied one end of a ribbon to the mobile and dangled the other end within his reach.

Again and again he tried to grasp the ribbon, until one day he succeeded in reaching it: With each tug, he made the mobile dance—and kicked his feet in victory.

The milestone inspired me to call his father at work.

Yet a far more amazing feat hung in the future: Our son grew out of his cradle and crib, and suddenly grew up—to become a father himself in January.

The cradle, too big for a small Boston-area apartment, mostly rests empty in an upstairs bedroom.

Still, I like to recall when my son and daughter filled it as infants and when my young grandson recently did.

More fascinating than the mobile was the sight of the baby in the spot where his father had slept.

Strange how a cradle, even one so old, remains a cradle, even while its inhabitants evolve into children, teenagers and adults.

"The night you were born, I ceased being my father's boy and became my son's father," Henry Gregor Felsen wrote in *Letter to a Teen-Age Son*. "That night I began a new life."

And so I saw my firstborn embrace his new role.

I'd previously known him as my son. Today, I know him as the father of my grandchild.

"Dear Miles," he wrote his firstborn last month:

"This is your first e-mail.

"I just wanted you to know how much I love you and think of you every day. I have been working so hard since your little life began that I feel like I have barely had the chance to see you. I miss you so much when I am away.

"Last night when I came home, you were already asleep. This morning, though, we had a few minutes together.

"You . . . always seem to recognize my voice. You also seem to like looking at the musical mobile that hangs over your changing table.

"I know you are going to grow up to be a smart, happy, strong and good boy.

"You have the most amazing mother in the world. She takes care of you every day in every way.

"So often you are both sleeping in exactly the same position—arms up near your heads and both looking in the same direction. I have often wanted to take a picture of this, but I will always have a picture of it in my mind.

"In just a few days, you will be 4 months old. You have grown and developed so much already. I am so proud of the little baby you are now, just as I know I will always be proud of the boy and man you will grow up to be.

"Take care, my son. I love you. / Your dad, Tyler."

A child outgrows a cradle but never a parent's love.

Attachment Parenting

"*My* parents were strangers to me from the moment of my birth," wrote 20th-century English poet Edith Sitwell.

Something tells me that my grandson will view his parents as anything but strangers. They subscribe to "attachment parenting," a style advanced by pediatrician and author William Sears.

The Baby Book, revised last year, is considered by many to be today baby bible, picking up where Dr. Spock left off.

Sears and his wife, Martha, a nurse, raised eight children, two of whom are pediatricians.

From my perspective, I knew something was different when I didn't spot a crib in my grandson's life.

Co-sleeping, or bedding close to a baby, is an integral part of the attachment parenting concept, as are breast-feeding and baby-wearing (carrying the infant a lot).

My daughter-in-law, Judith, was eager to try such methods.

She taught a Harvard University course on the behavioral biology of women. One aspect of the class examined how different cultures raise and treat children.

In traditional cultures, she said, babies are rarely put down. They are carried by their mothers most of the time and seemingly enjoy it.

I thought of my grandson squealing with delight in his carrier designed like a kangaroo's pouch, allowing him to sit facing the person holding him or be turned to look outward. Except when he's sleepy, he loves looking out and taking in sights and sounds. And without a doubt, he prefers the carrier to his buggy.

In many cultures, too, babies sleep right next to their mothers and also near their fathers, Judith said.

"The idea of putting the baby in another room came with industrialization and having homes with enough space that you could . . . . Yet, from an anthropologist's view, it's a fairly novel thing."

Sharing sleep seems to evoke more controversy than any other feature of attachment parenting, the Sears book notes.

"We are amazed that such a beautiful custom, so natural for ages, is suddenly 'wrong' for modern society," the pediatrician notes. "Some babies sleep best in their own room, some in the parents' room and some sleep best snuggled right next to mother. Wherever you and your baby sleep best is the right arrangement for you, and it's a very personal decision."

I confessed, "I'd be afraid I'd roll over on him," even if I followed all the safety guidelines.

"I had that fear, too," Judith said, "but I can't imagine now not being aware of where he is. I'm a much lighter sleeper now."

Now that the baby is able to roll over, a crib is in place for naps only.

The "new" attachment parenting is based on "learning to read the cues of your baby and responding appropriately to those cues," Sears says.

Seeing the process work so beautifully for my grandchild makes me wish I could raise my two children over again.

Instead, I'll settle for being an "attached" grandmother.

Birthmark

*D*uring my childhood, Mother would sometimes lift my hair to kiss the back of my neck.

"Right on your birthmark," she'd say.

Each time, to prolong the attention, I'd ask, "What's a birthmark?"

"Something you're born with. Not everybody has one," she'd answer, making it sound special.

"Each one is unique," she explained. "Yours is a pattern of little red marks. Sometimes it's hard to see; other times, especially if you're warm from play, it stands out."

As I recall, nobody else ever discerned the birthmark or, at least, ever mentioned it.

Even in her later years, when she caught a glimpse of the mark, it stirred a tenderness in her expression—as if she recognized me as her daughter after all.

Such small moments don't always come to mind when signing a Mother's Day card or selecting a birthday gift.

Later, after she's gone, the memories seep back.

They represent the marks of a mother that somehow imprint themselves.

So, too, do our children leave their impressions—helping to change us from the youths we were to the adults we are.

Instead of tying us down, they set us free: They open the windows to the world and its opportunities.

Parents realize how much they've learned by the time their offspring have gone off to start families of their own.

Working in the kitchen the other night, I thought of a time three decades ago—with my 6-year-old son and 3-year-old daughter bounding through the door.

Such imaginings gave me a sense of energy and youthfulness I hadn't felt in years.

After dinner, in the attic, I unearthed their old playthings before my grandson's first birthday.

Having sent a package of new clothes, I sought meaning in sharing family relics as well.

I discovered the wooden train and airplane, car and tugboat. And I found the cube with different openings—and the blocks that fit each one.

Future gift-giving possibilities include Legos, Lincoln Logs and a baseball mitt.

Yet I wondered what to give my grandson that might show a connection to me, his long-distance grandmother.

Across the attic beckoned my old "youth chair," which Miles could use before long.

It would provide another bond for us.

Then I realized the greater gift I had already received, proving my mission pointless.

During the summer, holding him in my lap, I saw tiny red marks on the back of his neck.

"That's his birthmark," his mother explained. "It shows up only when he's really warm."

Suddenly, I remembered his great-grandmother.

Only a mother—or grandmother—would notice such a thing; only she could find it endearing.

Then I kissed him.

Right on our birthmark.

Godparents

The recent wedding of our godson, Gabriel, in South Carolina presented a reason for celebration, with just a pinch of sorrow.

I was sad for missed opportunities that my husband and I had as god-parents.

We remembered his birthday, Christmas and each graduation with cards and gifts.

Still, despite the miles between, we could have been more involved.

During his childhood, why didn't we send letters and little surprises at times other than special occasions?

Godparenting styles range from the slacker type (mine) to the more-exalted model of C.S. Lewis.

"My dear Lucy, / I wrote this story for you," he says to his goddaughter, Lucy Barfield, in the introduction of *The Lion, the Witch and the Wardrobe*, "but when I began it, I had not realized that girls grow quicker than books.

"But someday you will be old enough to start reading fairy tales again. You can then take it down from some upper shelf, dust it, and tell me what you think of it. I shall probably be too deaf to hear, and too old to understand a word you say, but I shall still be / Your affectionate godfather, / C.S. Lewis."

Then there's the legendary approach of my friend Carole Banta, a godmother to some of the children of her godchildren.

She bakes Christmas cookies with them, then treats them to a lunch with balloons tied to the backs of their chairs and presents waiting on their plates.

For her youngest godchild, she flew from New Orleans to Dallas for godparenting training.

"It was life-changing," she noted. "The rector said: . . . 'If you . . . do not do one more thing for your godchild, pray for that child every day. Hold that child tight in your heart.'

"Praying for these children and thinking about them . . . makes you want to do the other things anyway."

Ted Sather, my godfather, grew up with my dad in Eau Claire, Wis.

By young adulthood, they'd tested their fishing lines in rivers such as the Chippewa, Flambeau and Mississippi.

My godfather fished with me, a 9-year-old, from a pier on Lake Michigan, where I discovered the joys of bait.

I waited for the perch to nibble. When the first one did, I was hooked.

Then came the hard part: removing the hook.

"If you catch a fish, you have to learn to do that and clean it, too," he instructed.

I dreaded the last step. Still, because I saw myself as a fisherman, I did it.

Years later, with his wife, my godfather attended the party for my high-school graduation, giving me a dictionary.

What endures, though, is the knowledge of how to catch and clean a fish—if I had to.

Since then, I've learned that time spent together means more than what one sends or gives.

The good news for our godson: Despite his unremarkable godparents, he has entered the seminary.

Time Recaptured

*I*n the spring, before the wedding of my godson, I joined his mother to examine the white dresses from her confirmation and wedding—along with her son's baptismal gown and bonnet.

How well I remember his christening.

"Why didn't we just sit and stare at our children?" I said, recalling that my son and daughter were there, too.

"Why did we ever hire sitters?" I continued. "If only we could have lived more in the moment."

We knew (but did we really know?): The time for raising children is finite.

Too often, with one foot in the future, we had to deal with the practicalities of parenthood.

Yet life does give second chances or at least a variation on them.

With my son and daughter-in-law recently moving to a new apartment, I baby-sat for my 18-month-old grandson.

What made the visit even more precious was the realization that it would last less than a week.

So, no matter how tedious or repetitive an activity became, I lived the experience to the hilt.

By the next time I see him, he will have changed.

And I don't want to wonder, when he is grown, why I hadn't just sat and stared.

On our first day together, he became fascinated with a fake owl that hangs on his aunt's porch to scare away pigeons.

How many times did he say, "Owl?" (with three syllables), navigating through the living room, dining room, kitchen and back hall to struggle through two doors and onto a stoop?

He would scurry over and stand beneath the pretend creature.

Holding the toy of the moment, as if to present an offering, he'd call the bird again.

Finally, he would reverse the route—then say, after reaching the living room, "Owl? Owl?" and repeat the ritual.

I don't exaggerate in suggesting that he did so at least 10 times a day, necessitating that he be followed every step of the way.

How often did we have "*agua*" or play "duck duck goose" or sing *Baa Baa Black Sheep*?

August afternoons called for trips to a shop for homemade ice cream.

Park, play, lunch, nap, park, play, dinner.

And so the days passed.

Each time I found myself sitting on the living-room floor to read with him—only to hear "Owl? Owl?" after we'd just said "Bye-bye, Owl!"—I'd willingly get up.

I didn't hesitate, aware that I couldn't revisit my days as a young parent when I put a sitter in my stead.

As any other grandparent would attest, such service brings a sweet reward: an impromptu hug; a pat-pat on the porch to imply, "You sit here, too"; or an open-armed lunge.

The best part of grandparenthood isn't getting to give back the grandchildren at the end of the day.

It's recognizing that they slow down time enough to allow for living in their moment, too.

In the
Fullness
of Time

*"Oh slow steady force unfolding the world,
You have blessed me and given me peace."*

"In the Fullness of Time,"
KAREN LOKVAM UPDIKE

Tia and Alberto's wedding day, June 25, 2005
© 2005 William Plowman

How Young Are You?

$\mathcal{I}$ am 48. My children, though not twins, are 28. And my mother-in-law is 40.

That's how young we feel.

As baseball player Satchel Paige once asked, "How old would you be if you didn't know how old you are?"

I remember my mother saying that she felt like a bride in her kitchen.

She felt like someone her real age, though, whenever she visited my sister to care for the grandchildren.

For a long time, I thought of myself as 28.

Eventually I traded up to 48, although 13 years have flown by since I actually experienced the milestone.

Both of my children think of themselves as younger, too.

"We're exactly the same age," my son thought when he heard a baseball announcer comment on an athlete who was turning 28.

"It was several seconds," he said, "before I remembered I am now 36."

One of his roles is that of an adviser to college students.

"I spend a lot of time around . . . (them) and do not feel like I am that much older—or that they are that much younger.

"They, of course, are smart and often converse like adults, but then something [occurs] that reveals their lack of . . . life experience or their lack of memory about anything that happened in the 1980s.

"This year's incoming . . . first-years were born in 1986, the year I started college."

"I think of myself as 28," added my 33-year-old daughter, a photojournalist and former lawyer. "I was single, on my own, looking for a job I

285

would like better than law and, finally, hitting upon photography. I did my first freelance assignment for a neighborhood newspaper.

"I think it was the first year in my adult life that I felt content, so that may be why the age sticks as how I see myself."

My sister-in-law Ann doesn't put a number on her age.

She knows just that she doesn't relate to what her birth certificate claims:

"I look at my skin, or I stand up after sitting for a long time, or I try to remember something that I thought I would never forget, (and) I know I'm 67.

"I love to run (in 5-kilometer races), and I know most 67-year-olds don't do that. I love to drive long distances. I love crossword puzzles—the more difficult, the better. I love to travel—the farther, the better. I love physical labor: gardening or moving furniture.

"Mother is such an inspiration . . . . If she can do all she does at 25 years older than I, I'd better get moving."

Her mom, who will turn 92 on Saturday, still walks 3 miles a day and plays 18 holes of golf a week. She feels "the same as I did when I was maybe 40. It's great," she said.

She hates "to look in the mirror . . . and see my thin hair or hear my scratchy voice, . . . but I guess that goes with age."

At nursing homes, she encounters "people there over 100—so 90 doesn't seem like anything."

Even my 61-year-old friend Sue, whom I've known for 35 years, views herself as only about half the age of our friendship.

"I feel about 16 . . . . I think being silly and doing nutty things—dressing up, wearing my goofy teeth, etc.—is something I thrive on. It gives me such a lift.

"The 60s can be so serious—health issues, friends passing—and I tend to focus on ways to lighten up."

So why do people consider themselves younger?

They settle on an age at which the events that took place "retain an emotional salience," said Columbus psychologist Jeffrey Smalldon, 51. "It is so easy to re-connect with those strong feelings."

In 1973 he visited Cambridge, England.

"That six months . . . was such a life-changer for me, such a pivotal period of time . . . . I have no trouble transporting myself back.

"That's the age that I go to, my early 20s—at a point when anything seemed possible."

And how young are you?

Beauty

$\mathcal{J}$ust when I thought I'd outgrown my angst over how I see myself and how others might see me, a *Newsweek* cover story—"The Biology of Beauty"—threw me a curve.

Now I'm worrying whether I have a waist-hip ratio between 0.6 and 0.8. (Is the size of my waist 60 percent to 80 percent of the size of my hips? Or was it?)

Healthy, fertile women typically have such a ratio—and an allure.

What would Mother Mary Ambrose think?

The mother superior of the Episcopal nuns who oversaw my high-school education once addressed the female student body:

"Remember that looks fade with time. Go through life emphasizing the interior decoration of your mind and soul."

Surprisingly, just a few weeks later, Miss America spoke at the school.

"Remember that you can become more beautiful all the time," said the reigning queen, seeming to dispute Mother Mary Ambrose. "Instead of reaching for potato chips while you watch TV, you can give yourself a good manicure."

Like many young women growing up today, I found myself lacking against the images that stared back at me from magazines and movies.

Why did you elude me, Beauty?

I once told my Spanish teacher, "Anna is so beautiful," after her daughter left the room. "She's young," Senora Villafranca replied. "Everyone is beautiful when she's young."

Recently, a friend gave me a T-shirt: "The older I get, the better I was."

What's amazing about growing older is that we start to realize how beautiful we were.

I wish I could gently shake young women by their shoulders and wake them from their Sleeping Beauty sleep:

"Don't waste a second doubting yourself or comparing yourself with others," I want to tell them. "Years from now, you'll come across an old photograph from the summer of '96 and marvel at your vibrancy. You'll wish you had accepted your gift, then lost yourself in something greater than yourself."

Today, I think Mother Mary Ambrose and Miss America both were right: I can honor all three—spirit, mind and body.

For too long, I denigrated myself. My legs, for instance, were too stubby and out of shape. By many standards, they were—and are.

Yet they still work, having walked the Earth for 53 years. I find my limbs—mapped by various veins, which they didn't have when I called them "ugly"—miraculous.

What a strange paradox: The older we become, with less to like about our physical selves, the more we like our true selves.

As time takes firm skin, stamina and fertility, it gives something in return: the liberating gift of self-acceptance.

We feel comfortable, integrated, whole. Instead of trying to be the same as everyone else, we learn to be our own best friend.

The process doesn't happen overnight. It can take a lifetime.

"Most people live, whether physically, intellectually or morally, in a very restricted circle of their potential being," psychologist William James wrote 90 years ago. "They make use of a very small portion . . . much like a man who, out of his whole bodily organism, should get into a habit of using and moving only his little finger."

In 1977, at age 63, Laura Schultz of Tallahassee, Fla., raised much more than her little finger.

"She lifted the back end of a Buick off her grandson's arm," Charles Garfield writes in his 1986 book, *Peak Performers*. "She usually picked up nothing heavier than her Pepto-Bismol bottle."

Garfield said in a speech that, when he interviewed Schultz three weeks later, she was depressed: Before the incident, she told him, she'd thought of herself as gray, dull, average. Too late, she was discovering her true power.

If only she'd known sooner, she said, how colorful and how beautiful her life might have been, she might have been.

Oh, Beauty, you are so much deeper than biology.

Apache Ceremony

*A*long with the history of women is each woman's history. The Apaches—whose most important rite is the Gift of Changing Woman—know this.

Last winter, a year before I learned of the ancient ritual, I was writing an essay about fallow fields. The phone rang.

"The lab results are back," my doctor said. "You've reached menopause."

I hung up, then reread my essay's opening words. Only then did I realize that my subconscious had been speaking about more than land.

Menopause is inevitable in women's lives. But, when it arrives, it brings not only a sense of commonality but also a feeling of isolation.

I experienced the same sensations one morning long, long ago. Why couldn't I go on just being me? I wondered at the time. The "me" I had come to know during the first 12 years of my life? Instead, a pair of unseen hands pushed me along, nudging me to be someone new.

Years later, the same shaping hands shook me in labor—like lightning through a tree—as I gave birth.

Between birth and death, we humans are always evolving. Sadly, some transformations are whispered about behind closed doors, or addressed in health class when boys see one movie and girls another, or discussed in pamphlets that parents leave on their children's bureaus or doctors hand out to their middle-aged patients.

Human changes so often are considered in terms biological. Little emphasis is given to spiritual rites of passage—defining doorways to self-growth and self-esteem.

This winter, the desert revealed a wonderful secret. While visiting Phoenix's Heard Museum of American Indian culture and art, I learned what the ancients knew—that mythology teaches us how to live. Rites and initiations help us understand new roles while letting go of our old selves.

The museum displays a dress and other artifacts worn by an Apache girl for the Gift of Changing Woman ceremony.

The four-day rite—still observed today—re-creates the beginning of the world. A young girl makes her transition to adulthood; isolation is replaced by a sense of community, as friends and family participate.

Standing by her side throughout the proceedings is her godmother—a woman selected by the girl's parents and admired by the village. She is someone the girl will strive to emulate.

The Apaches believe that Changing Woman was the first woman on Earth, the mother of all Apache people, who shapes and molds them with her hands. During the ceremony, which begins at sunrise, a girl comes to embody the deity's spirit, ensuring strength, prosperity and an even temperament.

She is given a staff that she places on the ground and runs around three times, to guarantee a long life. The staff one day will become her cane.

Thus, at puberty, a girl is reminded of her menopause. Nothing is forever. But all is connected.

On the night of the large bonfire and at sunrise the next morning, the Ga'an, or mountain spirits—four benevolent guardians who represent the four directions of Earth—bless the girl as she stands beneath the frame of a tepee, signifying a future home. East is painted black, South blue, West yellow and North white. A fifth, gray spirit represents fate, or everything that is unpredictable in life and nature.

Yet fate is always surrounded by the four gods, who keep the world in balance. They lead a procession through the crowd to show that they will accompany the girl on her life's journey.

Changing Woman's history is every woman's history.

Consider my mother: Once the youngest in her childhood "tribe," she is the only one at 79. Though fate has robbed her of her husband and a daughter, the four directions are with her still. She watches them from her window, stirring up the snow.

She—like me, like the Apaches, like all women—is shaped again and again by Changing Woman's hands.

Home Alone

On a neatness scale of 1 to 10, I hover around 5.

Not that I don't strive to be like Bree of *Desperate Housewives* and other Martha Stewart wannabes.

I was surprised, therefore, by how much I kicked back when my spouse was gone for a week.

Not feeling the need to fix supper or keep things in order, I threw myself into a backlog of projects.

On Monday, looking up from my desk, I noticed that six coffee mugs had taken up residence.

Thank goodness mold wasn't growing in any of them.

Still, I didn't see anywhere to put down the one I was holding.

Other intruders included a lone teacup, two empty water bottles and a pair of 5-pound weights. (Amazing how many curls one accomplishes while a dial-up service finds the Internet.)

On Tuesday, I didn't replace the folding screen that camouflages the bedroom treadmill.

Nor did I return the exercise machine to its upright position—all week. Instead, I walked over and around it.

Time saved.

On Wednesday, I realized that I'd stopped making the bed.

Far worse: The other half of the mattress had become an extension of a bedside table, holding a book (*Italian With Ease*), a couple of magazines (*People* and *The New Yorker*), a pair of reading glasses, an emery board and a box of notecards—and, best of all, the remote (which, finally, I controlled).

At least I recognized my decline.

Yet nothing could have prepared me for the shock that night when I detected a shadowy presence on the pillow next to mine. The culprit: an empty Go Lean cereal box.

On Thursday, after boiling water and adding steel-cut oatmeal, I turned the flame down to a simmer.

Going upstairs for something, I returned to the kitchen an hour later only to come upon the burnt remains of my unclaimed breakfast.

Late on Friday, feeling cold, I slipped on a down jacket over my pajamas.

With nobody to point out how ridiculous I looked, I went to bed in my "instant feather bed."

I ate most of my meals (if they could be called meals) in front of the television—some of them, even while standing close to the kitchen's small set.

What was I thinking? I asked my daughter-in-law when I recapped the preceding days.

She sent me the Deborah Garrison poem *Husband, Not at Home*, which reads in part:

"Her dinner a bowl / of cereal, taken cranelike, on one leg, hip snug to the kitchen / counter . . . She'll let the cat jump up / to lap the extra milk, and no one's home to scold her."

All week, talking to myself, I came up with the same lines that my children had used on me (and I had once used on my mother): Why make the bed when I'll just get back under the covers tonight? If I don't hang up my clothes, who cares? Why not watch television while I eat?

What had sown the seeds of my destruction?

I was simply alone, without even my grown children around—for whom I would have snapped back into my role as a homemaker.

Then, at the end of the week, I was almost late getting to the airport to pick up my husband.

Cleaning the house and preparing a dinner had taken forever.

Why bother, one might wonder?

As Charles Dickens says in *Martin Chuzzlewit*, "Keep up appearances whatever you do."

Karen's Cabin

$\mathcal{M}$y sister, fort builder of my youth, tamed the wild to her wishes. Karen fashioned treehouses, hide-outs and, with a ring of stones, campsites. Tagging along, I often followed her to a secret spot by a creek that she and a friend had dubbed "Nature." Drawing closer, she'd blindfold me—to avoid giving away its location—until we reached the spot.

And so, returning from a recent trip to Iowa, the two of us arrived at her rural Wisconsin cabin in the dead of night. A full moon and the stars captivated us until the call of screech owls sent me flying to the front door.

We had not come by way of a team of horses pulling a covered wagon with a cow tied to the back—as our paternal, Norwegian grandparents had done in a driving rain.

And although Karen's "postage stamp" of a place, as she calls it, doesn't have a telephone line, it is a far cry from the homesteader's log cabin with a dirt floor in Minnesota where Dad was born.

Her retreat rests on 80 acres in the county next to Dane, where Mother's Norwegian ancestors settled on the Koshkonong Prairie. Besides an old meadow spreading down to a winding creek, there are 20 acres of old woods, 30 of newly planted hardwoods and pine trees, and 30 of prairies. Added to the native bluestem grasses, which grow to almost 8 feet, are perennials such as blue flax, black-eyed Susans and purple coneflowers.

More than anything else, the getaway is the flowering of my sister's 40-year-old dream.

"Ever since I started riding again, I wanted a place (in an area) that I didn't think would get built up right away," she said.

Karen joined a friend—with a similarly reluctant, city-loving husband—in finding the land, plotting the road and building the cabin.

These days, both families take turns sharing the house.

My daughter likens the view, with hills and farms fanning the horizon, to vistas she saw in Germany.

The first time I entered the house, I felt as if I'd stumbled upon an enchanted cottage in a fairy tale—a walking stick by the door, the walls of Norwegian red and green.

The stone fireplace rises to the ceiling with its worn barn beam of a mantel. And the window seat, inspired by an illustration in a book of poems by Robert Louis Stevenson, runs the full length of a wall.

"Now that your parents are gone, and your family home has been sold, Karen's cabin feels like the Lokvam 'homestead,'" my daughter once said, sensing its symbolism even before I did.

Outside, the owls competed with coyotes. Inside, Karen and I visited, in front of a fire, on Mother's old couch, her pewter platters on the mantel. Nearby, my parents' maple breakfast table still held the wooden napkin holder decorated with Norwegian rosemaling.

Later, falling asleep upstairs, I recalled that my sister had compared the contour of her land to a loaf of Viennese bread. I pictured her campfire and picnic-table site on the ridge, the cabin a little below and, overhead, a huge splash of the Milky Way.

When I awoke, the first sight to emerge in the light of dawn was my old desk tucked in a window alcove. All I studied from there that day was the view down to the creek, where I spied a dozen cows grazing.

Downstairs, at the window seat, I saw the moon and morning star linger. As ground fog lifted from the valley, I felt connected to the land and those I hold close.

Delicately, in the stillness, two young deer leapt out of the tall grass and headed to the apple tree near the deck. I waited for them to rise on their hind legs and paw the branches with their hooves as my sister said a 13-point buck had done one evening. Instead, with nudging noses, they inspected the fallen fruit.

At the close of our visit, Karen left the gate open at the end of her road: "If you lock it," old-timers have told her, "that's a sure sign nobody's there."

Gradually, she reclaims the ways of country living—those that our ancestors surely once knew. My sister still leads me to places wild and free, still makes a fortress in the midst of nature.

Her "sunny, mote-filled cabin on a hill near Hollandale," as she calls it, has allowed us to come full circle and given our family a sense of coming home.

Grand Canyon

*H*ow could the sight of the Grand Canyon make a person feel so young?

One hundred years after President Theodore Roosevelt first viewed it, I glimpsed what naturalist John Muir called "God's spectacle."

A century barely matters, however, with a canyon whose walls reveal 2 billion years of geologic formations.

Nothing before had so impressed upon me the antiquity of Earth, the brevity of humanity.

In anticipation, like the ravens sailing above the South Rim, my heart soared.

Arriving at Grand Canyon National Park late one recent afternoon, my husband and I heeded a ranger's suggestion to drive a short distance to the first overlook at Mather Point.

We parked and walked but a few feet before we saw the unimaginable vistas.

We could hardly comprehend the magnitude, the towering buttes, the staggering decline.

Like a permanent parting of the Red Sea, the canyon features waves of rock seemingly frozen in motion.

A newspaper column cannot hold the Grand Canyon: The colossal South Rim represents "only a small dot" on the 1.2 million acres of the park. The mighty Colorado River carves the floor for 277 miles.

Posters and photographs fall short, too.

I hadn't really grasped the canyon until, standing before it, I felt its grasp.

As quiet as a prayer, its stillness inspires silence: Throngs of people whisper, as if in church, or speak not at all.

A shuttle ride away, at Hopi Point, we experienced the same hush—and, coloring the scene, a smoldering sunset.

Any word, overheard, was as apt to be foreign as familiar, giving the rim an international ring.

"Keep this great wonder of nature as it now is," Roosevelt pleaded in 1903, nine years before Arizona became a state. "The ages have been at work on it, and man can only mar it. What you can do is keep it for your children, your children's children, and for all who come after you, as the one great sight which every American, if he can travel at all, should see."

Why had we taken our children to Disneyland and Disney World when, instead, we might have made a pilgrimage to the Grand Canyon?

The natural wonder offers something far more fantastic than any fantasy: real mountains rather than Magic Mountain, live condors rather than mechanical birds of prey,

It also contains 287 species of birds, 88 of mammals, 25 of fishes and 50 of reptiles and amphibians.

And why had I waited all my life, 60 years, to go there?

The next morning, we didn't need an alarm clock any more than does a child on Christmas Day.

We rose at dawn to walk the paved path along the rim.

Passing the 1905-built El Tovar, the flagship hotel of Grand Canyon Village, we noticed the one corner that rests only 20 feet from the edge.

Carved on a lintel supporting a porch is the quotation "Dreams of mountains, as in their sleep they brood on things eternal."

Later, descending from the 7,000-foot elevation, I thought of that line from *The Titan of Chasms* by C.A. Higgins: We had come face to face with the eternal.

Words cannot hold the Grand Canyon.

Only the heart can.

Tia's 28th Birthday

*M*y daughter once was as young as the little girl who sat in front of me on a recent flight to Boston.

Now and then I heard the child sob, saw her small shoulders shake.

"She misses her mother," the flight attendants explained as they tried to help her make the tears stop.

I could hardly believe that the next day my daughter would turn 28—my age when she was born and my mother's age when I was born.

Such coincidental anniversaries of the heart don't inspire greeting cards, slogans or ready-made bouquets. Still, they explain my trips to celebrate with my daughter and, this weekend, my mother.

August gave birth to both of the women who shape my world.

At first I thought that my childhood, and later my daughter's, would last forever. At first I thought that my roles of daughter and mother represented separate scripts.

I see now that I slip back and forth between the two.

Are we defined not by what we are called but by our experiences?

And so on Sunday morning, almost three decades after giving birth to my daughter on a Sunday, I woke up in her apartment, struck by how fast everything had gone: One minute I was holding her in my arms, waiting for her father to bring the car around; the next minute I was watching the sun rise over the rooftops on Beacon Hill.

I have spent all my life as the daughter of a mother and half my life as the mother of a daughter. Yet, more and more, I feel like my mother's mother and my daughter's daughter.

Shortly before I married, when I was about to return to work in another city, Mom asked whether she might share something—a story about an older woman recalling when she and her husband had taken their baby home from the hospital.

Suddenly, as Mother read the tale, she burst into tears like a child. I sensed why but only intellectually.

My older heart, less green with every year, understands better: As I relive the scene, I still hear her apologies. Yet now, instead of my merely saying "That's OK," my feet frozen to the floor, I rush over, the way a mother might, to hug her trembling shoulders.

Strange how the years, more magical than any wizard, constantly reinvent someone.

If only I were a Michelangelo, I'd take my mother's hands and make them young again. I'd make her back as strong as Mary's in the Pieta. Instead of winter waiting at the gate, I'd make her hear the creek roaring into spring once more.

Most of all, I'd fashion her face to resemble her granddaughter's asleep on Sunday's pillow.

On her birthday, after we arose, my daughter led me beneath buildings that plow the sky, guided me on and off the subway, treated me to a swan boat ride in the public gardens.

She insisted on buying me a hat, placing it on my head and standing back to observe.

I cooperated, happy at the novelty of being fussed over.

All day she reached over to adjust the brim, pulling it down to the top of my eyebrows.

"See?" she said, pointing out others who wore a hat the same way. "Like that."

By the time she'd finished opening the small presents I'd tucked in my suitcase, her apartment seemed darker despite the sunny day.

I was there but not there, recalling parties on summer lawns, the wreckage of wrapping paper, pieces of toys from when time almost stood still.

On the ride to the airport, we talked about everything.

I told her the story we revisit each Aug. 1: Her 3-year-old brother awakened me in the middle of the night, hungry for a peanut-butter-and-jelly sandwich. In the kitchen, the full moon peeked in at us. Her brother went back to sleep, but I couldn't. It was "time."

And then it was time to board the plane.

Moments before, she'd made me laugh as she reminded me how, as a 3-year-old, she'd dropped croquet balls down the sewer to hear them splash.

I kept focusing on that long-ago day as the plane took off. I didn't want the flight attendants to see me cry.

"Do as the Romans Do"

*W*hen my daughter Tia offered to lead our family on a visit to Italy, I had no idea what to expect.

She suggested, for starters, that her brother, father and I pack as little as possible because we'd be "carrying our luggage and doing a lot of walking."

I should have realized that the trip would be better-suited to the under-30 set than the over-50 one. Instead, I basked in visions of Merchant Ivory films with myself as Helena Bonham Carter relaxing on a Tuscan hillside.

The night before we left, I called my daughter.

"Guess what," I boasted. "I've packed everything I'll need for the next two weeks in my gym bag."

"Go back and unpack half of it," she said.

I ignored her advice. Yet, if I'd known then what I know now, I might have avoided that mistake and four others.

Mistake No. 2: not grasping the meaning of "a lot of walking."

Day and night, Tia took us through ancient towns to train and bus stations, subways and sights, hotels and trattorie.

We climbed endless steps, too—in bell towers and museums, the Colosseum and art galleries, the Boboli Gardens and Palatine hill.

I had considered myself fit. Then, on the first day, when I was the only one who stopped a third of the way up the 276-foot Campanile in Florence, I couldn't fool even myself.

Not learning Italian before the trip was my third mistake.

I had ignored the language tapes and books at Christmas, rationalizing that my daughter, who practices her Italian every chance she gets, would see me through.

How the Italian face softened when she made an effort to try the other tongue.

"I'm so glad you speak Italian," she heard on more than one occasion. "My English is not so good."

When she had trouble finding the right word, Italians were patient, appreciative that she resisted the easier route of lapsing into English.

My fourth mistake? Talking too loudly. Throughout cities such as Siena, Florence and Venice, Tia had to remind us to speak more quietly in restaurants, on buses and in other public places.

When she pointed out the problem at breakfast the first morning, I stopped to listen, only to hear a faint murmur of voices and the clinking of silverware in a room full of people.

Last, I had assumed that shopping in Italy would be similar to that in the United States.

"Italy is one of the most ideal places in the world for window-shopping," Tia observed. "You enter a shop only when you see something in the window that you'd like to have or look at or know more about. You don't really browse inside the store, handling everything. . . . There are some department stores now, and the places where tourists shop are more geared to browsing. It's just something that I think a lot of people don't notice when they come here, and they end up rubbing people the wrong way.

"Likewise, you're not supposed to touch produce or fruit with your bare hands. Grocery stores have plastic gloves. At at an outdoor market, you're to tell the seller what you'd like; if you want three apples, he'll choose them and show each apple for approval."

Not everything she described is obligatory, of course.

"You could not do any of these things and still have a fine trip," she said. "They're just courtesies. In heavy tourist areas, shopkeepers have learned what to expect. . . . It's just if you want to surprise people."

She surprised me with her sensitivity, trying to "do as the Romans do" and to teach me to do the same.

Turning Tables

$\mathcal{R}$emembering a visit with my daughter, I couldn't believe how she kept her apartment so serene and uncluttered.

"Has she turned into a neat freak?" my friend Toni asked when we met for breakfast.

"Yes, it makes me want to throw out my stuff and start over. Even her fluffy white towels are rolled and arranged in a basket. I feel like a slob."

Toni identified with me at once.

"When I stayed with Cristin last summer, she wouldn't let me put down my wineglass—on a glass table, no less—without a coaster."

Where had the "I'll clean my room later" girls gone?

And when did our daughters become so meticulous?

Such a changing of the guard happens without ceremony, although a mother knows the moment as well as she knows her child.

Toni had the experience last summer: While attending a workshop in children's literature, she stayed for a week in her daughter's apartment—coordinated down to a silk tassel on the TV armoire.

Her daughter even wanted to conceal the suitcase.

"It seems my 8,704-cubic-inch travel duffel . . . bothered her principles of feng shui," Toni said. "We tried to hide it, but one-and-a-half closets that are narrower than my 32-inch roll-on wouldn't do the trick.

"So I kept it as neatly and discreetly as I could against her living-room wall. I was sure she was going to have it upholstered and tufted to match her decor."

My bulky luggage also interrupted "the flow" at my daughter's apartment, where sunlight splashed wooden floors, music filled airy rooms and flowers adorned everything: lavender in a blue vase, an arrangement on the bedside table, daisies where we dined.

She'd make my bed before I had barely emerged; she'd set the breakfast table and fill the espresso maker the night before.

Wherever we sat—for a meal or just for tea—she'd light a candle.

Toni was pampered, too.

"Every evening, after I returned from my classes, there was always a candle burning and soft music in the background."

(She discovered that the compact-disc player was hidden under a skirted table.)

"Shrimp scampi and seafood and pasta were often the meal du jour—no TV dinners for this mother. I was impressed and delighted. Her culinary skills must have come from some rare recessive gene."

Oh, babies, you've come a long way. These days, our daughters mother us.

Didn't I want to go on any of the rides? mine asked when she took me to a town fair. Or buy the little painting? She hoped I wouldn't regret either.

"I thought for sure Cristin was going to take me by the hand as she guided me past . . . the Boston Commons," Toni recalled. "How many times had I read *Make Way for Ducklings* to her?"

And other books—just like the character in the Strickland Gillilan poem *The Reading Mother*:

"You may have tangible wealth untold: / Caskets of jewels and coffers of gold. / Richer than I you can never be—I had a mother who read to me."

Best of all, our daughters have created a sense of home in the wider world. Mine gave up a law career to become a photojournalist.

Her firstborn serves as a third-grade teacher and reading specialist.

"On a hot and humid Cambridge day, in an old, non-air-conditioned classroom," Toni said, "I sat cramped in a child's chair and listened to my teacher-daughter regale me with tales of her students, show me their language and art projects, and read me their stories.

"Richer than I you can never be—I had a daughter who read to me."

A Romance Language

*I*talian is among the Romance languages, but the language of love is universal.

Do the stars start the conversation? Or do the starry-eyed initiate their fate?

Whatever the answer, after two paths converge, they continue as one.

A decade ago, while teaching in Germany, my daughter decided to pick up Italian.

Each vacation found her traveling to the Tuscany region to enroll in a class.

Even after returning to the United States, she periodically studied in Italy.

Then, while living in Connecticut, she practiced speaking the language with a group of elderly Italians.

Tia later joined an informal supper club in which younger Italians and Americans honed their linguistic skills.

Two years ago she met Alberto, an electrical engineer from Florence.

"Forget about it," one of his friends told him afterward. "She's interested only in learning Italian."

Until she met Alberto.

Today, they are not only engaged in speaking each other's native tongue (often starting a sentence in English and finishing it in Italian) but also engaged.

"Maybe today is the birthday of the person you'll someday marry," I would tell Tia as a child. "I wonder whether he lives down the street or in another state?"

Only time, completing the picture, answers such questions.

I never dreamed that her future husband was growing up in another country. Or that *Happy Birthday* was being sung to him in Italian.

Or that, in 2005, he would celebrate two weddings with my daughter—one in her country, the other in his.

Fulfilling the long-ago musings, Tia presented a cake to him on his June 30 birthday.

"New blood is good for families," she had once observed. "It's like opening the window for a breath of fresh air. It keeps them from becoming set in their ways."

I finally see the wisdom of her insight: Love transforms not only the lovers but also the other people in their orbit.

Buon giorno, buona sera, buona notte—"good morning," "good evening," "good night."

Throughout the day, seeking to learn the language of my future son-in-law, I listen to compact discs. From morning to night, I stay plugged in.

The idea that he is known as "fearless in the kitchen" inspired me to clean every cupboard and drawer before his first visit to mine. It also prompted me to try new recipes—although he never follows them, even when making, say, English muffins or sticky buns for the first time.

"With Alberto in the family," Tia said, "you'll never have to cook alone again."

During my last visit to her apartment, Alberto arrived with two bags of groceries.

I watched him make pasta for a soup he was creating.

Along with plenty of side dishes, he also fixed *bistecca* wrapped in prosciutto and trout seasoned with horseradish sauce.

Later, as stars brightened in a night sky, the three of us indulged in his homemade chocolate biscotti.

His meal was amazing, even more so because it was prepared in a kitchen with barely a pot and a spoon.

"Why is that, Tia?" he asked, half-teasing.

"Because," I said, "if she ever wanted to move to Italy, she wanted to leave at a moment's notice without worrying about a lot of possessions."

"Instead," he said, looking at her as if no one else existed, "Italy came to you."

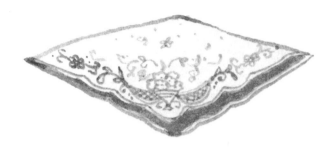

Wedding-Dress Shopping

Life is full of dress rehearsals.

And so I found myself shopping with my daughter for her wedding dress.

While she selected samples with help from my daughter-in-law, I held my infant grandson—the perfect antidote to welling tears.

I wasn't sad so much as moved.

In fact, I remembered how my mother bristled when someone would sigh, "Isn't it sad how the kids grow up."

"That's how it's supposed to be," she'd tell me later. "What would be sad is if children didn't blossom into adulthood."

Therefore, with my newly engaged daughter, I'd gone off in high spirits on the female rite of passage.

I couldn't help reliving her days playing dress-up with a friend next door.

And suddenly Tia was trying on styles as a real bride-to-be.

Almost half a century ago, the whole family had accompanied my oldest sister on a similar mission to the same place—Priscilla's of Boston.

The rest of us crowded into a fitting room while Dad waited without.

"This is a cool fort," announced my little brother, crawling undetected under a hoop skirt.

Laughter tumbling down through five decades reached me on the recent Sunday afternoon. I recalled the beautiful dress that my sister chose—the one I wore six years later.

"Just think, if you get your gown here, then we . . . ," I started to say to my daughter.

Before I could finish, she emerged from the fitting room in a gown that made even my grandson's eyes grow wide and mine blur.

We all agreed that she had found just the right one.

"Here," said the saleswoman, helping my daughter with a pair of white pumps.

I couldn't help thinking of the tiny, red-leather Mary Janes that a friend had sent at her birth: How much time would pass before she'd grow into them, I'd thought.

The saleswoman then adorned her head with a tiara and two veils, one covering her face and the other reaching the floor.

For a moment, none of us spoke as Tia stood on a riser in front of a three-way mirror.

I realized in the chapellike quiet how like a veil her future has become.

As her mother, I know her past—from the moment of her first stirrings, her heart beating next to mine.

From now on, though, separate experiences in the scrim of years will shape her. When the shorter veil was lifted, what awaits her seemed to float free.

I thought of the white lace handkerchief that my English teacher had given to me to carry at my wedding.

When she appeared in the receiving line, I blurted out half a thank-you, half an apology: "But I didn't even cry."

On the recent Sunday I did, picturing the joy of giving it to my daughter on her wedding day.

"As your matron of honor, and as perfect as the dress is, I'm not going to let you get it today," my daughter-in-law announced—to the saleswoman's regret but my daughter's relief.

Tia had asked us both beforehand not to allow her to buy a gown on her first outing.

"You have a whole year, and you should take more time to look," her sister-in-law added.

As all mothers know, the perfect daughter—unlike the perfect dress—doesn't have to be sought.

Luckily, she arrives in our arms.

Well-"Tamed"

Who has not looked about a crowded airport and seen all types of people—fathers, mothers, sons and daughters—who seem familiar but aren't?

The lack of recognition reflects an absence of shared history—or bonding, or, as the fox in *The Little Prince* says, "taming."

"What does that mean—*tame*?" asks the little prince.

"It means to establish ties," answers the fox. "To me, you are still nothing more than a little boy who is just like a hundred thousand other little boys . . . . To you, I am nothing more than a fox like a hundred thousand other foxes. But if you tame me, then we shall need each other. To me, you will be unique in all the world. To you, I shall be unique in all the world."

At age 4, Antoine de Saint-Exupery—the future author of *The Little Prince*—lost his aristocratic father to a stroke.

He grew up in a castle with his mother. Was he affectionately called "the little prince"?

"The young man adored his mother, who indulged her gifted . . . son," essayist Duncan Elliott writes. "They corresponded throughout his life, and the letters speak of a love and sweetness special even for the mother-son bond."

"One only understands the things that one tames," the fox informs the little prince in the Saint-Exupery fable: "(Men) buy things already made at the shops. But there is no shop anywhere where one can buy friendship."

To "tame" a friend, the fox explains, requires rites—"what make one day different from other days."

As our Thanksgiving rite approaches, we pilgrims in an America "on alert" are making plans.

The bond of family drives us: a grown son to the father who played chess with him every evening or a grown daughter to the mother who once helped her create a winning Halloween costume.

Such shared moments—preparing for the first day of school, participating in sports, going on a family vacation—inspire bonds.

So, at Thanksgiving, we have to gather with family—or at least friends.

"You are beautiful, but you are empty," the little Prince says to the roses who look like his rose. "But in herself alone, she is more important than all the hundreds of you other roses: Because it is she that I have watered, because it is she that I have put under the glass globe, because it is she that I have sheltered behind the screen, because it is for her that I have killed the caterpillars . . . . Because she is 'my' rose."

In a travel diary, on a night flight to London in 1992, my mother next to me wrote of her rose:

"Only the Atlantic is below. Soon it may be Greenland. I wonder why they 'suspected' me at the airport—examined everything and every part of me. What are they expecting? I am only a brokenhearted widow, missing my husband more than anyone will ever know."

Saint-Exupery, a pilot who helped chart the skies, knew the flight pattern of a soul, too. He would have understood her descent into sadness as much as her rise out of it, soaring higher to reassure her family.

"It is only with the heart that one can see rightly; what is essential is invisible to the eye," the fox tells the little prince.

The time spent on our roses, our family and friends, is what makes them so important to us.

Any parent, tucking a child into bed, knows; any child, watching a parent go out the door, knows. And so does any mother, anticipating a Thanksgiving homecoming.

She wants to know, too, exactly when her brood will arrive.

"If you come at just any time," the fox says, "I shall never know at what hour my heart is to be ready to greet you."

309

Christmas Past

*C*hristmas past was present-less.

Almost.

During the summer, a New Orleans friend who had always sent a smoked turkey asked, "Do you still want to exchange holiday gifts?"

I worried at first. Then I recalled that she had agreed with other friends not to get caught up in the annual frenzy.

In early fall, a Toledo friend suggested, "Let's not do Christmas presents anymore."

Again I worried: Had I made a bad choice of gifts the year before?

"I know you love me, and you know I love you," she said. "We don't need to keep giving each other presents to prove the point. I'd rather you take any money you might spend on me and do something nice for someone else."

For the first Christmas ever, she said, she and her family wouldn't exchange gifts, either. I thought of mentioning the idea to other friends.

Before I did, however, one in Nashville, Tenn., sent an e-mail message that she was having my mailbox decorated as a holiday gift.

In a reply, I thanked her—and made a suggestion for 2005.

"I remember your husband saying that you and your closest friend give each other the gift of no gift," I wrote. "Should we do the same?"

I'd barely hit "send" before I received her response.

"Oh, yes! Only true soul mates can give the present of no presents," she said.

And so, in 2004, my family also inaugurated such a tradition—with two exceptions.

We welcomed with gifts the two newest members: our 11-month-old grandson, Miles, and our future son-in-law, Alberto.

I was concerned about actually doing what we had often said we would try—emphasizing not presents but our presence.

I shouldn't have given it a thought: I found "gifts" everywhere, as Miles spent his first Christmas in our home, as Alberto ushered his parents from Italy to our celebration—and as each family member reached the door.

For our 12 days of Christmas, nine of us gathered.

No smoked turkey? I was prompted to roast one myself—grateful for the gift of electricity.

The fragrance, an added bonus, filled our home on Christmas Eve.

We made the annual gingerbread house, too—yet Piero, our daughter's future father-in-law, showed us, among other new touches, how to hold powdered sugar on a spoon, blowing it onto the gingerbread to depict the effects of a snowstorm.

And, in honor of the upcoming June wedding, he placed two candy canes to form a heart on the back of the house,

Our foreign visitors also delighted in little Miles, giving him a copy of *The Three Little Pigs* in Italian.

"Bravo," Alberto and his parents said each time Miles pulled himself to a standing position.

"Bobo settete!" they exclaimed as they played peekaboo with him.

Piero joked that, upon his return to Italy, he would miss the toddler more than his own son.

On Christmas night, the tree aglow and the house bathed in candlelight, I was carrying platters to the serving table when I suddenly spied a crawling Miles underfoot.

From the living room, everyone saw the hostess somersault over her grandson.

The best present: Miles wasn't hurt. Neither was I.

Instead, I'd provided some unexpected entertainment.

How should I explain our recent Christmas? The first one when we didn't exchange gifts, we had the most.

June 25, 2005

*U*pon hearing about runaway bride Jennifer Wilbanks, I wondered why her mother hadn't fled instead. That I could have understood, what with the 600 invitations, 14 bridesmaids, 14 groomsmen and an over-the-top wedding reception waiting in the wings.

If the idea to flee did cross the woman's mind, she probably wasn't the first mother of the bride to entertain the notion.

Yet, just as in childbirth, once we're caught up in planning our daughters' weddings, we can hardly turn back.

And just as in the throes of early motherhood, when we endured sleepless nights, we wake up often—thinking about printers and caterers, florists and musicians.

Each child grows in her own way, and so does each wedding. Yet the baby steps along the journey would be missed if the mother went missing. I wouldn't have heard my daughter say, for example, how she wished to carry a bridal bouquet of gardenias.

Did she know that her paternal grandmother had chosen the same for her wedding?

No, said Tia, pleased at the coincidence.

With her groom, she also selected June 25 for the wedding—only to learn afterward that my parents had married on that date.

Later, when she mentioned what accessories she wanted to wear, I had my mother's long white gloves to pass along—for "something old."

My daughter had already chosen her wedding dress when her other grandmother offered the lace gown she'd found in 1935 at the Higbee department store in Cleveland. Not only did the heirloom fit Tia to a T, but she also seemed made for it. And, in a way, she was.

Unsure of what to do, she settled on a surprise: She would wear her new dress for the ceremony, then slip into the vintage gown just before she and her groom were to cut the cake.

Happily, my sister-in-law Ann had come upon her parents' cake topper to round out the tableau.

During the reception, my 10-year-old great-niece crept into the changing room.

"How did you know Alberto was the one you wanted to marry?" Grace Ann whispered as I helped my daughter into her grandmother's dress.

As the three of us left to rejoin the reception, I asked Grace Ann to carry her great-grandmother's train. I wouldn't have missed my great-niece's visit or being with my daughter for anything, nor the surprised expression of my mother-in-law, 92, when she spotted her treasure.

A home movie from the 70-year-old wedding flickered in the background, mirroring the couple cutting their cake in 2005.

How quickly the bride in the black-and-white images had become the oldest person at her granddaughter's wedding. And how fast our daughter had taken her place as the bride.

Soon we were seeing off the newlyweds. I handed them a New England pie basket (just as my mother had given my husband and me) filled with wedding cake and other treats. And in that moment of separation, I felt closer to my mother, closer to my daughter.

As I watched Tia vanish into a waiting car, I thought of the tiny white outfit I'd dressed her in for the trip home from the hospital. Wasn't it only yesterday that I waited for her father to bring the car around as I held her in my arms?

Italian Fairy Tale

*I*n a life as unpredictable as fiction, any day might be as magical as a fairy tale.

Perhaps, when my daughter was young, a good sprite whispered in her ear to try out other languages as she grew up.

Her love of Italian, after all, is what led her to Alberto.

Tia married him four months ago in the United States.

Little did I realize then what their second celebration, last month in Italy, would include.

Pieve di San Pietro a Romena, a late-11th-century church built on a former Etruscan and Roman place of worship, lies in Casentino, in the upper valley of the Arno River.

Gentle slopes and the ruins of medieval castles fill the picture-book Tuscan landscape, rivaling any I saw during a story hour in childhood.

Behind a tower, one could imagine, Rapunzel waits to let down her golden hair.

On a sunny morning at an inn, I again helped Tia into her bridal dress.

Her second wedding day was surely a dream, I thought.

The groom and his mother drove ahead—and, later, his father, Piero, set out with the bride and her parents.

Tall and slender cypress trees, climbing the hills on tiptoe, showed the way.

As we passed through villages, children held on to their mothers' hands and pointed at the bride through a car window.

A cell phone rang. The caller: Alberto.

He suggested that his father pull off the road and wait: Ten minutes before the start of the 11 a.m. wedding, not even the priest had shown up—nor any of the guests, except our son.

Custom, as Piero explained, would have considered it unusual for a bride to reach her wedding on time, let alone early.

So we stopped, then drove about, until the groom phoned again, saying we should continue on our happy journey.

Upon our arrival, Alberto presented Tia with a cascading arrangement of white roses—a bouquet selected by his mother, Silvana.

Her gesture was "the modern combination of two traditions," Alberto later explained.

"The mother of the groom gives a special present (the flowers) to her new daughter, and the fiancé waits outside the church and gives (this) one last present to his beloved before becoming a family—a present so greatly appreciated that she'll keep it with her even during the ceremony."

The guests who had gathered outside clapped in greeting.

Friends and family then took their places inside the ancient church, site of so many ceremonies for Alberto's relatives. Violin music filled the sanctuary; daylight shimmered through long, slender mullions; candles flickered.

After renewing their vows, the couple were showered in rice.

The reception site overlooked Poppi Castle, where Dante Alighieri once stayed and wrote:

"The little streams that flow from the green hills of Casentino, descending to the Arno, keeping their banks so cool and soft with moisture, forever flow before me."

So does the image of the wedding couple as they cut a ribbon to enter the dining room. So does the five-hour Italian feast, where music played and children, beyond the opened doors, frolicked.

First one, then another and another, found a four-leaf clover in the cool, soft grass. Each in turn gave the green gift to the bride and groom.

In the afternoon, a light rain sparkled in the sunshine. Showers symbolize prosperity, said many of the guests, coaxing the newlyweds outdoors.

A tardy bride, four-leaf clovers and a fortuitous sprinkle promise good fortune in such a fairy tale. My wish for them: *"Possano d'ora in poi vivere felici e content"* (May they live happily ever after).

College Reunion

$\mathcal{F}$orty-four falls ago, wearing a black skirt and white blouse, I posed near the banister for a commemorative photo. Moments later my parents drove me from Wisconsin to Northwestern University in Evanston, Ill., to begin college. Mother eventually told me that she was never more surprised than when, after they'd helped me move into Willard Hall and taken me to dinner, I burst into tears while saying good-bye.

"After all," she said, "you'd studied in Mexico that summer and didn't once appear homesick in your letters."

True enough. Yet the day had turned to dusk, when thoughts naturally fly homeward, and the two who meant the most to me were leaving. Unlike a summer excursion, my arrival on campus signaled, as it does for many college freshmen, the demise of the world as I knew it and the need to find or forge a new one.

The heartache continued over four years, even as I hoped college would become, as many said it would, the best years of my life. Instead I worried, would I measure up?

I studied hard, I had some fun, but if anyone had asked me, would you rather be here or home, I would have chosen home.

The Charles Deering Library, started in 1929 and completed when my mother-in-law attended Northwestern (1930-34), was patterned after

Kings College in England. By the 1960s, the library's collection already contained more than 1 million volumes.

What I valued most in the imposing edifice, however, was a cozy niche — the phone booth built to blend in with the lobby's paneled walls. My lifeline, I'd enter it often during study breaks—hungry for a word from home or pep talk.

One evening, when I placed the call, coin after coin tumbled out, over-flowing my cupped hands. When Dad answered, I told him of my newfound riches.

"The money isn't yours. It belongs to the phone company," came his response.

There was no swaying him, so I stood there afterward, begrudgingly dropping the money, one coin after the other, back into the slot.

I hadn't been inside Deering since the 1960s. Yet, this fall, two close friends and my husband and I returned for our 40th class reunion, held in the library.

Seated across from me at dinner in the vaulted reading room upstairs was a former homecoming-queen candidate, Jane Poor MacWilliams. I hadn't known her personally but recognized her. We enjoyed getting acquainted and together found the courage to approach a third woman, Marsha Schwartz Landau, whom I also hadn't known yet had admired from afar. When we told her how highly we had regarded her campus leadership, she was visibly moved.

Another woman went out of her way to praise our friend Bill for his help in a business class they shared.

That's what reunions allow, I realized: a chance to say "Thank you."

I was filled with unexpected joy. What I did that evening is what I wish I would have done all through college: reaching out to the new, instead of longing for the familiar.

Sorry to leave, I traveled down the stairs into the lobby. Suddenly, I remembered—and turned to the left. There it was, after all the years. Grabbing the phone booth's handle, I peeked inside. Only a maze of cut wires greeted me. Yet, even if I could have called my parents, there'd have been no one now to answer.

Still, I remembered Dad's long-ago lesson, proud of his stance. I recalled my mother's voice, too.

How I wished I could have thanked them again for the sacrifice they made in covering the tuition for both my undergraduate and graduate-school education.

For the first time, fortified with what I'd just learned, a part of me wanted to go back and start over.

Yet my mother-in-law, Molly Murbach Chapman, got it right as a college freshman and, again, this fall at 93. Such an attitude may explain her longevity:

When asked how she felt about moving from her home into assisted living, she said, "I think of it as another adventure—like going off to Willard Hall at Northwestern."

Halloween Ghosts

The year draws to a close, its leafy remains reminding us of spent days.

So, too, does a piece of childhood depart, slipping away as a stranger steps in.

More "ghosts" are afoot on Halloween than meet the eye.

As children, my friends and I sensed a rattling of bones in the rustling of cornstalks, the scraping of tree limbs and the creaking of shutters.

Our thoughts turned to the graveyard we hurried past on our way to school.

Only the brave took a shortcut through the cemetery. Those who did swore they'd seen "Pete the Bottle," a town legend, still sleep against a tombstone. We worried, too, about the "moth man": With sharp knees and pointy elbows, he resembled an insect. He rode a rickety bike along a wooded path, carrying his specimens inside a case balanced on the handlebars.

When he showed us the moths and butterflies pinned to cotton, we gasped at their fate.

What if we were to run into him on Halloween night? And we never, in our greed, went trick-or-treating at the forlorn-looking house in which the inhabitant was said to strangle cats.

As if we weren't scared enough, the parent-teacher association heightened our fright with its haunted house.

That the "eyeballs" were made of grapes—or the "brains" of spaghetti—didn't matter: We wanted to be afraid and even liked to be.

319

Yet the holiday had its non-scary side—devouring cookies and cupcakes in the classroom, bobbing for apples at parties, buying wax lips and candy corn at the corner store.

And, year after year, we fantasized about costumes.

One such discussion caused the demise of Halloween as I knew it.

I was talking to my mother and Aunt Alma when I blurted out, "I can't decide what I should be this year."

"You're not going trick-or-treating, are you?" Alma asked. "Why, I think that's terrible when older kids go. Halloween is for little ones."

"A lot of kids my age trick-or treat," I said in self-defense.

"It isn't right—teenagers acting so rowdy, frightening children," she insisted, then addressed Mother: "You're not going to allow her, are you?"

"But I'm not a teenager; I'm 12," I moaned, hoping that Mom would take my side.

"Perhaps you should decide whether or not you feel too old," suggested Mother, ever the diplomat.

I realized how little I knew Alma, who visited a few times a year from upper Wisconsin.

Suddenly she struck me as the type who might peer out a window, awaiting a footstep on her lawn, so she could hurry to the door and shout: "Stay off the grass! Can't you read the sign?"

Still, I went ahead that year—dressed as the Tin Man.

The problem was that I felt hollow, too: With every door that opened, I wondered whether I was being seen through the eyes of my judgmental aunt.

Gone was the carefree squealing from house to house. Instead, behind my mask, I hid a new self-consciousness.

Later, even my "loot" lost its appeal—when I sensed that I'd taken candy from a "child."

These days, as a mother and grandmother, I always feel a closeness to the awkward trick-or-treaters at my threshold—those who shift from side to side.

With one foot steeped in childhood, the other headed for adulthood, they can't help wondering, like ghostly specters, where they belong.

Thanksgiving Chairs

*J*ust as the Pilgrims had a thanks-giving celebration, the societies in their wake seek a steppingstone to gratitude.

Something as simple as a chair or table, from year to year, might serve as an anchor in an ever-shifting scene.

Even in the depths of Alzheimer's, my mother rallied at the sight of her ladder-back chairs—which had come to reside in my home 30 years earlier.

"They are so familiar to me," she whispered, as if trying to recall the names of once-close friends.

Clustered in my house, they probably reminded her of family members once gathered around her—especially my father and a sister, who had died.

That year, after helping to clear the Thanksgiving dishes from the dining-room table, she offered to wash them, too.

"No," I said, pulling out a ladder-back, "you sit here and keep me company while I do them."

I remember that still life as vividly as a snapshot that my 11-year-old sister took one Thanksgiving, showing our young dad standing behind a ladder-back at one end of the table and Mother behind hers at the other.

321

A few seconds later, we'd form an audience as Dad carved the roasted bird.

My mother-in-law has many such memories from the years when she raised four children with her husband in California and Ohio.

Her recent move into an assisted-living center meant that her dining-room furniture, bought in 1945, wouldn't fit.

When one need ends, another often comes along: Her table and chairs, buffet and tall chest have found a home in the dining room of my daughter and son-in-law.

They'll welcome family in Massachusetts for this Thanksgiving.

When changing hands, furniture often reflects the change in people.

My daughter was struck by the sight of her grandparents' possessions.

She envisioned her grandmother behind her grandfather, resting her folded arms across the top of his chair while he lingered at the table.

She recalled how he encouraged everyone to write predictions for the next year, seal them in envelopes and tuck them in a buffet drawer to await their opening 12 months later.

She remembered not only the cornucopia centerpiece but also the overflowing love and laughter.

In a moment, she had navigated from a highchair to a seat at her grandparents' table, then to the position of hostess.

One recent week, I mailed the youth chair—which once held my three siblings and me, and later my two children—for my grandson to use.

He'll join the rest of us at the Thanksgiving table.

After the feast, as always, we'll go backstage to clean up.

I already know my role because of a dress rehearsal during the summer.

At my daughter's birthday dinner, I helped clear the dishes and started to rinse them.

"Here," she insisted, pulling out a chair: "Sit and keep me company while I load the dishwasher."

I sensed how Mom might have felt when I thought I was granting her a favor.

A chair not only provides a resting place but often reveals our place within a family.

Thanksgiving brings a chance to show gratefulness for all the parts we've played.

And for all the players.

A Blue Basket

*D*ecember 2005: Beneath my desk sits a blue basket. It took up residence in January when I returned home after a month's absence. Sorting through the mail late that night, I saved the best for last: Christmas cards. With dying embers before me, the ticking of the grandfather clock over my shoulder, I opened and read all of the greetings in one fell swoop before placing them in the basket.

The crush of news and mingled memories left me overwhelmed. And the words "The hopes and fears of all the years" from *O Little Town of Bethlehem* kept reverberating in my head. Photos of newborns, new houses and weddings leapt out, while other cards related Alzheimer's and death, divorce and lost jobs—the seesaw of "gain" and "loss."

Of all the messages I read that wintry evening, the one from my cousin Kay made me want to unwrap Christmases past, not just the ones from my youth, but especially those from my children's.

At age 28—as a divorced mother of three little girls—Kay had married Orvin, a 48-year-old widower with four daughters and a son. Instantly, she became the mother of eight. And on their first Christmas morning together, their dog gave birth—to eight puppies.

"Two years ago, when we sold the home where we grew together as a family, our children gave us a beautiful letter," wrote the couple, married for 34 years:

Then, after the death of their daughter Tammy, their "hearts were too heavy" to pass it on. They waited until Christmas 2004 to share the letter. As I read it, the walls of my family room appeared to fade away. I envisioned Kathy, their oldest, wide-eyed when she saw her father open the violin that her new mother had given him.

I pictured her, too, reaching a hand into the ceramic Santa cookie jar and relishing the "food everywhere—fridge, porch, garage, root cellar, table and in us! . . .The gorgeous fires Dad made, plus the colorful, crackling pine cones; carols around the piano."

Most of all, she treasured "hugs and kisses, the genuine love and friendship. . . . Dad and Kay created the kind of Christmases everyone talks about and Norman Rockwell paints. They last a lifetime."

"First of all, you have all been supportive of my bad times," Tammy wrote, before turning to the good memories: "Santa coming in and trying to fool. . .us (we caught on). Actually, having Kay step in to help all of us (Dad especially)."

Their first Christmas as a family, when they appeared in the town newspaper, also stood out for Jimalee—as did the "aroma of lutefisk and lefse (Norwegian fare, and) wiping butter off my chin; eight stockings hung under the mantel . . . . Mom dancing the Norwegian jig with Dad on the fiddle. The year of animal slippers from Grandma Evelyn. Family prayers with so many thanks. 'Sister Act' with kids on piano, guitar and oboe."

Sister Valerie loved picturing "the cat Rascal refusing lutefisk, all of us on the stairway and banister. . . striped footie pajamas. . .the kids playing piano and singing, Dad playing the fiddle."

"Filling up an entire pew at church" made an impression on Storm, the lone brother, as did "taking over Herreman's Restaurant on Christmas Day, and watching one family and a man with a fiddle change the . . . spirit of total strangers."

As each of the eight conjured up their favorite visions, I ached to go back with them. No longer relieved that the holidays were finally over, I couldn't wait until this Christmas to try to aspire to what Kay and Orv had achieved.

Cousins and in-laws, childhood and college friends are spread to the four winds—save for the basket where I've kept their greetings.

Today, after reviewing its contents once more, I return the container to its spot under my desk. As a wedding photo slips loose from a card, I tuck the image back inside.

Though divorced last month, the bride and groom are still together in my Christmas time capsule.

Also alive are the hopes and fears of all the years.

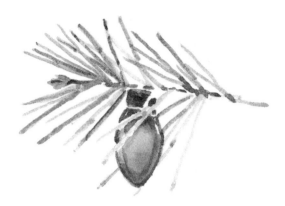

Christmas Blue

"*W*ho put the lights away last year?" a frustrated Dad would ask as he wrestled the tangled strands onto a Douglas fir.

Yet the simple act of encircling, then lighting, the Christmas tree would transform not only him but also the rest of the family.

As a young child, I was dazzled by the multicolored bulbs.

I had seen red, green and yellow shine in traffic lights, of course, and white glow in a lamp or the beam of a lighthouse.

Blue, which I glimpsed only during the holidays, most enthralled me.

Beneath the high altar of Christmas, I'd focus on one of the cobalt bulbs—inching so close to the tree that I could feel the heat upon my nose.

The color trapped the tint of twilight, the shade of Mary's robe and the hue of hills where shepherds kept watch over their flocks by night.

Usually rambunctious, I would often sit cross-legged, like a Tibetan monk, staring at the blue light.

Its magic breathed life into the figures of a Nativity scene.

Or its prism conjured up tundra and Santa's workshop.

I wanted to be nowhere else but under its spell.

I'd listen to *Billy the Brownie* on the Magnavox with Nippy, our cocker spaniel, curled up next to me.

Or I'd pore over each gift time and again, wondering about its contents as the scent of wrapping tape mingled with evergreen.

Whenever bells jingled and the front door opened, with cold air coiling to the back of my neck, I'd strain to determine whether my place of worship should be abandoned.

Dad, ever an advocate of fresh air, would rouse me from my reverie by announcing an ice-skating outing.

And I'd join my sisters, skimming over the frozen pond until our toes turned numb.

Or we'd go tobogganing, the snow often falling even as our long sled was unlashed from the top of the car.

"Keep your hands in your laps," Dad would yell, his legs pumping to the edge of the hill before he hopped aboard.

We had so many perfect landings with him at the helm. When we tried without him, we'd frequently turn over, the snow caking in the collars of our boots and mittens.

Afterward, pushing through the back door, I'd throw off my outerwear, helter-skelter, stepping on crumbs of snow that felt like cold nickels in my socks, and go back to my vigil by the tree.

Although I couldn't open any gifts until Christmas, a blue bulb would unwrap my imagination.

And, these days, it reflects my Christmases past and those of my children, too: Like snowflakes out of the blue, the happy times come swirling back.

My grandson's first Christmas tree recently took up residence in his living room.

At my arrival, he ran to the balsam fir and pointed, exclaiming, "Lights!"

I wonder what he'll see in blue or whether he'll choose a different color over which to muse in the heady days when presents are yet to be opened and Santa is only a sleigh ride away.

Love Remains

*W*here does love go? And hate?

Do feelings, once spent, evaporate, rise to meet the clouds, then rain again on the landscape of the heart?

A bridesmaid in three weddings, I've seen two of the marriages end in divorce.

When love died, where did it hide? It must have re-emerged somewhere because each of the four has since married another.

Where does grief lurk? I've seen surviving spouses recover—some enough to remarry; others enough, at least, to smile and laugh again.

Where does bliss reside? And sadness? Do they get recycled, too?

Does joy wait in sunlight for another time? Does sorrow, like the moon's path on water, skim the surface before diving deep?

Do quarrels gather, grumbling in cryptlike rooms, before their release in crowded prisons or dusty flats, or at a table for two?

After war or mayhem, where does roiling emotion run? Does it collect in mighty rivers, welling the high banks, only to burst forth and fill the world in another generation?

Does raw emotion drip in pools, hide in closets, hover in halls?

Can homes remember the glad feelings and bad? Can a parlor recall the faint echo of toe-tapping fiddlers or of a sinking heart?

Do the trees at Gettysburg still hear the impassioned words of Abraham Lincoln? Does the Lincoln Memorial reverberate with Martin Luther King Jr.'s "I have a dream"?

Pride, avarice, envy—have they remained the same since the Greeks first warned of their dangers? Each day, the newspaper tells of another fall from grace.

Does breathing, or walking, get harder as we grow older because of the accumulated weight of spent emotion filling the atmosphere, bending us low?

Does the passion that brings life into the world—and art and music and literature—keep re-entering new lovers, new lives?

Does what made Walt Whitman write stir the poet down the street?

Is some of Tristan and Isolde in everyone?

I watched a niece reading to her 2-year-old and saw a curtain lift. They were feasting at the banquet I once shared with my children and my mother shared with me. I felt so close to an answer, I could not see.

Several days later, a waitress took my order.

I was struck by all the living that she and I, two strangers, had experienced to reach that ordinary exchange—all the sunrises and sunsets, the new moons and full, the birthdays and holidays, the years of school, the times of being included or left out, the tedious tasks, the joyful moments, the illnesses, the recoveries and near misses that allowed us to survive and arrive at that intersection in time.

The meeting was unique, yet the routine ritual of taking an order and giving one is continual. So is the complimenting or complaining, the satisfaction or dissatisfaction, that results.

So is the ritual of reading to a child. So is the ritual of falling in love.

Assembling and reassembling itself, universal emotion lives on—as if, in our lifetimes, we are lent our feelings. We borrow them like books from the library.

Others who come after us recirculate the same ones, finding in them their own interpretations, insights and meanings.

Recirculated, recycled, like books, like rain, it's all the same, I thought as I sat in the restaurant.

Where does love go?

For all I know, love remains.

Front lawn,
7th Avenue

Karen and Mom

Chris and Dad,
3rd Avenue

Sonja's
wedding day

Chip, Tyler and Tia

Tia and Tyler

Tyler and
Judith's
wedding day
©2001 Albert
Cook

Tia and Alberto's
wedding day
©2005 Albert Cook

About the Author

*K*irsten Chapman is a prize-winning essayist whose articles appeared in *The Columbus Dispatch* for 21 years starting in 1984. She was twice selected winner for Best in Ohio: Essays in the Ohio Excellence in Journalism competition hosted by the Press Club of Cleveland. Her previous book, *The Way Home*, was praised by *Dispatch* columnist Mike Harden, who wrote: "There is about the work of Kirsten Chapman an eloquent but quiet grace. She is a fine and gifted writer."

In 1991 she co-authored with Babette Sirak the book *Love Affair, The Story of the Sirak Art Collection*. That same year her essays began to appear in *The Dispatch* and, in 1995, continued in a weekly column until Christmas Day 2005. For six years (1994-99) she was a contributing columnist to the *New York Times* Syndicate's former New America News Service.

Her writing has earned the Best Newspaper Editorial Award and Best in Category Award in the American Legion Auxiliary's 1993 Heart of America national media competition; first-place awards in Best in Ohio: Essays in the 2006 and 2002 Cleveland Press Club's Ohio Excellence in Journalism competition; and a first-place award in Column Writing in the Ohio Newspaper Women's Association 2002 Writing Contest.

Her work has also won four first-place awards for column writing, and a first-place award for short feature writing, from the Central Ohio Chapter of the Society of Professional Journalists.

In 1998 she published a collection of personal essays in *The Way Home* (Third Tree Press). She received B.A. and M.A.T. degrees from Northwestern University.

She and her husband, Erie (Chip), are the parents of grown children Tia and Tyler, the parents-in-law of Alberto and Judith, and the grandparents of Miles.

About the Illustrator

*D*esigner and artist Patti Sharpe focuses on illustration and watercolor, finding inspiration in nature.

She has illustrated *The Way Home, Scottie the Snail, Search for Golden Dolphin* and *Entertaining With Longaberger*. She has also created works for private collections as well as clients in the civic and medical fields.

With a degree in botany from Miami University, she began her career at The Limited, designing for Bath & Body Works, White Barn Candle Company and Limited Too.

Patti and her husband, Don, and dog, Jade, live on a farm in Marion County, Ohio, where they work to preserve habitat and support wildlife. Their adult son, Dan, lives nearby in Columbus.